Ms. Mentor's Impeccable ☞ Advice for Women in Academia

Ms. Mentor's Impeccable ☞ Advice for Women in Academia

Emily Toth

PENN

University of Pennsylvania Press

Philadelphia

10 9 8 7 6 5 4 3

Published by
University of Pennsylvania Press
Philadelphia, Pennsylvania 19104-4011

Library of Congress Cataloging-in-Publication Data

Toth, Emily.
    Ms. Mentor's impeccable advice for women in academia / Emily Toth.
        p.   cm.
    Includes bibliographical references and index.
    ISBN 0-8122-1566-4 (alk. paper)
    1. Women college teachers—United States—Miscellanea.   2. Women
graduate students—United States—Miscellanea.   3. Women college
teachers—United States—Social conditions.   4. Women graduate
students—United States—Social conditions.   5. Women college
teachers—United States—Conduct of life.   6. Women graduate
students—United States—Conduct of life.   I. Title.
LB2332.3.T68   1997
378.1′2′082—dc21   97-6259
                                                              CIP

To B.T.

Contents

Preface

Ms. Mentor was born in late 1991, when Emily Toth stewed and bubbled with a thwarted desire to change the world of academics for women—or at least tell the younger generation Some Sordid Truths.

Having spent nearly a quarter-century in academia, and having survived all those years as an out-front feminist, often being a feminist when feminism wasn't cool . . . Professor Toth felt she had much to say to younger women. She wanted to share information about opportunities and ostracisms, truths and trickeries, pitfalls and platitudes (such as "this university values teaching ever so much" and "we're a meritocracy, of course" and "we treat everyone equally, even women").

But Emily Toth found that many a new academic woman said, in effect, and with an admirable independent spirit: "Please, Mother, I'd rather do it myself"—find my own way, make my own mistakes. Having eschewed biological motherhood herself, Emily Toth found it ironic that her advice could be brushed aside by those who weren't even—wretched truth—her own daughters.

She is not, of course, disparaging the entire younger generation. Many a woman newer to academia used Emily Toth's counsel wisely; some were also grateful, publicly. One or two sent expensive posies. Yet Emily Toth longed to reach a wider audience—and so was hatched Ms. Mentor, a crotchety spirit who never leaves her ivory tower, from which she dispenses her perfect wisdom on all things academic. Like her counterpart Miss Manners, Ms. Mentor is impeccably knowledgeable and self-confident, and knows much more than anyone will ever ask.

Where E. Toth failed, Ms. Mentor would succeed.

And so "Ms. Mentor," a column of advice to women professors, graduate students, recovering academics, and those who love them, made her first appearance in the spring of 1992 in *Concerns*, the journal of the Women's Caucus for the Modern Languages. Ms. Mentor dealt with, among other things, what to wear to academic conventions—a subject that got her denounced in certain circles for "triviality." (But she still believes that the personal is political: poufy sleeves are not powerful.)

Soon letters started pouring in to Ms. Mentor, and not just from women in the modern languages. Readers were sharing her column and passing around dog-eared photocopies. A graduate student in forestry wrote; medical students chimed in; at least one affirmative action officer fulminated (Ms. Mentor adores fulminations). And so Ms. Mentor decided she would best reach her sage readers by writing an entire book of advice containing her ruminations and fulminations, gossip, anecdotes, and (of course—for this *is* academia) subjects for further study.

How many of your questions are "real?" is a question often addressed to Emily Toth when she goes abroad and it becomes known that she is in close direct communication with Ms. Mentor.

To which the answer is: All Ms. Mentor's queries are "real," for all are about real-life problems. Many are letters sent directly to Ms. Mentor (c/o Emily Toth, English Department, Louisiana State University, Baton Rouge, LA 70803). Others are questions posed to Emily Toth or to her vast network of friends, acquaintances, meddlers, scouts, critics, and needlers—all of whom are continually looking for new problems to solve, new diseases to cure, new worlds to conquer.

How many of your stories are "true?" is the other most-posed question—to which the answer is: All. Ms. Mentor leaves out a few identifying details, but the rest is all accurately reported. She reminds her sage readers that, given a system in which so many people have lifetime job security, many bizarre things can happen. Yet among the untenured, Ms. Mentor's major audience, there are indeed punishments for unconventional acts.

Ms. Mentor recalls, for instance, the crusty liberal arts dean who drove home unexpectedly one snowy afternoon and was greeted at the door by his very nervous, hand-wringing wife of twenty years. Brushing her aside, the dean strode to his clothes closet—which proved to be inhabited by a very untenured, very naked assistant professor of political science, who was making good use of his time by reading an old issue of the *New York Times*.

The assistant professor did not receive tenure, and out of this story Ms. Mentor has struggled for many years to derive a moral applicable to women in academia. She still has not succeeded—but finds it nevertheless an excellent tale, well worth retelling.

Ms. Mentor does, of course, attract other kinds of objections, the main one running something like this: "You are a mindless, bourgeois tool of capitalist patriarchy. Instead of encouraging community, you support individualistic solutions. You should be enabling your readers to work to overthrow . . ."

At which point Ms. Mentor tunes out, for she is not in the business of overthrowing capitalist patriarchy: her aims are far more modest, but much more immediate. She wants women to have power in academia NOW.

And so, rather than rock throwing (with which she does have some sympathies, however), Ms. Mentor prefers that women learn the fine arts of self-defense—and achieve the fine protection of tenure. A solitary woman, railing against injustice, has no power at all. But a team of women, all tenured, can speak with one voice and make the changes that will stop sexual harassment, achieve equal pay, get respect and money for Women's Studies, combat homophobia and anti-Semitism and class and race prejudices, allow paid leaves for child care and elder care, support accessibility and disability rights—and all the other things that are called "women's issues" and should really be human rights, and human responsibilities.

But only tenured professors have the power in academia—and so women need to get tenure. Ms. Mentor can help them, and will.

For only after tenure, can they really do what Ms. Mentor tells them to do.

Acknowledgments

Ms. Mentor's birth was attended by many midwives whose contributions of biting anecdotes, sharp ideas, raucous laughter, and delicious gossip should be lauded. Some prefer to remain demurely anonymous, but the first supporter Ms. Mentor can celebrate publicly is Joan Hartman, the editor of *Concerns*, who has never sought to change a comma of Ms. Mentor's, even at her most ranting. Ellen Cronan Rose and Ellen Messer-Davidow, Emily Toth's predecessor and successor as president of the Women's Caucus for the Modern Languages, also egged on the creation of "Ms. Mentor."

In the wider field of academia and its environs, Annette Kolodny, Susan Koppelman, Robin Roberts, and Martha Ward deserve special commendation. They are Ms. Mentor's dearest chums, yentas, nudges, listening posts, and coconspirators.

Others whose ideas have especially enhanced Ms. Mentor's include Marleen Barr, Emily Batinski, Marilyn Bonnell, Stephanie Bressler, Mary Lynn Broe, Ellen Cantarow, Jane Caputi, Mary Wilson Carpenter, Sabrina Chapman, Barbara Davidson, Cathy N. Davidson, Carmen del Rio, Barbara Ewell, Cynthia Fisher, Elizabeth Fisher, Daniel Mark Fogel, Molly Freier, Linda Gardiner, Carol Gelderman, Lynne Goodstein, Suzanne Green, Mary Hamilton, Elizabeth Hampsten, Suzette Henke, Barbara Hillyer, Dominique Homberger, Florence Howe, Dorothy Jenkins, Leola Johnson, Rosan Jordan, Mike Judge, Andrea Lapin, Nancy Love, John Lowe, Wahneema Lubiano, Mary Jane Lupton, Deborah Martin, Michelle Massé, Carol Mattingly, Kenneth McMillin, Sally Mitchell, Janet Palmer Mullaney, Dana Nelson, Margaret Parker, Mary Perpich, Annis Pratt, Susan Radis, Gerri Reaves, Angelita Reyes, Lillian Robinson, Audrey Rodgers, Sue V. Rosser, Hal Ruddick, Adelaide Russo, Nina Schulman, Kimberly Clarke Simmons, Dale Spender, Susan Swartzlander, Bette Tallen, Linda Wagner-Martin, and Barbara Wittkopf.

The Women's and Gender Studies faculty of Louisiana State University should be cited for their energy and aplomb. The Economic and Social Justice Research Group of Baton Rouge NOW and the Women's Studies Consortium of Louisiana have contributed ideas and indignation.

The late Dorothy Ginsberg Fitzgibbons, Emily Toth's mother, was her first mentor. Emily Toth also owes much to other family members, including Sara Ruffner, Theresa Toth, Dennis Fitzgibbons, Ellen Boyle, and the late John Fitzgibbons. She further acknowledges that all her academic mentors were men, and fine ones: Philip Klass, Richard Macksey, Daniel Walden, Stanley Weintraub, and Philip Young.

Pat Browne and Arlene Caney duly scheduled a Ms. Mentor session every year for half a dozen years at the annual American and Popular Culture Association convention.

Beauregard and Bunkie Toth contributed feline self-assurance: they mentor or maul every human they meet.

As a role model, living legend, and goddess of etiquette, Miss Manners, Judith Martin, is without peer. (Ms. Mentor has never met her, but worships her from afar.)

Patricia Reynolds Smith, the sagest of editors, jumped at the chance to aim Ms. Mentor at a wider audience, through the good offices of the University of Pennsylvania Press. She has been the perfect editor for Ms. Mentor's quirky humor and crotchety ways. Mindy Brown, Jennifer Malloy, Kym Silvasy, and Carol Gaines ably midwifed *Ms. Mentor's Impeccable Advice for Women in Academia* into print. Eric Halpern wisely directs the Press.

Nicole Hollander, artist extraordinaire, created a cover drawing worthy of a goddess—or Ms. Mentor.

Finally, Bruce Toth has lived with Ms. Mentor's teeth gnashing and phrasemongering for some five years, and Emily Toth's for nearly thirty years. He finds them both witty and wise, which is the best sign of his own good taste.

Graduate School:
The Rite of Passage

Anne, a straight-A student through high school and a summa cum laude from Bryn Mawr, has fallen in love with art history. She's trekked to every odd little church in every corner of Italy and says her soul is more Italian than American. Friends have found her lying down by the hour, staring at the ceiling of the Sistine Chapel. A boyfriend even broke off with her because, he said, "You love Michelangelo—even though he's dead and gay— more than you love me." Anne can't deny it. And now, after five years of waitressing in Europe and discovering that tempestuous romances don't satisfy her soul, Anne wants to go to graduate school. She wants to get a Ph.D. in art history.

Beth has worked for several years in a biology lab, doing routine testings and samplings. But she loves to read novels. She continually regrets that her college major was General Studies, with just "Intro to Lit" and a few low-level science courses to certify herself as a medical technologist. She'd wanted a job that she could fall back on and pick up anywhere, since her husband's job requires a family move every few years. They also have two young children. But now Beth is thinking she'd like to do "something for myself." She'd like to go to graduate school and really study literature in depth, not just as a fan.

Cassie comes from a family of intensely practical doctors and lawyers who've always considered her an oddball: she's obsessed with human motivations and peculiarities. At family events, when everyone else is talking money, Cassie is gathering gossip. When the doctors discuss hearts and the lawyers discuss writs, Cassie wants to know all about who, what, when, where, why, and how. Cassie majored in mass communications, but found her courses too technical, not satisfying her curiosity. She's figured out that what really grabs her is anthropology—comparative cultures—a field in which academic jobs scarcely exist. So she's considering graduate school in history.

Anne, Beth, and Cassie all need impeccable advice from Ms. Mentor, who will allow her sage readers to eavesdrop.

A Ph.D., Ms. Mentor declares, should be pursued only by those who love what they are doing. They should burn with curiosity and wonder; they should delight in discovering new things. Otherwise the graduate school apprenticeship is too long, and the required studies often dreary. Graduate students have little power and much stress: as fellowships and assistant-ships dry up, poverty becomes a way of life. And at the end, given the dismal job market in virtually all fields, most Ph.D.s will not follow in their professors' footsteps, even if they want to.

Still, Anne has the burning drive; Cassie has family money to fall back on. But Beth must be able to stay at one university for years of study. Then she'll need to move, possibly several times, to remote and distant places where jobs happen to open. Even with good child care and a husband willing to share a commuter marriage, her options are limited. It's not uncommon, now, for a new English Ph.D. to take five years to find a tenure-track job.

This is not to say that Beth cannot be an academic. But Ms. Mentor would place her bet first on Anne, with her passion for her subject, her real-world experience, and her willingness to sacrifice. Cassie, though, may find history to her liking—if she discovers mentors who share her passion for gossip and narrative. But Beth, so far, knows only about reading literature for pleasure, and Ms. Mentor fears for her.

Will Beth be able to embrace the jargon of literary theory—or will it make her mewl and twitch?

For Anne, Beth, Cassie, and all their fellow students, graduate school will be a series of rituals, some dating back to German education a century and a half ago. (There are those who think Ms. Mentor was present at the creation, but she denies it.)

All graduate students today, in lockstep or death grip, enroll in required seminars and classes—some exciting, some deadly. If they're in science, they'll do labs and fieldwork. If they're in applied practical fields, they may do internships or clerkships or residencies. They may need to be proficient with certain languages or computer programs or machines. They may be sent to ask strangers eccentric or peculiar questions, which their sociology or statistics bosses will then manipulate, via numerical hocus-pocus, into conclusions about human behavior.

Graduate students may also be coaxed into doing other very odd things for their major professors. A group of food science graduate students at a Big Ten university were once seduced into swallowing huge quantities of hot sauce so that their professor could photograph, with fiber optic equipment, the effects on their stomach linings. (The students who suffered the most were those who took aspirin.)

Similarly, some science graduate students at Johns Hopkins University were once enlisted to help protect their major professor's prized gardens from rabbit incursions. Following his directions, the students hied themselves to the Baltimore Zoo, where they beseeched the zoo keepers to give them tiger dung. Then they hauled it out to their professor's estate, where they spent the rest of the day slathering it about his carrots and marigolds.

They did get Big Macs for lunch.

More mundanely, though, students are required to take oral and written exams, sometimes several in different subject areas. Then, finally, they're turned loose to write theses or dissertations—the stage at which the uncommitted are most likely to drop out, and disappear.

If, as sometimes happens, graduate students

- cannot bring themselves to do one more reading assignment—or
- cannot get out of bed to go to the library—or
- get nauseous at the smell of a lab or the thought of a rat—or
- spend hours, days, or weeks in useless housekeeping chores, such as folding sheets or curtains, while avoiding all academic work—or
- fuss and dither for months, never finding a dissertation topic that really grabs them . . .

Those are all danger signals. Academia may not be for them, and dropping out can be the smartest thing to do. It is never a sign of failure.

For at every stage, Ms. Mentor proclaims, graduate students should be asking themselves: "Am I leading up to what I want to do?" and "What are my goals for this week, this month, this year?" and "Do I want to do this for the rest of my life?"

If Anne finds something new about Michelangelo; and Beth discovers a forgotten novelist whose work anticipates Edith Wharton's; and Cassie forges ahead with an historical study of several kinky anthropologists' lives—then they will have the intellectual excitement that will keep them learning and growing, getting their doctorates and making genuinely new contributions to the world of knowledge.

Then it will all be worthwhile, and Ms. Mentor hopes their parents will live to see the great day. She herself will cheer and sing and perhaps even flick her tambourine.

But not all of Ms. Mentor's correspondents reach that pleasant pinnacle, as sage readers will now discover.

Up Against the Balls

Q: One of my most outspoken professors (I'm in political science) told me that "most of the guys who go to grad school these days don't have the balls to go into the real world." Assuming that "guys" means all of us (he usually includes women), is he right?

A: Ms. Mentor has always been intrigued by the idea that one needs "balls" in order to do anything other than the work for which they were intended—i.e., the propagation of our species and the recreational pleasures of the bearer thereof.

She recalls Mary Ellmann's clever dissection, in *Thinking About Women*, and Kate Millett's, in *Sexual Politics*, of Norman Mailer's claim that a writer can do without anything "except the remnant of his balls." Besides wondering, as feminist critics have a habit of doing, where one would place a pen—or, these days, a computer—in a testicular vicinity, Ms. Mentor . . . well, she thinks it all quite silly.

Still, your query, like all those Ms. Mentor selects, deserves a thoughtful reply. If your professor's claim is to be taken literally—that most of the people in grad school lack balls—that is certainly true in the humanities, where well over half of incoming graduate students are women. In political science, however, nearly 75 percent of graduate students receiving Ph.D.s are men. Ms. Mentor thinks it unlikely that they are all eunuchs.

Ms. Mentor therefore understands your professor to be saying, in a crudely symbolic way, that guys "with balls," those who enroll in the "real world" rather than in graduate school, have the qualities attributed to true masculinity—such as courage, intelligence, and resourcefulness.

Ms. Mentor thinks it fortunate and delightful that all women, whether they are in graduate school or not, have those qualities.

Plotting One's Courses

Q: My department's director of graduate studies, when he advises students about classes to take, has an unfortunate habit of placing course lists in his lap—so that the advisee has to look at his crotch. I am interested in getting a Ph.D. in rhetoric. I am not interested in his crotch.

Last time I went to ask about my program of study, his crotch was—well—bulging.

I am grossed out.

A: Do you have a sympathetic woman professor who can subtly tell Dr. Crotch to knock it off?

If not, there is no easy way—given his power over your career—to confront him honestly and openly. What he is doing is a kind of sexual harassment, a "micro-inequity" that is difficult to combat. If you try, by filing a complaint, you might be accused of "making a mountain out of a . . ." Well, you get the point.

As there is no clean way to confront Dr. Crotch, Ms. Mentor sighs and offers a sneaky way. One might, for instance, leave an anonymous note in his mailbox: "We, the graduate students, suggest that you not put course lists in your lap when you're advising us. We do not like to look at your crotch. Thank you!"

This should do the trick, especially since Dr. Crotch will have no idea who sent the note. He will suspect everyone. But if the note does not change his behavior, and if—as is often the case with Dr. Crotches—he is hyper-heterosexual or even homophobic, you can torment him with a second anonymous note: "We, the grad student guys, love it when you hold the course lists in your crotch. Keep up the good work!"

After such a truly dirty trick, the superstraight male who won't change his behavior, pronto, is beyond hope.

Don't Know Much

Q: I have returned to graduate school to get a Ph.D. in women's literature. When I was originally an undergraduate back in the 1950s, I chafed under what I have learned to call the requirements of the patriarchy—to read and appreciate literature by men that demeans or makes invisible women and girls. Back then, I just called it being bored by the bullshit.

However, I was what was then referred to as "well educated": I was well read in the literature, history, and philosophy of the white boys. I'd had my three years of Latin and two years of French, I'd done a research paper in high school every year since ninth grade, I'd taken English classes where we'd been required to read one novel, one play, and some poems every month that school was in session, etc. I'm sure you're familiar with the Old Curriculum. After all, Ms. Mentor Knows All.

Now, forty years later, I return to a completely different world. And I don't like everything about it, you can bet. One of the main things I don't like is the loss of the concept of the educated person. Most of my professors, who are at least one generation younger than I am, seem so unbelievably limited in *what they know*, in *what they have read*. I don't understand why that is. I hope I am not being ageist, but I do believe that my range of knowledge when I was their age was broader and deeper.

I love all the new things I am learning in Women's Studies and women and literature courses, but one of the things I love most of all is comparing those things with what I already know, adjusting my understanding of the true nature of reality, history, etc. But it is really weird to see that my co-students and *most of my teachers* don't have any basic other knowledge to add to this new material.

These are a bunch of observations, and I know they can easily be written off as manifestations of one or another sort of -ism, some social disease of the politically incorrect, but inherent in this set of observations are some questions. I know that in your wisdom you will discern the questions I am too chicken to ask outright.

What do you think, O Wise Ms. Mentor?

A: In other words, does Ms. Mentor think the current generation is dumber than yours? Well, probably. Certainly every older generation thinks so, and Ms. Mentor is as old as the hills.

Usually, though, each generation's knowledge is different. Your fellow students almost certainly know television and popular music ("media texts") better than you do. They, and your teachers, may also be more skilled at speaking and writing the jargon of postmodernism ("indeterminacy," "discourse," "slippage"). You, like Ms. Mentor, may think much of that jargon is silly, pretentious, and senseless—but it is part of today's concept of what makes an educated person. (Ms. Mentor has more faith in Karl Marx's claim that any great idea can be expressed simply.)

Your underlying questions may be varieties of the bright young person's typical observation when starting a first full-time job: "I'm Surrounded By Idiots." It is true, unfortunately, that many of the things you value, or at least know well, are no longer valued very much by anyone, including the self-satisfied white males who sanctified them in the first place. You can deplore that, but you can't do much to change it.

What you can do is steel yourself and embrace the "discourse." Or you can regard it as an anthropologist might, as a quaint set of bizarre native customs. Simply from living longer, you know a great deal of history and psychology, both of which should encourage you to view everything with an analytical, if not jaundiced, eye. You may decide to learn what you like, and in the privacy of your own room, write satires about the rest.

Ms. Mentor has been doing that all her life.

Ungraded, Degraded, Misgraded?

Q: With the exception of one professor, all the professors I've had so far in graduate school return my papers with an A grade, but no comments. And they don't discuss the papers with students in office hours, either. Is this the kind of feedback that will prepare me to publish rather than perish? I'm worried.

A: Ms. Mentor will begin by commending you for your superb perceptions. You have psyched out what pays in academia.

At research universities, where graduate students are trained for whatever paltry positions might someday emerge, teaching is the daily work that is often unmentionable. Meeting classes is talked about, wryly, as the dues that faculty pay in order to pursue the really prestigious fun: publishing books and articles; poking holes in others' obscure or obtuse arguments; posturing at conferences or flaming opponents over the Internet; or pursuing administrative posts through which to protect or punish.

In research universities, teaching provides many psychic rewards (which few faculty will admit), but prestige and money come from writing. If your professors are particularly candid, or rude, they may claim to be modeling correct professional priorities for you: students are little swarmy things to be swatted away in the interests of Pursuing Knowledge and Power, which come through publishing.

Ms. Mentor hopes that once you are a professor yourself, you will not subscribe to the publishing-is-all-that-ever-matters creed. But to aid you in achieving that blessed state, Ms. Mentor suggests these ways to wring some feedback out of invisible or recalcitrant pedagogues:

- Use the graduate student grapevine to finger the most responsive professors. Often they are newer and younger and filled with zeal and grand ideas. (As Jill Ker Conway notes in *True North*, she was advised to take her Harvard classes from junior faculty. They hadn't already put all they'd ever know in their books; they weren't burned out.)
- If there is no grad student grapevine, create one: a graduate student organization, or brown bag lunches, or coffees. These are not just for gossip or mutual moaning (though those are valuable). Grapevines can spawn writing groups, support groups, and pals who'll help one another get jobs and opportunities.
- Create or join a writing group, with ground rules: How often should the group meet? What should each member be expected to bring or distribute beforehand? How precise should comments be? (Global? A paragraph at a time? Grammatical nitpicking?) If face-to-face writing groups aren't possible, try e-mail (writers' magazines have some suggestions).
- Read up on a subject, at least two journal articles, before tracking down a professor and asking polite, specific questions *before* writing each paper: "Can you suggest other useful sources on this subject?" or "Have I neglected something important?" or "Why does Koppelman say this?" Vague or whimpering queries—"How should I write this paper?" or "I don't know what you WANT!"—are hard to answer and wearisome, and

drive less responsible faculty to evade office hours. (Sometimes such professors can be tracked down in bars near campus. Those are not the best venues for academic feedback.)

As for post-paper feedback, Ms. Mentor adds these tips:

- You may ask the professor: "Would you be willing to read an article I want to submit to a journal?" (It's even better to name a specific journal.) The article may be substantially the same as your class paper, but your strategy will free the professor from feeling hounded to justify a grade. (That, too, often drives professors out of the office and into the bars.) Asked to read a journal article, your professor will have been seduced into feeling that s/he is doing real professional work—and you'll get your comments.
- You may send your papers to journals that provide feedback—such as *PMLA*, *Legacy*, and *Signs*. You will, of course, have studied the journals beforehand: How detailed are the articles? What writing styles are favored? What documentation is used? Do the journals prefer wide syntheses or close readings? How intricate and how tactful (or tactless) are the arguments refuting previous researchers? What seem to be the political stances of journal writers and editors? Given the odds, your work is likely to be rejected, but you may get back detailed, informative critiques.

The critiques may also, sometimes, be scathing, but Ms. Mentor urges you to preserve your ego strength despite the slings and arrows of graduate school. Find people who love you for yourself and won't snipe at you about your GRE scores. Treasure nonacademic friends who ask real-life pointed questions that deserve good answers, such as

- "Why are you clubbing some old dead guy for his racism? He can't mend his ways now"—or
- "Why study a wife beater like Melville? Even Hawthorne wouldn't get it on with him"—or
- "So you're a sanitary engineer. Is our local water safe to drink?"—or
- "Why did that creepy Bettelheim hate mothers so much?"—or
- "So when will you find a cure for AIDS?"—or
- "Why do these smart professors write such long and windy sentences?"

Ms. Mentor exhorts you to flee from those who demand, "What are you going to do with your degree?" They're too depressing.

Finally, Ms. Mentor reminds you that professors' grades and comments are not the main education one acquires in school. Grad students, like all apprentices and underlings, learn best by doing. Through writing papers and reports, you teach yourself to put together ideas, come up with theses, and discuss and demonstrate them with quotations and conclusions, numbers and notations, theories and speculations. Professorial comments, whether ego-satisfying or soul-shattering, won't teach you to be an independent professional generating your own momentum.

Ms. Mentor, who is often the recipient of clumsy though well-deserved flattery, acknowledges that graduate students do need to please their elders. But the motivation to think, research, and write must come from within— not from the hope for more good grades or strokes. An academic needs a strong, independent drive; intellectual curiosity; and an unconquerable urge to write and publish.

Professorial feedback, Ms. Mentor concludes, is but a garnish. The meal—preferably lush and sweet and spicy, not chewy or stringy—is what you concoct yourself.

Ms. Mentor, of course, always brings the sage.

Class Conscious

Q: I'm in a history graduate program, and many of my classmates strike me as pompous, moneyed bores. (OK, I'm in an Ivy League school, and I do come from a preppie background.) Do academics ever escape their ancestry?

A: Rarely. In fact, few Americans stray far from their original class position. First-generation college students rarely get Ph.D.s and become academics, and few, if any, of those will be hired as faculty in the Ivy League, where the nasal "preppie honk" is still a favored accent. Someone who attended Cleveland State (for instance) will be considered quite exotic among people who all matriculated at Princeton, Harvard, Stanford, and the like. Ms. Mentor knows one academic in Oklahoma who grew up in foster homes and one in Illinois who is the child of migrant workers, but the typical academic is the offspring of a college-educated, suburban nuclear family.

Ms. Mentor recommends that you read *Working Class Women in the*

Academy: Laborers in the Knowledge Factory, edited by Michelle M. Tokarczyk and Elizabeth A. Fay, and take to heart their descriptions of how the poor feel among the elite.

And should you tire of the pompous, moneyed bores about you (Ms. Mentor yawns and twitches when she thinks of them), you can always urge them to join you in a few hours a week of volunteer work for a battered women's program, or Planned Parenthood, or Habitat for Humanity, or a soup kitchen, abortion clinic, literacy program, or progressive political candidate.

In short, you can do your bit to revive the historical tradition of *noblesse oblige*. Ms. Mentor believes fervently that it behooves the rich, wise, and powerful to aid the less fortunate. That is why she shares her perfect wisdom with the masses. You, in your own way, can follow her lead.

Fat Chance

Q: I'm a grad student in education, and I'm very fat. I know women of size have problems with job discrimination and hostility, and my classmates all seem to be thin, white, suburban, and athletic, and obsessed with their weight, to the point of anorexia.

I'm used to anti-fat comments from people who don't know anything about metabolism or set points or the fact that more than 95 percent of diets fail. Even Oprah Winfrey's weight yo-yos, and that's far more unhealthy than being "overweight." But I didn't expect educated people to still believe foolish myths about fat (it's a matter of poor willpower) or disease (fat will kill you—tomorrow), or to monitor every mouthful they eat with self-hating comments ("I hate myself for eating all this chocolate"). I get angry sometimes; mostly I get bored.

But I'm also worried about what this means for my academic future, as a fat woman who won't—and can't, anyway—get skinny. I've tried all my life, with starvation diets, self-punishment, killer exercise, and even some secret surgery. Nothing works, and I know that fat activists are right: if we're fat, it's because it's in our genes.

My adviser is a skinny woman who punishes herself to get that way. Yesterday she told me that if I don't lose weight, I might as well quit grad school, as it'll be wasted on me. Is she right?

A: While Ms. Mentor was fuming over your letter, she was hearing about olestra, a recently approved substance with the mouth feel of fat but not the calories. Apparently it just slides through the intestines, pirating away needed nutrients, and causing "unfortunate" side effects (say the popular media): explosive diarrhea and "anal leakage," visible on the underwear of tasting volunteers.

Ms. Mentor hopes that by the time you read this, olestra will have been banned. But she thinks it more likely that several I-must-be-skinny-at-all-costs women will be permanently injured, malnourished, or dead. And the promoters of olestra will have fattened their profits at the expense of women.

"I Must Be Thin" strikes Ms. Mentor as a deadly mantra, one women should resist. It siphons away mental energy; it leads to ridicule and abuse and prejudice, for beauty standards have always depended on scarcity and difficulty. In poor societies, fat is in; among rich people, thin is in—so that U.S. women who can afford to dine grandly brag instead that they've learned to starve themselves. Ms. Mentor has heard that some women actually interrupt delicious dinner parties to denounce their own thighs.

And now universities, seemingly in cahoots with the sadistic designers of airline seats, have added a new torture. The latest brand of classroom furniture installed at, among other places, the University of Oklahoma and Louisiana State University, features seats that are only fourteen inches wide. The distance between the seats and their attached writing surfaces is so small that pregnant women and male athletes literally cannot fit inside the desks they're supposed to sit in.

(For further information about the madness of thin people, Ms. Mentor directs her readers to a marvelously funny 'zine called *Fat? So!* available for $12/year from Fat! So?, P.O. Box 423464, San Francisco, CA 94142. NAAFA, the National Association to Advance Fat Acceptance, can be reached at 1-800-442-1214, and they can share some surprising facts—not myths. Ms. Mentor also recommends the classic book *Shadow on a Tightrope: Writings by Women on Fat Oppression*, edited by Lisa Schoenfielder and Barb Wieser, and a new encourager: Cheri K. Erdman's *Nothing to Lose: a Guide to Sane Living in a Larger Body*.)

But all this does not answer your real question: Can a woman of substance be an academic?

To which Ms. Mentor responds: Yes, but you must be sly and choose your battles. Usually it is not worthwhile to try to educate the scrawny self-punishers about the uselessness of dieting: that will just frustrate you. You can leave around *Fat? So!* and NAAFA leaflets; you can give them to your adviser, if you think she's open to seeing fatophobia as a form of bigotry. If not, shrug and try to be amiable: you still need her approval.

You can also make yourself feel better by bedeviling and misleading the fatophobes around you:

- If you have a boyfriend—most fat women do, since men like a lot of woman to hug—flaunt him.
- Now and then, wear darker clothes: the skinnies will be bamboozled into thinking you've lost weight. Loose-fitting dresses rather than pants will also confound them: they can't easily see and judge your body. (A tip: under skirts, you can wear divided slips for comfort.)
- Silence patronizers ("You'd be so pretty if you'd just lose weight") by claiming you're on a slow, medically approved diet. They don't have to know that your basic four food groups are whatever you like best—such as chili corn dogs, sour cream and onion-flavored potato chips, Godiva Chocolates, and Budweiser.
- Tell the skinnies that you're "part bulimic." (You know which part: you like to binge, but you never purge.)
- Use the sterotypical role of Fat Woman as Everyone's Jolly Pal to get inside information. People will tell you secret stuff you need to know— not only gossip, but who really runs the show in your academic department. That's enormously useful.

Ms. Mentor also recommends finding a self-loving Women of Size support and exercise group: they'll be women to eat and laugh with. Call whichever local hospitals are touting the so-called ills of menopause: they'll be looking for ways to hook women. And use the Net for support and discussion groups.

Meanwhile, in grad school, Ms. Mentor recommends that you work most on your writing. If you write well, with lively and interesting prose, you can get to the point where no one knows or cares what you look like. The great women's rights advocate Elizabeth Cady Stanton was fat, and deliberately so; Gertrude Stein was monumental; Colleen McCullough, author of *The Thorn Birds* and other books, strides around and collects her millions in a muumuu.

Ms. Mentor cannot guarantee that all this will cure fatophobia and get you academic success, but she does know that activity is always better than brooding—just as eating is always better than starving. Toffee beats tofu.

And eventually, as Americans grow older and simply can't have tiny bodies, women of substance may be seen as a wise avant-garde. Ms. Mentor likes to imagine an alternative world in which anytime a woman starts to worry about calories or eating, she tells herself, "Eating well is a contribution to women's well-being and therefore to worldwide feminist revolution and the betterment of all." Then she chows down, with relish, on those chocolate chip cookies and gooey fried cheese nachos and mile-high ice cream pies.

Imagine a world of happy, well-fed, self-loving, intellectually alert women instead of the bulimic, the cranky, the anorexic, or the walking-dead-from-dieting.

That would truly be revolutionary.

Dissertation Dilemma

Q: I'm choosing a dissertation topic, in literature. What should I keep in mind to be marketable?

A: Ms. Mentor is reluctant to contribute to her own growing reputation for fogeyism, for possessing antiquated ideas. Yet she cannot divest herself of the belief that pursuing one's own intellectual interests is the only valid reason to be in graduate school. And so, in her well-mannered way, Ms. Mentor periodically rails and sputters at the idea that dissertation writers must put "marketability" first.

Ms. Mentor hereby declares: Academia does not pay well enough for people to sell their souls in that way.

She further advises that before choosing any topic, you should undertake a serious self-study. Now, Ms. Mentor is not recommending therapy (or gynecology). Rather, she means for you to start a diary, write letters to yourself, and initiate thoughtful chats with nonacademic friends and family, in order to ask yourself truly:

WHAT DO I WANT FROM ACADEMIA?

Some possible answers:

- To follow my intellectual interests.
- To do new research about women, or people of color, or lesbian writers.
- To get a job with a clear structure of deadlines, rewards, and punishments.

- To continue the life that gives me ego boosts, since I've always been good at schoolwork.
- To make a good living as a professor.

The last is the worst reason, as the job crunch deepens and salaries fall even further behind those of other professionals. Many university faculties are now more than half part-timers, underpaid and without benefits. Some community colleges in the Northeast now consider a typical teaching load for a "part-time adjunct instructor" to be three courses per semester, $1500 per course, no benefits, no chance for tenure or promotion. (This information is available in the *Chronicle of Higher Education*.) Older professors are not dying or retiring at the expected rate, and when they are, they are often not being replaced at all.

You need better reasons to stay in school. For some students, familiar routines are powerful pulls: they need deadlines and grades, carrots and sticks. Overwhelmingly busy with reading, students too rarely ask, "What for?" (beyond the fact that it's assigned). Few grad students will dare say, "This is boring." As Leslie Fiedler pointed out a generation ago, academic types generally have a huge tolerance for boredom and an equally enormous fear of risk. The real world is scary. Stay in school and do your homework.

(In reality, there are many highly structured 9-to-5 jobs, such as technical writing, that pay better than academia does. They don't require homework, and technical writers also don't risk being publicly heckled by teenagers.)

Further, Ms. Mentor probably does not need to tell you that graduate school rarely provides ego boosts: one of its unspoken functions is to make students squirm. Even in his youth, at Johns Hopkins University, Professor Stanley Fish was famous for telling classes that "Studying literature should be painful. If it isn't, you're not doing it right." His then-colleague, Professor Eugenio Donato, used to accuse the rare smiling student: "You think literature is pretty."

But Ms. Mentor assumes that you have signed up for the rigors of graduate school, accepting years of poverty, for the best and most valid reason: driving intellectual curiosity. There are things you want to read and know and learn, and as you approach your dissertation, you get to ask yourself:

- What am I really interested in?
- What do I want to do with my life?

The topic you choose will determine which jobs you can aim for, and what you can teach, and what you will be expected to write about for publication. If you select Charlotte Perkins Gilman, for instance, you will be "marketable" in Women's Studies; American literature, nineteenth and twentieth centuries; and possibly nonfiction, autobiography, and cultural studies. You may love Renaissance poetry, but you will have to bid it adieu as a subject for scholarly inquiry.

What not to do. Ms. Mentor shudders at the current proliferation of cross-century dissertations, such as "The Rhetoric of Ignatia Quicksilver as Applied to the Works of Shakespeare, Henry James, D. H. Lawrence, Toni Morrison, and Beavis and Butt-head." Supposedly the student— should she live to complete such a sweeping, impossible dissertation— will then be deemed qualified for jobs in Shakespeare, Renaissance drama, nineteenth- and twentieth-century British and American literature, the novel, modernism, rhetoric, African American literature, cultural studies, postmodernism, gender studies, and Ignatia Quicksilver.

(Ms. Mentor finds it particularly offensive that many a white graduate student who's written one chapter on Toni Morrison—and who hasn't?— purports to be an expert on African American literature. That insults African Americans, who have a distinct, rich culture and literature very different from white folks'.)

In reality, the student with the conglomerate dissertation will come across to hiring committees as a jill-of-all-trades who may be hired for "generalist" positions, but those are usually non-tenure-track instructorships. If she wants a Real Job, she needs a Real Subject for her dissertation: an author, a period, a genre, a critical approach, a community of authors more closely meshed. She needs to demonstrate, through her dissertation, that she knows something well, something that she's passionately interested in pursuing.

Time matters, too. Ms. Mentor advises you to choose a topic that you can complete quickly. No vast syntheses; no biographies (they take too long and require too much money and travel). No need to write the definitive word. Just the completed one.

With well-focused subjects, some highly motivated students can write their dissertations in a year. Ms. Mentor did hers in just under two, she thinks—although they used different calendars then, in the Pleistocene era. It is not uncommon for dissertations to take four years, some of them part-time while the student is teaching, working at another career, or involved with family.

But some students take up to eight years or more—an ominous sign. Often they were never really inspired in the first place, and now they are dithering and procrastinating. Frequently they are people who genuinely do not enjoy writing—or who would rather write lampoons and letters than literary criticism. They prefer real life to lit crit, and that is a perfectly rational choice.

They should stop punishing themselves, Ms. Mentor decrees. There is no shame in not completing a dissertation, for the average person changes careers five to ten times in a lifetime. The shame is to continue in something one does not love, just because one has begun it. Smart folks stop.

Meanwhile other smart folks, the incorrigible literature lovers, try to find subjects that enthrall them. If you're one, what should you write on?

Ms. Mentor suggests that you think about which authors, genres, readings, have kept running around in your mind long after the courses and teachers were forgotten. Which ones did you talk about incessantly with your friends? Which ones are you still quoting? These are the ones you'll enjoy rereading and rereading. What do you not know about these authors and texts? What would you like to know?

Further, are there writers whose papers are in your university library, barely touched by human hands? Does your local historical society have materials you could work on? Is there something genuinely original (and therefore more exciting) that you could do?

You should continue your search until you find something that tickles your fancy, for you will be working with it a long time. This will be your only chance to write a book on a subject dear to your heart and have it critiqued by experts.

Ms. Mentor also recommends that you read some completed dissertations in your field (the university library will have those written locally). Besides seeing how a dissertation is shaped by a thesis (point of view), you will be pleasantly surprised by how awful some of them are. "I can easily write something that mediocre," many a grad student has told herself, chuckling with pleasure. This is extremely gratifying.

Finally, you should think of choosing to do your dissertation as a gift to yourself and the world, not as a punishment meted out by some horrific schoolteacher martinet in your head. And if the obvious person to direct your dissertation is horrific, you should not work with that person. Life is short. Choose a director who's congenial and helpful, and who's well published in your field: your director's connections may help you get a job.

Ms. Mentor believes that her wise readers should choose pleasure over pain. If living an interesting life inspires them more than the prospect of committing literary criticism, then they should choose life.

Early Publishing = Premature Perishing?

Q: Do I need to publish to get a first job? Should I be sending my seminar papers to academic journals for feedback, or will their manuscript readers get annoyed with me?

A: Ms. Mentor already knows what numerous learned worthies are thinking: there's too much bad stuff published already. You may be right in thinking you're not ready, and that you shouldn't clutter the mails, the Net, the journals with your naive maunderings. You should give your ideas, and your prose style, time to mellow and grow. What you send out should be substantial, long-mulled-over, and gravely wise. That is the only way to make an important mark, rather than selling out to the trendy, or prostituting yourself to the marketplace.

Ms. Mentor characterizes the above sentiments as Senior Scholar Claptrap and Entrenched Pseudo-Wisdom. For you it's also unrealistic, suicidal advice.

Yes, indeed, in an ideal world one would not publish a semicolon before it was ripe. But in the real world, a half-baked, or even raw, book is not uncommon. And a publish-no-thought-before-its-time academic, is an unemployed academic.

You cannot wait to be brilliant. You need to make yourself known as soon as possible.

Luckily for you, the human memory often blurs distinctions: people will remember your name, but not whether your work was splendid or shameful. You should be delivering conference papers, and writing book reviews; you should be volunteering to edit manuscripts, judge contests, arrange conferences, chauffeur visiting scholars and writers. You should be sending stuff around, whether it's published or not; you should list on your vita all the pieces that are "in circulation." When an article is turned down, you should study the readers' reports, revise, and send it out again within a week.

You must be ambitious; you must aim to publish early and often. That is the only way you'll distinguish yourself from the hordes of people who apply for every tenure-track job—sometimes as many as two thousand for every one job in the humanities.

Without publication, Ms. Mentor guarantees that your career will truly perish.

The Professor Passes the Last Course

Q: My dissertation director dropped dead in the back seat of a taxi, and I have two chapters still to go. Now what?

A: Ms. Mentor, who reads Miss Manners faithfully about proper behavior, sends condolences on your loss. The passing of a professor is always tragic.

Ms. Mentor recalls the terrible case of a young man named Cameron, who was actually present, hailing the Number Ten bus, when his dissertation director—as Cameron put it—"started spitting out black stuff and then croaked." Cameron persisted in telling this crudely entertaining tale for weeks afterward, until he became known (behind his back, of course) as "the Asshole with the Albatross." He took a leave of absence to collect his thoughts, and Ms. Mentor does not know what became of him.

You, though, presumably do not want to quit. You want to salvage your dissertation and your academic prospects. And so Ms. Mentor suggests that you meet as soon as possible with your department's chair of graduate studies for advice about possible other directors. You may already have someone in mind, someone else on your committee, but the graduate chair can give you practical advice—what forms will you have to file?—and other information about professors' interests.

Further, if your original director left a lukewarm reference in your file (that sometimes happens), the graduate chair can have it removed, lest it taint your future possibilities.

(Do not make the mistake made by "Jim," a highly promising graduate student in New York, who had almost completed his dissertation when his director died suddenly, leaving behind a tepid reference letter for Jim. Out of sentiment—or perhaps a strangely rigid loyalty—Jim did not attempt to have the letter removed. As a result, he was never able to get an academic job. Later Jim married a troubled young woman who was receiving interplanetary radio bulletins through the fillings in her teeth—and when last heard from, Jim was supporting them both by selling mortuary slabs in Ohio.)

Ms. Mentor wants you to be wiser, about past and future. For your new director, you will be tempted to seek out someone you like. You've sustained a loss; you'd like comfort. But you most need someone who'll give your career the biggest boosts.

Avoid your original director's enemies (you may not know who they are, but the graduate chair will). Avoid those who've opposed your original director's methodology: if you're a socialist feminist, you don't want someone who scoffs at "that pseudo-Commie crap." Avoid outright sexists and the very territorial: they may want you to rewrite your entire dissertation so it's theirs, with no trace of your original director's hand.

Meanwhile, Ms. Mentor urges you to continue writing. Keeping busy will be consoling and also reassuring to whoever steps in as your next director. You'll be able to show that you're not someone who needs handholding but someone who's a colleague in training. You need a mentor, not a master or a mother.

It is perfectly all right, however, to continue to need Ms. Mentor's impeccable advice.

Every wise academic does.

The Job Hunt

It used to be that, 'round about the time he was finishing his course work and starting on his dissertation, a young man's fancy would turn to his future employment.

And so, he would talk to his major professor, who would call his friends at a select number of schools and find out who needed, for instance, "a man in American literature" or "a new fellow in economics." The major professor would recommend "my brightest student, a fine young man." By the following fall, the young man would be teaching, possibly at an Ivy League university or a fine Seven Sisters college. Most likely he would remain there, easily tenured along the way, for his entire career. Now and then he might publish an article or a review or a poem, but he would not be pushed to do so. Nor could anyone in a small college be expected to do publishable scientific research.

Rather, he would always spend some of his leisure time sipping sherry with students (some of whom might also be his bedmates). He would also pride himself on his taste, culture, and intellect.

Had she known such a young man, Ms. Mentor would have shuddered in his presence, and she would have loathed his major professor. For both were pillars of the establishment that kept out women, and Jews, and open lesbians, and people of color, and anyone else who wasn't, in the terms of the day, "our kind."

Before the 1960s, American colleges were mostly for "our kind," not for the masses. Although the G.I. Bill opened college to many a (male) veteran who might not otherwise have attended, there were still few graduate schools. Many colleges kept blacks out entirely; most colleges also had quotas on Jews and women (who might be restricted to 20 to 40 percent of the student body), and most women students did not finish college. According to Betty Friedan in *The Feminine Mystique* (1963)—a book that Ms. Mentor still highly recommends—some 60 percent of women college students in the 1950s dropped out to marry. Many, presumably, were pregnant, in those days before the Pill (1960) or Roe vs. Wade (1973).

When Stephen Ambrose, later to be the biographer of Richard Nixon and the major historian of D-Day and much more, was finishing his doctorate at the University of Wisconsin in the 1960s, he received twenty-five job offers.

Today, a Stephanie Ambrose would be delighted with *one*.

Ms. Mentor wants women to grow and learn and thrive and share their knowledge—but academic women also need to be realists. There are very few jobs, and the job market for professors has been in an almost continuous slump for a quarter-century. Yet applications to grad schools continue to rise, especially from adults who've been out of school for some years. Often they give their all as teachers and graders and scholars-in-training—and then, there are no permanent positions for them.

The job hunt itself is now a full-time pursuit, for which graduate students need to budget hundreds of dollars for photocopies, dossiers, postage, telephone calls, and travel to the academic conventions where "job markets" are held. There, crammed into overheated hotel rooms, new Ph.D.s may have just thirty minutes with an interviewing committee—half an hour to sell themselves and their life's dream.

Later, in on-campus interviews, would-be assistant professors must be neat, smart, personable, good-humored, thoroughly knowledgeable, and fully alert and engaging, sometimes for two full twelve-hour days that may include meeting up to fifty different people. And even then, offers may be long in coming—or positions may be canceled, thanks to acts of God or state legislatures.

And so aspiring academics are also mortgaging their psyches. They must consider living apart from loved ones who also have careers; they must be willing to be academic gypsies.

In the humanities, it is not uncommon for Ph.D.s to spend five years or more as part-timers or adjuncts or temporary replacements before they finally get on the blessed tenure track. The same is true for post-Ph.D. scientists who spend years moving about as "post-docs." In 1995, for instance, the National Academy of Sciences Committee on Science, Engineering and Public Policy revealed that among chemistry Ph.D.s only about one in five—21 percent—held an academic job.

Although she has many marvelous powers, Ms. Mentor cannot change the American economy, nor conjure up jobs where there are none. But she can help bright new academics—those wise enough to read her—to use their talents effectively. She also recommends that they read and study Mary Morris Heiberger and Julie Miller Vick's excellent book, *The Academic Job Search Handbook* (University of Pennsylvania Press, 1992, 1996).

Then Ms. Mentor will advise them, as in the following exchanges.

Wow! A Clown!

Q: I've been told that vitas and job applications need a "WOW" factor—something with a unique flair. My grad school classmate who wrote her dissertation on the Marquis de Sade plans to wear leather to interviews; another who wrote on menstruation swears she'll have the nerve to wear a white dress with red spots.

My dissertation, though, is just on Elizabethan comedy. I've been a school grind and library rat all my life, except for the crazy summer I spent as Bozo the Clown at an amusement park, where I learned to smoke marijuana and finally got fired when I was found half-dressed and dazed underneath the Thunder Coaster.

How can I wow a hiring committee?

A: Ms. Mentor would say that you do have a wow factor, right under your nose (right where you wore your Bozo honker). She suggests that you delete the part about the dope and the Thunder Coaster, but keep the rest: it's the funny little bit that will make your application letter stand out.

Hiring committees these days have to be ruthless. With five hundred to a thousand people or more applying for each spot, the first screeners—who may be temporary contract employees—have to throw out the dull, the unsigned, the misspelled, the mal-addressed, and the indecipherable, as well as the cringing, the flaky, the morbid, the fanatical, and the psychopathic.

Then hiring committees start their serious reading.

They're hoping desperately to be entertained, entranced, or tricked out of the misery of reading hundreds of letters that sound alike. "I am applying for . . . ," "I have studied . . . ," "My dissertation attempts a synthesis . . . ," "I argue that, contrary to previous theorists . . . ," "I would be happy to meet with you. . . ."

And so Ms. Mentor advises you to announce early in your letter that you have a special something for the job. For instance: "My field is Elizabethan comedy, which I've studied in theory—through my academic work—and in practice, in my summer job as Bozo the Clown. I've found that being Bozo helped me understand the performativity . . ." ("performativity" being one of the chic buzz words for the lit crit crowd . . .).

You can state that playing Bozo the Clown taught you about teaching, which is, after all, a lot like standup comedy. Through your Bozo work, you learned a kind of public polish that aided you when you taught first-year composition . . . And helped you with acting out scenes when you taught Introduction to Literature. . . . (Did it help? Well, say that it did: you'll sound like an engaging teacher.)

A good application letter is a performance with one goal: seducing your audience into interviewing you. Candidates who've sent letters on perfumed or hot pink paper or with words cut out of the newspaper also do get attention—but they're often regarded as unprofessional, and their efforts get posted on mailroom bulletin boards. (Some are even turned over to the police.)

Your letter, though, has a good chance of getting you the coveted interview, whereupon Bozo will help once more. Most academic interviews can be dry: "Tell us about your dissertation"; "What would you like to teach at our university?"; "What are your research plans?"; "What do you see yourself doing five years from now?" Especially after a day of convention interviews, hiring committees will be wiggy with fatigue—at which point someone who can make them laugh may make them weep with relief.

You can be the dashing-but-dignified young woman who amuses and delights even the most jaded codgers with tales of Bozo, the *commedia dell'arte*, and Shakespeare. And be sure to mention *A Midsummer Night's Dream*. To most English Department academics, the character Bottom represents their greatest fear as they stand before a class of adolescents, trying to teach: What if they notice that I'm wearing the head of an ass?

In short, Ms. Mentor congratulates you on having a genuine wow factor, on being able to produce the humor and entertainment that are so lacking, and so wildly appreciated, in these difficult academic times.

Were Ms. Mentor on a hiring committee, you'd undoubtedly be her first choice.

That Old Soft Shoe—Will Nothing Else Do?

Q: Once I finish my Ph.D. (in the social sciences), I figure I'll have spent twenty-two years in school, working up to a first job as a university professor. Yet most hiring is done first by letters (most candidates are screened out), and then with half-hour interviews at our major organization's annual meeting.

I figure I can write a super standout letter that can nab me an interview. But then my whole academic future—including whether I even *have* an academic future—hinges on my "performance" for, say, twenty-eight minutes. Isn't this like being a standup comic (or a bank robber)? Is this the way to run a knowledge industry—making us flit and swoop and strut our stuff like Fred Astaire or Madonna?

I almost wonder if I shouldn't just mail off a videotape of myself dancing, singing, and spieling on my own behalf.

A: What you describe is, indeed, the commencement of a professorial career: the new Ph.D., fresh from the rigors of intellectual competition and bursting with new ideas and enthusiasm for teaching and learning, has to perform a successful dog-and-pony show for half an hour in order to get her foot in the door.

If she fails her audition—and most of those interviewed won't get the role—then it's quite possible that the career and the life she's worked for through all the years of straight As and honor rolls and scholarships and fellowships may all wither, turn to ashes, go down the tubes. (Ms. Mentor's readers may supply their own favorite metaphors.)

Is this fair? No.

But out of injustice, says Ms. Mentor feebly, can sometimes come opportunity.

Not getting an academic job is not the end of the universe as we know it—although after twenty-two straight years of schooling, you may think so. If you'd asked Ms. Mentor's advice much earlier, she would have told you not to leap from college into grad school. Ms. Mentor feels it is much wiser for everyone, even valedictorians and summas and magnas and dean's listers, to dip at least a toe into the Real World. Scholars need the experience of full-time wage earning, office politics, handling bureaucracies and paperwork, dealing with impossible or good bosses, as well as car owning, cat feeding, apartment renting, cooking and cleaning and being adults.

In short, Ms. Mentor would have preferred that you do a real-life research project—"What do I want to be when I grow up?"—rather than plowing straight on through school.

But that is all water under the widget. Now your hurdle is the interview—your audition.

When Ms. Mentor first surveyed the field some fifteen years ago, there were over one hundred fifty books on interviewing, but very few on how to *be* interviewed. More useful, Ms. Mentor found, were business management texts that told candidates the power spot to sit (to the right of the most powerful person in the room); the best time to schedule one's interview (between 9 and 10 A.M. on the second conference day); and odd pitfalls to avoid, such as invading an interviewer's space by placing a handbag or coat on his turf.

Most helpful, though, are advice books for actors on how to audition. Much of what they say about body language and eye contact and firm handshakes applies. Smile; sit comfortably but neither lewdly nor nervously (wear a longish skirt); look directly at everyone; don't fiddle with jewelry, clothes, or lint spots (a good reason not to wear black). Be rested and well-fed (don't skip breakfast); be lively and enthusiastic.

Practice your spiel—the description of your dissertation. Do mock interviews with fellow students, roommates, and faculty members. Get them to ask you obvious, strange, illegal, and rude questions (you'll find samples in letters to Ms. Mentor). Have a couple of clever sound bites, work on looking poised and nonchalant, and remember what actors say about sincerity: once you can fake that, you've won it all.

Likability sells first, and then knowledge. Be ready with well-researched questions about the school (you'll have studied their homepage and their catalog). Know the names of faculty in your field. Suggest what you can do for the department and the school: where you fit in, what unique talents you can offer.

And afterward, if you don't get the job, do not blame yourself. A now-famous biographer once lost a job at Amherst solely because at her Modern Language Association convention interview, the hotel room's fireplace went berserk and began spewing black smoke into the room—whereupon our heroine had an uncontrollable coughing fit and could not complete the interview.

Sometimes real life intervenes. You won't interview well if you've just had a death in the family, or your wallet's just been stolen. (That happened to a young woman Ms. Mentor knows, and she wonders if an envious classmate was sabotaging her interview.)

But self-blame is useless, and Ms. Mentor urges you to persevere. Actors *do* get jobs, and so do academics, and much of it is a matter of technique. With practice, you will get better. Ms. Mentor can guarantee that.

Not Moby Dick

Q: When our annual job market convention comes up, I'm going to be seven months' pregnant, and unmarried. (Suffice it to say, the father of my child is a very generous, handsome rogue who likes to spread his seed into every available furrow.)

Given the fact that I may look like a whale and won't want to answer questions about my "husband," should I

A.   Not bother to go, since I won't get a job anyway?
B.   Go, and hope for the best?
C.   Lace myself up tightly, claim to be fat, and hope I don't have a conniption fit?

A: Ms. Mentor votes for B, but acknowledges that you do have a problem: many a hiring committee won't see past a big belly to appreciate a big brain.

Still, the convention will be your only chance this year. If you do get interviews, prepare a few little jokes about the forthcoming event and claim you have perfectly reliable child-care arrangements (whether you do or not). Your mission is to neutralize the obvious question: Are you a mom or a professor?

Sometimes, truly, lying works best, such as claiming that you have a husband who's a freelance writer who'll be doing child care at home.

But Ms. Mentor does not encourage you to lie. She only presents alternatives, and trusts you to make the best choices.

Just avoid having a conniption fit. It will make a permanently negative impression.

A Matter Of Morals

Q: "Tell us about your morals," said a group interviewing me at our job market convention. I told them I was raised among Pentecostals and snake-handlers (true), but that now I go to a Presbyterian church (rarely), and don't smoke or shoplift. I didn't mention that I do drink wine and that I have sex with my boyfriend in a non-missionary position.

What kind of question is that: "Tell us about your morals?" Is it legal? How should I have answered it?

A: Ms. Mentor is reminded that a decade or two ago, one very Christian university became famous at the Modern Language Association convention for asking such questions of job candidates. It seemed that a faculty member had recently absconded with a student—and her morals—and his ex-colleagues didn't want it to happen again. Naturally, of course, the university became notorious at MLA for being the only school whose interviewers mentioned Sex.

Are such questions legal? Probably, although they do border on asking about "creed," and maybe marital status as well.

How should you have answered them? Ms. Mentor thinks you did fine. You were honest and tactful, considering the provocation.

Whether you could actually fit into such a community, if the job is offered, is another question—but you haven't asked that. So Ms. Mentor, with her usual prudence, will remain silent.

Without Cane, Yet Able

Q: I'm worried about how best to present my disability during job interviews. I have a degenerative hip condition, and I've been advised not to walk long distances, stand for long periods, or climb stairs. However, in a pinch, I am able to do all these things, and on good days my limp is not immediately apparent.

I'm worried that at interviews people will see me sitting down at every opportunity, and taking the elevator whenever possible, and assume I am lazy. In fact, one college where I teach as an adjunct has expressed concern (behind my back, of course) over my "low energy level." Since I actually am very energetic (otherwise I'd never be able to work full-time and complete a dissertation), I believe they are reacting to my disability.

I don't want interviewers to get the impression I'm lazy, but I don't want to be constantly explaining, "I'm using the elevator because I'm disabled." I could try to "pass" by climbing stairs, etc., but I'm not sure dishonesty is a good idea. (Besides, I might hurt myself.)

Have you any advice for me?

A: Ms. Mentor was particularly pleased to receive this missive, for it lets her point out a fact that few people want to face: Anyone who does not have a disability now will either have one later, or be dead first.

Thus disability rights are everyone's cause. Ms. Mentor recommends the excellent book *Feminism and Disability*, by Barbara Hillyer, and advises all pre-disabled individuals to get to know the Americans with Disabilities Act (1990), the civil rights bill for the disabled. (A Q & A later in this book discusses the ADA in greater detail.)

Besides inspiring Ms. Mentor to remodel her ivory tower to make it more accessible, the ADA has pushed colleges and hotels to come up with ramps, elevators, parking spaces, and many an ingenious modification to let folks with disabilities gad about just like the pre-disabled.

You, however, have a mostly hidden disability, which your colleagues interpret as laziness rather than as a handicap. That's not altogether bad: to an employer worried about health costs, you are not a "problem." Moreover, your ability to do many things at once—finish a dissertation, teach full time, and correspond with Ms. Mentor—shows you to be well organized and energetic.

But what about job interviews? Most academic conventions, held in hotels, won't present problems—for rare is the candidate with so many interviews that she does not have time in between for caffeine, rest, snacks, or scheming.

On-campus interviews, though, can blow your cover.

In an ideal world, of course, you'd simply announce that you have a disability, perhaps adding that since Elizabeth Taylor and Liza Minnelli also have hip problems, it's obviously a special scourge besetting glamorous women. (If you can say this in laughing self-deprecation, you'll be regarded as quite witty.) In an ideal world, potential colleagues would see your need for rest as another charming quality in a brilliant woman.

But in the real world, Ms. Mentor knows, you might be stereotyped not as lazy, but as "crippled," with all the unspoken bigotries that evokes. You might be patronized, or your disability might be used (covertly) as an excuse not to hire you: "Can we afford . . . ?" The Americans with Disabilities Act, like Affirmative Action, encourages well-intentioned people and smites the most egregious, but it cannot tell Ableist U. that they must hire you.

And so what you have is an educational challenge: How do you teach possible bosses to see past your disability to your many unique talents? How can you make your disability unimportant—or even turn it into an advantage?

You've already mentioned the simplest way out: to pretend you don't have a disability at all. But that entails risks ("I might hurt myself"). And over a two-day visit, you know you'll need to sit down often, while your hosts might be expecting you to hoof long distances in snow and ice.

You could be "found out."

Here Ms. Mentor reminds her learned readers that academia today is a tough world. Your choices aren't really whether to be hired "as disabled" or as "not disabled." The real question for any job candidate is: How can I get hired at all?

And so Ms. Mentor proposes a different strategy for your consideration: hiding in plain sight. Rather than concealing your disability, you might decide to flaunt it, by getting a crutch or a cane—a wooden one, so that your disability seems temporary. You can casually tell hirers ahead of time that you've been injured and will be using a "sympathy stick." The point is to make the disability visible—but transcendable.

Before your talk, you can prepare small talk and little jokes about your new implement. You can freely say that since you've had the crutch or cane for only a couple of weeks, you're not completely comfortable with it. You hope that everyone will sympathize; you don't know how long you'll have to use it.

In a presentation, you can tell your audience, "I wish I had two legs to stand on." If it's germane, you can comment on famous characters with disabilities—on Lord Byron's clubfoot, or Alexander Pope's crooked spine, or the Hunchback of Notre Dame. You can note that Charles Dickens's Tiny Tim and his crutch are still trotted out to do good every Christmas. (If you feel, as Ms. Mentor does, that Tim is a mawkish little twit, surpassed only by the truly insufferable Barney—you should keep that critical insight to yourself.)

You can even complain with gentle humor, "I wanted to get ribbons for my crutch in your university's colors, but they didn't have them where I live." Ms. Mentor predicts that your hosts will find this enormously flattering—and before you leave campus, someone will almost certainly come up with the ribbons, and maybe even a pennant.

Is this deceptive?

Has anyone lied?

No. And you will also have shown possible future colleagues that people with disabilities aren't freaks, self-pitiers, cripples, or fragile pieces of glass. Your good humor about your disability cannot help but be winning, like the cagey wit of Lily Tomlin's paraplegic character Crystal. (When a kid asks, "Are you a ride?" the wheelchaired Crystal says she's the best ride there ever was. And unlike walkies, she never has to worry about getting hurt.)

Ms. Mentor recommends that you listen to Lily Tomlin's routines, memorize them, and filch lines shamelessly: telling a story well is one sign of a good teacher. Unless your hosts have hearts of stone and souls of steel, those who meet you will root for you. They'll feel good watching you succeed; they'll be kind to you; they'll laugh with you.

You'll also have won in the main challenge for all job candidates, disabled or pre-disabled: How do I stand out from the crowd and make them want me?

When the hiring faculty makes its decision, you'll be memorable: "the woman with the crutch and the terrific sense of humor." They'll like your style; they'll congratulate themselves on having the good sense to hire you despite the "handicap" they witnessed. (And if they don't offer you the job, some of them will feel very guilty. That's good.)

But even Ms. Mentor cannot guarantee that you'll be hired—whether you hide your disability or flaunt it. Some faculties are hopelessly dour and sour, dedicated to shooting themselves in the foot. Two decades ago, for instance, the University of Wisconsin rejected a stellar junior candidate because they felt she was "too lively"—and she now edits the major journal in American literature.

But for now, Ms. Mentor emphasizes, all you need is a foot in the door. After that, your hip and the rest of you will follow.

Any university will be lucky to have you, and for your best asset: your brain.

Telephone Tremors

Q: As a job seeker, I've experienced a new form of hiring torture: the telephone interview. I have come close to only two tenure-track jobs in two years. Both have used telephone interviews to narrow their field of candidates from ten to the three they would invite to campus.

The first phone interview came at 8 P.M., with a male interviewer who introduced himself and asked if this was a good time to talk. He mentioned the name of his school, and quickly reaching for pen and paper, I wrote a note to my companion to retrieve my application file. I had applied to 104 colleges that year and had absolutely no recollection of this particular school. The conversation went poorly; the interviewer was not in my discipline (he held a fine arts degree in photography); and I didn't know the needs of his institution. I vowed never to let myself be taken by surprise like that again.

So, the following year, I developed a strategy. If a phone-interview call came out of the blue, I would politely express great interest in the caller and the institution, but say that this was not a good time to talk and suggest that we arrange a convenient time for the next day. Then I'd have twenty-four hours to get to the library, read the catalog, and prepare my answers.

Another call did come, and I used my line. The caller assured me that this was not a phone interview—just a check to see if I was still interested and available. Of course I was, and wanted to sound enthusiastic. But then the conversation became very uncomfortable, though I tried to remain open and friendly and buy myself time to do my homework.

The caller (a woman) wanted to know if I had questions: in particular, did I need information about elementary schools in the area? Did I plan to buy a house? She was obviously fishing for information about my marital and family status.

As I later learned, the college is in a tiny, insular community with fewer than thirty faculty. I wonder if an unmarried young woman would have been a threat to this interviewer or the college community, for it was clearly a screening call. The interviewer asked no questions about my qualifications or experience, and though I politely asked twice to talk at a better time, she kept insisting that this was not an interview.

She finished the half-hour phone call by assuring me that the committee did not yet have a process for narrowing the field of candidates and that they would be contacting me within the next week. She arranged for the school to send a large packet of information, which I read carefully; I also studied the catalog on microfiche. But after hearing nothing in ten days, I called the school and was told that three candidates had been invited to the campus and I was not one of them.

Was there anything I could have done? What can I take from this to be better prepared for the next round of hiring?

A: Ms. Mentor was deeply saddened by your letter. Torture by telephone—now you hear it, now you don't—is very cruel.

Yes, of course, Ms. Mentor knows why departments do such things. They are screening candidates; they cannot afford to invite all the good ones to campus; and it's as good a method as any in their eyes.

But it's not.

No one would expect to be given a syllabus and told to teach a Shakespeare class five minutes later; no one should be expected to summon up, after 104 job letters, the perfect recollection and exactly matching enthusiasm that an interviewer wants. Nor should "cold" calls be made, without previous appointments. And illegal questions—seeking information about marital status—should be barred. The only job seekers who do well under such circumstances are the glib, the mendacious, and the idiosyncratic who do somehow memorize everything. (Such unusual beings used to be called "idiot savants.")

But as there's no way to stop diabolical departments, the best you can do is to be always prepared.

Ms. Mentor advises you to get a big accordion-style, alphabetized folder, into which you file all 104 job applications, each with its original job description. Then get on the Internet and download each university's homepage—and each department's, if there is one.

Print out the homepages, highlight in different colors the essentials, and file them with your applications. For each school, you can also attach two or more positively phrased questions to ask, such as, "Yours seems like an excellent collection of environmental studies courses. Do you encourage faculty to continue developing new and interesting courses?" or "You have a very large popular arts program. What do your students find especially attractive?" or "I'm impressed with the internship opportunities for students. How are those arranged?"

(Ms. Mentor hopes that sage readers will see the value of positive questions: they flatter the interviewer. Conversely, "What are you racist fart-knockers doing about your piss-ant legislature?" won't get you hired at a state university.)

Now you're prepared for all calls—if you keep the accordion folder within reach at all times. Should you sleep with it? Should you get call-waiting? Probably yes, sighs Ms. Mentor, for if you're not available, conscienceless callers will go on to the next person.

Ms. Mentor also grieves: this is no way to treat future colleagues. When you do land a tenure-track job, Ms. Mentor hopes that you will not forget what you have endured. For only those who are hired can, in the future, make hiring humane.

Wifey

Q: I followed my husband to his faculty job, in the humanities, at a research university. I wasn't finished with my dissertation, and so I took an instructor position in the same department. Now I've finished my Ph.D., but no one sees me as anything but His Wife. How can I improve my status and get a tenure-track job?

A: You are a "trailing spouse," a "deflected woman"—terms used by Nadya Aisenberg and Mona Harrington in their excellent book, *Women of Academe: Outsiders in the Sacred Grove*. They point out that following hubby's job is the single biggest way to derail your own career. But you didn't ask Ms. Mentor's advice in time, and now all she can do is offer two suggestions:

1. Find out if instructors ever do ascend to tenure-track assistant professorships in your university. At most schools, it's impossible, but if you know someone who did it, find out how. (Often there's a rich but unsavory story associated with people who make such a leap: rumors of sexual favors, bribes, and blackmail abound. At one Middle Atlantic university, the wife of an assistant professor in English reportedly went down on her

knees, slobbering and crying over the department chair's hands, begging for a tenure-track job—which she got.)

2. Write and publish a book, to make yourself eligible for tenure-track and tenured jobs elsewhere, and resign yourself to a commuter marriage. Do not be "place-bound" as a "captive spouse."

If you were in science, there would be ways you could work under (the terminology is unfortunate) your husband: you could be a research associate on his grant, for instance. You might even seek your own grant money. But such niches are not available in the humanities.

Ms. Mentor wishes you well in what is really a very small universe of choices.

One Trick Lady

Q: What happens if I hedge about my marital status or sexuality in a job interview?

A: Ms. Mentor recalls the old saw from Archilochus, the wild and wily seventh-century (B.C.) poet: "The fox has many tricks; the hedgehog only one. A good one."

Sting 'em before they sting you is indeed one approach to illegal questions, and many a job candidate has fantasized doing just that:

> "You've got your nerve asking if I'm married, you slimy pigface! Just because no one would ever marry your ilk!"

> "Of course I'm a lesbian! Especially if you're one of the alternatives!"

> "How dare you ask me that! I'll sue your butt off!"

But in real life, one has to be foxy, not prickly.

Interviewers legally are not supposed to inquire about a candidate's race or sex (although those are usually obvious)—nor about marital status, national origin, religion, or handicap. In some states, sexual orientation is also a no-no (it should be an illegal question everywhere, opines Ms. Mentor).

But when they hold all the cards, interviewers who want to can ignore the rules. And if a candidate even says, meekly, "Do you know that such questions are illegal?" that's an obvious criticism of the questioner, and there goes the job.

And so Ms. Mentor concludes, with regret and distaste, that unless you can afford to turn down a job, the only way to handle illegal questions is to answer them. Indeed, any female candidate must be prepared for unlawful, strange, or intrusive queries.

Ms. Mentor recommends these responses:

"Yes, I'm married, and my spouse is a freelancer." That answers the university's worry about whether the spouse will be expecting the department to procure him a job. Once a position is offered, the candidate may indeed want to negotiate a job for her partner. But at the first interview, the best strategy is to make the spouse not part of the equation at all.

—or—

"No, I'm not married. I'll be going to a new job alone (or with my children)." Or (with an engaging smile): "I'll be coming with my cats (or with my golden retriever)." Pets are often a better selling point than children.

—or—

"I've always considered my sexuality a private thing." But (1) "I do have a partner, a freelancer who'll be coming with me." *Or* (2) "I live alone, don't date students, and like to think I get along well with everyone in my university community."

All these answers are best said with a calm smile. For a woman in academe, there is no perfect marital/sexual status: everyone knows that even nuns sometimes forsake their vows.

The best you can do is to be dignified, precise, and good-humored—exactly the kind of person everyone wants to hire. Then your marital/sexual arrangements, disabilities, or other problems will fade away in the eyes of the interviewers. The department, in its collective wisdom, will *have* to have you.

Mrs. Higginbotham-Vanderlingen-Schnickelpuzenski

Q: I'm finishing my dissertation soon, getting married, and going on the job market. What name should I put on the dissertation?

A: Ms. Mentor believes all women should keep their original last names ("maiden names") throughout their lives. When your name stays the same, your high school classmates will always know that It's You doing those wonderful or notorious things. Then they can swell with pride, writhe with envy, or spread vicious but delectable rumors when you win your Oscar or Nobel prize.

Changing your name with marriage sends the wrong message (that you're your husband's property). It's also impractical, since the average American marriage lasts less than seven years. Elizabeth Taylor, after all, has never changed her name.

Worst of all is a hyphenated name. No one will ever quite catch what your name is; they won't know where to alphabetize you; and your paychecks will always be mislaid. You will be unmasked as someone who flaunts her heterosexuality. Hiring committees will know you're married, which to them smells like "a problem": what to do with hubby. Often they'll solve the problem by just not interviewing or hiring you.

A rose by any other name . . . no, says Ms. Mentor. Keep your own name. It smells the sweetest.

Black's Not Me

Q: I am an African American woman who's getting a doctorate in Victorian literature. At our last academic convention, I had the most interviews of anyone in our department—eleven, in fact—and I even had half a dozen job offers before I left the conference. And *every one* of those offers was for a job teaching African American literature.

Now I'm certainly proud of my race, and I believe Black Is Beautiful, but it's not my intellectual field. I like African American literature to read for pleasure, but my dissertation is on Charlotte Brontë. What can I do about this blatant and absurd tokenism? Should I just figure that *any* job is a foot in the door, and that I can always publish my way back to Charlotte Brontë?

A: Ms. Mentor says Yes.

You are lucky enough to be in the only sought-after cohort in literary hirings: African American scholars, especially those working in African American literature. This is your chance to turn the tables and get a genuine employment advantage.

Ms. Mentor advises you not to turn down any university right away. Find out what they're offering. Will they agree, in writing, that you'll teach at least one Victorian course a year? Will you get released time to read up on African American literature, and to mentor black students? Will you have a research assistant and a grader if you're expected to teach large classes?

Can they guarantee you a Tuesday–Thursday teaching schedule so you'll have the other days free for research and writing? Will they agree in writing that your publications in Victorian literature will count toward tenure, along with anything you might publish in African American literature? Does everyone understand that you're developing a research agenda in two fields, not one?

And whatever salary they offer, ask for more. Raises are a percentage of what you're already earning, so start as high as you can.

And by now there are undoubtedly some readers who are thinking, "How crass! How materialistic!" But Ms. Mentor thinks all women should earn good salaries and should be rewarded for what they bring to their jobs. You bring a great deal, and you should get paid handsomely.

Charlotte Brontë, who wrote so eloquently about the poverty of governesses, would definitely approve.

Space Of My Own

Q: After three years as a post-doc (I'm in chemistry), I've finally been offered a tenure-track job at "Z" State University. But the research I do requires a great deal of equipment, which has to be housed in lab space. I'm not sure that Z State has the money or room for it all. As a woman in my small subfield, I have no female colleagues—nor, for that matter, do I have any male mentors. And so I turn to Ms. Mentor: How do I make sure that my research—which, I know, will be the major way I'm evaluated— isn't skunked from the start by equipment screwups?

A: Were it not considered pointless in our practical modern era, Ms. Mentor would wish for everyone to study such subjects as philology and literary criticism. Books are so easy, so cheap, so sturdy, and so portable. You can even mark them up with pencils and never lose your data.

But enough ancient musings.

Ms. Mentor, who often exhorts women to go into science, is full of admiration for the pioneers who are so often The Only Woman in the Lab,

The Only Woman at the Table. Besides coping with sexism, sexual harassment, and all the other discriminations bright women are always heir to, women in science are often isolated from any peers at all. (They are, of course, infinitely superior to their male colleagues. They've had to be.)

And so women scientists must create their own networks, which many are doing admirably. The Association for Women in Science (AWIS) has some six thousand members; the Society of Women Engineers is thriving on many a campus; and rare is the science journal that does not have a "Special Issue on Women" at least every year or two. For pleasure and enlightenment, Ms. Mentor also recommends the writings of Sue V. Rosser, virtually the only scientist who is also a director of Women's Studies. Her works (listed in Ms. Mentor's bibliography) are exceptionally good gifts for the "sensitive men" on your list.

But now, having done what a proper researcher should do—reviewed the literature, declared her theoretical perspectives—Ms. Mentor will answer your question about equipment and lab space.

It all comes down to money, of course—and right now you're in the best position you'll ever be to get what you want. Once a university has offered you the job, it's a courtship, and you get to negotiate the terms of the marriage. When the salary's mentioned, pause and say, "I'd like a bit more." (They're not going to flee: they've decided they want you, and a new job search is much too expensive.)

Also say, "I'll need some commitments to do my research effectively"—whereupon Z State will ask, "What do you need?"

At that point you brainstorm. Although you have no official mentor, Ms. Mentor points out that you can find a whole network of informal ones. Get on the Net and ask other scientists what you should ask for (but be tactful: Z State faculty can be on-line, too). Consult your dissertation director, your post-doc bosses, and anyone else who's ever supervised your research. They've presumably written you good recommendations, and you flatter them by asking their advice.

Make a list of everything you *might* need, including software, personnel, and office supplies. Ask for more than you need. Ms. Mentor knows one new Ph.D. in veterinary medicine who, to her own amazement, was allocated a research associate paid for with "hard money" (university funds). Everyone else had to make do with whatever grant-funding ("soft money") they could raise on their own, but our heroine got the associate line: she was new, and she asked.

Send your wish list (but *don't* call it that) to the department chair or dean negotiating with you, and ask politely for a written commitment. *Unless you cannot afford the delay, do not sign your contract until you have a written commitment for the lab space and equipment you need.*

When you arrive at Z University, Ms. Mentor warns you, you may not have everything you were promised (such is the world of shrinking science today: it's more often incompetence or lack of funds, rather than sexism). Still, you will almost certainly have less lab space than you wanted, and possibly less equipment. But the letter of commitment is your contract to ask for what you're entitled to—nicely, but repeatedly.

If Z really is not coming through, start quietly researching alternatives. (You can, of course, file a grievance or sue—but only if you want to make quick and deadly enemies.) Try creative solutions instead. A Southern engineering researcher, desperate for extra space, got a new lab at a local half-empty research park, where the staff said they were "honored" to have her with them. (They even gave her a free parking space.) An East Coast researcher with mounds of equipment arranged for extra, unused space at a closing-down U.S. Navy facility. In both cases, the researchers gained new friends, appreciators, and recommenders for grants, tenure, or other jobs.

Although you may spend your whole career at Z University, always keep alert to other opportunities: sabbaticals, retrainings, institutes, conferences. Get to know powerful senior professors. Especially in science, where peer review is the norm, one must Be Known.

Too, the world of science is in a ferment today, as government funding folds. You're among the most talented and lucky ones to have a tenure-track job—plus you're wise enough to write Ms. Mentor for advice.

Surely you're on your way to being a star.

Sneering and Sniding

Q: I've just been subjected to the world's snidest job interview. How can I get revenge?

A: Ms. Mentor presumes that you are seeking an assistant professorship, for the truly snide job interviews rarely take place on the senior level. (There, people turn smarmy instead.)

Ms. Mentor can also imagine the nature of the snideness. Condescending and sexist remarks; maybe racist or homophobic ones, too. Your age or appearance may have been a matter of comment; your marital status may have been discussed; and you may have been asked inappropriate, embarrassing, or crude questions about nonprofessional matters.

(A job candidate at a former teachers' college in New Jersey was once asked her opinion of pantyhose. And then the interviewer told her, in graphic detail, what he thought about undergarments that kept him from getting at . . . , whereupon the candidate stood up abruptly and said she needed to go to the bathroom. When she returned, that particular interviewer was no longer in the room.)

Since many of the snidest questions are illegal, and all are unethical if not rude, Ms. Mentor suspects that you would like her to roar: "Sue the scumbags!" But Ms. Mentor cannot do so. She would never utter the word "scumbag" (she prefers "malefactor," "miscreant," or "ill-bred ding-a-ling"). She also knows that a lawsuit would be a waste of time and money.

There are, of course, other forms of revenge, some civilized and some not. A harmless treat is to rent *9 to 5* (Jane Fonda, Dolly Parton, Lily Tomlin) and chortle at the superb revenge fantasy sequence. Less benign is to send strange or unexpected gifts in the mail. A literary character—perhaps in an Erica Jong novel?—once got satisfactory revenge by sending used tampons to a swain who mistreated her. More recently, a singer in the band L7 threw a used tampon at a disrespectful audience member. Ms. Mentor shudders at the indelicacy.

There are also grandiose ways to kill with kindness. An acquaintance of Ms. Mentor's once sent a disliked relative a life-sized Mexican statue of a donkey, which threw the recipient into a tizzy: Was the donkey a tacky piece of kitsch or a rare find in folk art? Was it an insult or a tribute? The stymied recipient gnashed teeth for days.

But your response should be simpler, and unfailingly gracious. Do write notes to all the miscreants, thanking them for their interest in you. If acquaintances inquire, you can suggest the truth through subtle aspersions: "They were interested in me, but—well, you know the ____ Department at ____ University. Personalities *do* always get in the way." Be enigmatic; smile ruefully.

Ms. Mentor implores you not to tell the story publicly until you have tenure at a place where you intend to stay. Academia is small, and word does get around, and there will always be someone who wants to blame the victim (you) for whatever happened.

Nevertheless, you *can* manage to make the story known. Tell your closest friends (and your mentor, if you have one) exactly what happened, in minutest detail. Then *they*—not you—can spread the word, and the ill-bred ding-a-lings will quickly become the subject of sly innuendo and wicked satire. You can also write up the entire event, a few details changed, and send it to *Lingua Franca*, *Concerns*, or another suitable journal, to be published anonymously or pseudonymously.

But what if you get the job offer? It can happen, even after an interview from hell. *And what if it is your only offer?*

Ms. Mentor says to take the job and love it: consider it a stepping stone. You can learn about teaching and have time to publish; and it's much easier to get a job once you've had one. (At the university where Ms. Mentor currently parks her ivory tower, almost every new assistant professor started out with a temporary job somewhere else.) From the malefactors, you can learn how to conduct yourself gracefully in an adversarial culture. On your own, you can continue to apply for jobs elsewhere—but in the meantime, collecting a paycheck may be the best revenge.

And once you're safely tenured and happy somewhere else, you can always think about sending them a donkey.

The Conference Scene

A distraught reader writes to Ms. Mentor:

> I gave a paper—my first—at our major professional conference. It's very prestigious, and hardly any graduate students' papers are ever accepted. Yet not one of my professors attended my session. I was crushed. Is there any explanation for their behavior?

Indeed there is, and this was the start of Ms. Mentor's reply:

> Ms. Mentor hopes that you did not spend any time crying into your pillow. Mourning for boors is a waste of one's time, faculties, and tear ducts.
>
> Ms. Mentor also deplores the absence of your professors at your *début*—the understudy becomes a star!—although she is not surprised. Ms. Mentor is a venerable and jaded soul, who knows that too many entrenched senior professors see the younger generation not as followers in the pursuit of pure knowledge, but as upstarts who need to be humiliated or ignored. Especially among academic men, it is an Oedipal drama, in which the fathers and sons try to crush each other.
>
> Women, though, need not act in that play, and it is a far, far better thing to learn to work the conference scene for your own knowledge and pleasure.

Still, you may ask yourself, or Ms. Mentor: Why *do* senior professors so rarely attend other people's conference presentations? Do they know it all?

Do they have back trouble, so that they cannot bear more than a few minutes in the spindly, grotesquely uncomfortable chairs that pass for furniture in most convention hotels?

Ms. Mentor suspects it's something else: that senior professors are playing their own version of Scarlett O'Hara's Approach to Life. As Margaret Mitchell notes early in *Gone with the Wind*, when her heroine is just sixteen: "Scarlett O'Hara could never long endure any conversation of which she was not the chief subject." Similarly, many a full professor cannot bear any presentation in which he and his work are not at the center.

(Here Ms. Mentor murmurs to her astute readers that this is the same behavior exhibited by the famous Hollywood director who reportedly spent several hours—well, forty-five minutes—in a monologue about his own greatness, only to turn to his hapless audience of one and say, "Well, enough about me. What do *you* think of my latest picture?")

Most senior professors would rather be stars—either as presenters or as subjects of the admiring papers of young graduate students. Such adoration being hard to come by, most wind up opting out of the big national conferences in favor of smaller, invitational ones. Those are also valuable for another reason: they're more apt to pay their speakers, since the honor is not sufficient reward.

What are the rewards for attending an academic conference?

There is intellectual stimulation. Academics go to conferences to share their research findings, compare notes on what they've discovered, and ask pointed and useful questions about the research of other scholars. This goal is usually achieved among scientists, for whom conference papers have standard formats (such as poster sessions) and visual aids (especially slides) that cannot help but produce a coherent, well-organized presentation.

Ms. Mentor has, in fact, often been enlightened at the conferences orchestrated by scientists, who even provide entertainment for "the wives" (although they no longer make the purpose so obvious). At the American Association for the Advancement of Science meeting in New Orleans, for instance, a session on the Scoville Scale for the hotness of peppers inspired hordes of conference-goers to try to outmacho each other at local restaurants. (Only one actually managed to finish a habañero pepper, 300,000 on the Scoville Scale. An ordinary bell pepper is zero; a tabasco pepper is 9,000 to 12,000.)

But enough of Ms. Mentor and her bite—although with the proliferation of regional cuisines in the U.S., new taste treats are another good motive for attending academic conferences in faraway places. Many wise organizations do make a point of meeting in cities that offer good eating and good touring, such as New Orleans, San Antonio, and San Francisco.

Ms. Mentor also reminds fledgling scholars that conferences are your professional orientation, and you must attend them. Yes, she knows that many a graduate student or new faculty member will say, "I can't afford to pay my own way," but in truth, you cannot afford not to. Conferences are the places where you make a professional name.

The fortunate graduate student will have a mentor to teach her the ropes, but even without one, she can learn the protocol from the major academic journals in her field, as well as the weekly *Chronicle of Higher Education*. She should get into the habit of reading "the *Chronicle*" regularly, and preferably in public.

For every conference that is not thoroughly invitational, there are calls for papers and proposals issued months (sometimes years) ahead of time— in journals, in flyers posted on graduate school bulletin boards, in targeted mailings, and more recently on the Net. The deadlines and procedures for paper proposals must be taken seriously and literally: if they want an abstract, send an abstract; if they want the complete paper, send a complete paper. Follow directions carefully, be neat, use good white paper and dark print, and you will not be summarily weeded out.

What else separates the rejects from the accepted papers?

Ideally, all accepted papers are well organized, with new but solid information that's presentable within twenty to thirty minutes. Solid papers do not rely on snoozers, those vague platitudes and blowhard generalities that make your eyes glaze over, such as: "The new Computer Age technologies present challenges for us all . . . ," or "We live in a time of transition in which our political system must evolve to meet the challenges of global . . . ," or "Brazil (or anywhere) is a land of contrasts . . . ," or "We must stop this carnage on our nation's highways."

How can you guarantee that your paper's accepted?

Sometimes, yes, it is a matter of politics—of who knows whom—and you can only get to know the Big People by attending conferences, or by insinuating yourself into their vision via a mentor.

But where the competition's open, as it usually is, papers that are accepted in the sciences are ones that show methodological rigor and present significantly new information.

In the humanities and social sciences, some fields reward the creation of new jargon. But at the most intellectually stimulating and entertaining conferences, the most-favored papers are those containing at least two of Ms. Mentor's Three Major Requirements: Gossip, Humor, and New Information.

Some organizations even change, wisely, to suit Ms. Mentor's requirements. For instance, the Modern Language Association, once noted for stuffiness and pomposity, has now become notorious and lewd, with such papers as "Jane Austen and the Masturbating Girl" and "Emily Dickinson's Clitoral Imagery." At other literary conferences, scandalous and rediscovered gossip about the long-dead and formerly respectable has become especially welcome (sometimes it's called "The New Historicism"). "Why Did George Eliot's New Young Husband Throw Himself into the Venetian Grand Canal?" is a crowd-pleaser; and so is "Would Kate Chopin Get Tenure at LSU?" Secrets always sell.

If you are an entertaining and enlightening presenter, conference and panel organizers—and audiences—will love you. They may hire you. And you may, within a couple of years, even get paid for speaking.

Conference presentations are significant. Especially among grad students, they're often the subject of great interest and debate.

But the major purpose of academic conferences is to network, gossip, and conspire with one's peers. *Always wear your name tag at a conference, and have business cards made and ready to share.* Out of conference meetings come jobs, recommendations, knowledge, and (yes!) more conferences. For each year a few of the luckiest or most tenacious graduate students do manage to meet the big stars in their fields and impress the Great Ones with the youngsters' devotion and possible future importance.

But returning to the original query: Ms. Mentor thinks it would be kind and gratifying if professors did attend the presentations of their graduate students. Some do. Some even offer warm praise, not just gruff critiques.

After all, professors should know that the graduate students at Hometown University are *not* competition. They are *not* after the jobs of the Hometown faculty.

They're after everyone else's.

Fashionable in Academia?

Q: My first big-time academic conference is coming up this year. What should I wear?

A: Ms. Mentor knows that many readers will consider this question frivolous, not in keeping with the high dignity of the scholarly calling. But they will be wrong.

Presentation of self is vital in academia, and it is still possible to dress for success—or for failure. (Interested scholars are referred to Susan Faludi's *Backlash* for the ways in which the "dress for success" suit was replaced by the little-girl look, to the great detriment of women.) The best clothes for a professional woman to wear to a big-time academic conference are dresses or skirts that no one will notice or remember: not too tight, not too short, not too colorful.

Ms. Mentor sympathizes with a not-uncommon urge to be acutely fashionable or flamboyant, but she advises young women in particular to resist that urge. It is difficult for many academic men, who do the hiring and judging, to take young women seriously. It is impossible if the young women are not dressed in a mature, even slightly frumpy manner.

A Polite Rejoinder

After Ms. Mentor published the above answer in *Concerns* in 1992, she received the following response from a reader whose missive was signed "Chic in Canada":

Reader's Reply

I cannot resist commenting from my particularly anti-ageist perspective that your otherwise delightful advice in the "Ms. Mentor" column about how the prospective job candidate should dress is inappropriate, and perhaps positively risky, for the female candidate who actually is "mature." The middle-aged female job candidate should, in my opinion, *avoid* looking "frumpy" at all costs—or should I say, even to the tune of considerable "cost." A frumpy-looking, middle-aged candidate is almost sure to be immediately typed as frumpy-dumpy in her politics and scholarship as well.

My advice is that any candidate past the age of thirty should abide by the three "E's" when dressing for interviews: she should appear earthy, ethnic, or elegant, whichever style she thinks she can carry off the best. The earthy and ethnic styles tend to create an excellent impression these days, but if, say, the candidate happens to be small, blond (perhaps even streaked with gray!), and Caucasian, they may not work for her.

In any case, I advise her to strive for a quietly—and not too obviously expensive—elegance of style. Her outfit should be dignified, chic, reasonably "with it," but not ostentatious or attention-grabbing in any way. But not frumpy or, horrors, really *mature*. Her "outward" appearance should, on the contrary, represent her "inward" youthfulness of mind. . . .

The Conclusion

Following the above communication, Ms. Mentor and "Chic in Canada" had a *tête-à-tête* (an international fashion summit) and reached a *rapprochement* on the subject of the proper attire for academic conference interviews.

They agree that understated elegance can be valuable; that miniskirts are always incorrect, because they look childish; that pants can be risky, for conservative schools; and that dressing as a Wall Street banker (gray flannel, little tie) will seem too powerful, and therefore out of place, in academia. Ms. Mentor retains some skepticism about "earthy" and "ethnic," especially if "ethnic" means turbans and swirling fringe, but she and "Chic in Canada" agree that colorful scarves are tasteful and welcome accessories.

Ms. Mentor and "Chic in Canada" also welcome additions to their dialogue.

Squelched

Q: I've been gagged! The paper I proposed for a literary convention was accepted, and the organizers put me on a panel of four people, scheduled between 1 : 30 and 3 on the second afternoon of the conference.

Presenter One (male) took forty-five minutes; Presenter Two (male) took thirty; and Presenter Three squeezed hers into fifteen (even leaving off one page). And I didn't get to give mine at all.

Presenter Three, who wasn't at fault, apologized to me. The others, and the panel chair(man), acted like I didn't exist. I slunk into the bathroom and blubbered, and spent the rest of the conference feeling vile. Should I have screamed during the first presentation? Should I send a nasty letter to Presenter One, or the chair, or the organization?

And what should I do with my paper?

A: Ms. Mentor thinks there should be a Bill of Rights for conference speakers and attenders, comprising these points:

1. All papers must be interesting, preferably containing gossip, humor, and/or new information. (Presenters in the hard sciences are exempt from having to present gossip; those in anthropology are required to do so.)
2. All papers must be delivered in a dynamic, energetic, animated style. No droning or muttering, ever. Sniffling and gum chewing are discouraged. Arm motions are welcome.
3. Presentations must take no more than the allotted time (in the humanities, usually twenty minutes). If four presenters are scheduled in a ninety-minute time slot, no one will take more than fifteen minutes, so there will be time for audience questions and interaction.
4. Anyone who is boring or goes overtime must be terminated by the panel chair, by any means necessary.
5. Anyone who violates this Bill of Rights will be banned from all conference panels and presentations for one year following the offense.

In your case, the chair and Presenters One and Two were all at fault for not sharing. (Some people genuinely do not know things they should have learned in kindergarten.)

The chair should have kept track of time and passed a note card ("You have two more minutes") to Presenter One when it was close to the end of his slot. A neon-bright orange or fuchsia card is particularly effective.

Since the chair did not do so, you could have passed such a card yourself, either to the chair or the presenter. That violates protocol, but it would wake them up. Or you might have pointed to your watch. Or raised your hand and said politely, with a rueful smile: "I'm afraid we won't have time for my presentation. . . ."

Beyond those polite gestures, you would have to get nasty—and once you have tenure, perhaps you'll consider doing so. You might kick the chair; or you might have a resounding coughing fit; or you might hold up a sign saying, "Stop! In the Name of Love!" (Admittedly, few people have such a sign handy. More's the pity.)

Or, if you'd simply like to undermine and upstage the presenter, you can start putting handcream on your hands—slowly, deliciously, with sensual gestures.

No one will listen to the presenter at all.

In the future, though, Ms. Mentor suggests you ask an audience friend to be ready to interrupt, or to make a "Time" sign if earlier presenters go overtime. Or make a dramatic throat-cutting gesture. You can also speak to the chair ahead of time: "Can you make sure no one goes overtime? I'd hate to have to rush. . . ."

Meanwhile, all is not lost, for you do have an already written paper, ripe for another conference. You may want to retitle it, and ask to be first in your session, but for your vita, you'll get "extra mileage" for your work.

As to revenge for this conference: should you communicate with the organization or the chair or Presenter One? Ms. Mentor thinks they're not worth the time you'd spend, but you *could* send them all copies of this answer from Ms. Mentor. (If you're wicked or cowardly, you could mail the copies anonymously from another city. Or half a dozen from different cities. You could create a chain letter, or even a homepage.)

Perhaps it's the impatience of baby-boomers-growing-old, but Ms. Mentor has noted some amusing trends in recent conference panels. When a presenter is boring, the other presenters have not hesitated to show their displeasure—by rolling eyes, playing with rubber bands, cracking knuckles, belching or twiddling or scratching, or even taking short naps (this practice, common in Japan, is a fine import). Audiences have also revolted—with interruptions, and even with hooting and heckling.

Best of all, some chairs are taking responsibility for the interest and entertainment value, and are obviously asking themselves, "Are the purposes of this session being advanced by allowing the presenter to continue?"

In one case Ms. Mentor witnessed, the chair listened politely, only drumming fingers, to ten very long minutes of blather and drivel. There were still at least five minutes to go when the chair, with much rustling, passed a card to the presenter: "Time's up. Stop Now."

The presenter did. Some audience members, earlier bored to tears, now wept with relief.

Others, recognizing what the chair had done, broke into impromptu applause.

Fallen Woman

Q: One of the famous profs in my field just pursued me sexually at a conference. I won't tell you what I did, but what does Ms. Mentor think I should have done?

A: Well, Ms. Mentor presumes you "fell," as they used to say in the nineteenth century. She hopes you practiced safe sex and that you got some pleasure from the illicit encounter. She could tell you that you shouldn't have done it (he's married) OR that you should have (following one's desires, rather than one's duties, is rare enough for academics). Or Ms. Mentor could provide professional readings of the situation (he can help you get tenure; he can preclude your ever getting a job at all). She hopes you put your career first.

But the question you are really asking, she suspects, is something else: What next?

Well, that depends.

Are you a job-seeking graduate student, or a tenured professor in an endowed chair, or something—what?—in between? Will Dr. Famous Prof ever have the opportunity to hurt or harm your career? Will this encounter help or hinder you in journal article acceptances, grants, contracts, or fellowships? Or will the waters close over it, as if it never happened?

And will he call you tomorrow?

And will this turn into a relationship like that in Gail Godwin's novel *The Odd Woman*, in which the heroine meets her lover annually at the Modern Language Association convention and then returns to her best friend's roaring, shrieking disapproval: "Five furtive fucks a year, and you call this a relationship?!"

Ms. Mentor hopes that your newfound relationship, if you have one, will be more fulfilling. And more frequent.

Ms. Mentor also urges you to keep her fully informed about all the particulars of this entire affair. For research purposes, she does have a need to know.

All By Myself

Q: Is it worthwhile for independent scholars to go to academic conferences?

A: Ms. Mentor will begin by defining terms, for "independent scholar" is a recent euphemism, originally meaning "unemployed Ph.D." Now it refers to the huge cohort of people in the humanities who do attend conferences year after year, continue to write articles and books, form organizations and support groups, and consider themselves scholars on a par with those holding tenured and tenure-track jobs at universities. (Indeed, their writing is often as good or better than that of the tenurees, for they're not so bound to please their colleagues with impenetrable jargon.)

They flourish especially in the humanities, but barely exist elsewhere. People holding Ph.D.s in science may be academics, or researchers in industry, or entrepreneurs with small medical technology businesses. Those with social science Ph.D.s may work as consultants or researchers for schools, government agencies, advertisers, and pollsters. But they rarely write unless they're paid for it.

"Independent scholars" are more like "public intellectuals" or "people of letters." In the past, their ranks would have included such figures as premiere anthropologist Margaret Mead, who received tenure only late in life; novelist Mary McCarthy, who rarely taught but whose sharp tongue and rapier wit were revered and feared for half a century; and Sir Francis Galton, the nineteenth-century British gentleman scientist who studied such phenomena as fingerprints and the statistical efficacy of prayer. These independent scholars followed their own bents and indulged their own curiosities, and today, in academia, they would be considered oddball, eccentric, perhaps even loony.

Would they have been welcome at many academic conferences? Possibly not—for much of what passes for intellectual discourse today is far narrower, and less entertaining, than what they attempted.

But should *you* go to conferences?

Yes, if you ever hope to get an academic job, or if you'd like to reassure yourself that you don't want one.

Yes, if you have any ties to journalism: the satirizing of pedantries, especially those of the Modern Language Association meeting each December, is particularly prized.

And yes, sometimes there are sensations no one should miss—such as, in early 1996, the appearance of Professor Donald McCloskey at the San Francisco conference of American economics professors. One of the founders of the caucus of feminist economists, Dr. Donald McCloskey had now become, complete with red heels and blonde wig—Dr. Deirdre McCloskey.

As for Ms. Mentor, who never would have expected economists to kick up their heels in that way, she also recommends a few conferences for intellectual stimulation and entertainment value, for academics and independent scholars alike.

At the annual conference of the Popular and American Culture Associations, for instance, papers are given on a world of formal, strange, or bizarre topics: literary criticism, Buicks, pornography, Vietnam, chewing gum, voodoo, rap music, Dear Abby, roller coasters, Dolly Parton, the *National Enquirer*. Anyone can give a paper on anything, and often does. The sessions are spontaneous and rarely without some merits, sometimes unintentional. "PCA" can be the most hilarious of meetings.

Ms. Mentor also recommends the annual meeting of the Oral History Association, a loose group that welcomes scholars of wide stripes (historians, political scientists, literary critters) as well as "real people": archivists, activists, genealogists, fans, and the interestingly obsessed.

Oral History presentations are all about real people, including (in recent years) Foreign Service wives, biographers' discussion circles, best-selling writers who could not cope with success and drank themselves to death, civil rights and antiwar activists and their opponents, educators and anti-educators of women, and tidbits about the foibles of movie stars.

Several years ago, at the Cleveland meeting, one Oral History presenter revealed that the great fruithead Carmen Miranda did not wear underpants.

Such information being essential to understanding the great issues of our times, Ms. Mentor will conclude with an answer to your initial question: Yes.

Conventional Blues

Q: Why is going to the MLA convention so depressing? Call me what I am: "Hoarding Prozac."

A: Your query arrived, as luck would have it, on the day that Ms. Mentor received her Modern Language Association convention program. She scanned the program, felt dyspeptic, put it aside, and clicked on MTV—which gave her the chance to shimmy and howl along with the video of AC/DC's raucous heavy metal anthem: "We're on the highway to hell!"

She felt much better afterward.

But that does not really answer your question—except to suggest that there's something about MLA, the largest academic organization in the world, that drives people to MTV.

First, MLA traditionally begins on December 27, a time at which no one looks her/his best. MLAers usually arrive tired from enforced Christmas togetherness, clad in dingy brown or black, and anticipating major aggravations. MLA hotels, usually in cold Northern cities, are often understaffed for a convention of such weightiness. Check-in time overwhelms the desk; elevators break down; phones give up the ghost.

Further, MLA attendees are all people who were in the National Honor Society in high school. They're grown up and often successful—but they know they're still dweebs. At MLA, they're all still thinking: "I'm inadequate, and everyone'll find out."

Yes, Hoarding Prozac, everyone at MLA seems smarter than you are—or at least more confident, more articulate, or better at name-dropping. In the foreign languages, they speak the language better than you do, and the people in French dress better than anyone else.

Also, since MLA is the professional summit for those in the modern languages and literatures, some souls invariably choose to strut and fret and rattle their statuses. In paper sessions, audiences grow testy, and tact flies out the window: "You've completely failed to see . . ." or "Your argument is fatally flawed by your . . ."—whereupon the presenter, on the defensive, grows louder and windier. Others wade in, fumes fill the room, pomposity and snideness abound, and the young are usually savaged.

Most academic veterans have been trashed at least once at MLA. While most such duellos are fought by men, Ms. Mentor knows an intrepid young feminist trio who, two decades ago, presented an MLA session on "Menstruation and Literature"—after which a very loud audience member spent seven minutes denouncing them as "hopelessly sexist" for writing about women instead of people. "I, for instance, am writing on farts . . . ," whereupon the Loud Lady pulled out a filebox full of notecards on farts, flatulence, and related subjects. (Now, of course, all of that could easily be kept on a disk. Much progress has been made.)

(Ms. Mentor here inserts a bibliographical note for gentle scholars: the "Menstruation and Literature" papers eventually became part of *The Curse: A Cultural History of Menstruation* by Janice Delaney, Mary Jane Lupton, and Emily Toth [Dutton, 1976; Illinois, 1988]. The MLA session is also alluded to in Gwen Davis's novel *Ladies in Waiting*.)

But resuming Ms. Mentor's answer to Hoarding Prozac: Although MLA is touted as the place to meet old friends, many mature feminist scholars attend irregularly—leaving their agemates, sans gossip, feeling irrelevant and melancholy. Since scholars have always been taught to kick those who came before them ("Professor Pink has utterly failed to interrogate Gaskell's transgressive love-hate relationship with pandas"), the feminist scholar of a certain age is apt to feel that she is a football as well as a weathered presence. This is not enjoyable.

Ms. Mentor leaves for last the most dispiriting facet of MLA: its role as the "slave market" for job hunters, who become more and more hysterical each year as the shortage of positions deepens. At MLA, desperation is palpable. The halls smell of it.

So, Hoarding Prozac wonders: *Why would anyone go to MLA?*

Ms. Mentor, ever the teacher, reminds sage readers of the traditional reasons for going to any academic conference: to learn stuff, to present a paper, to seek a job, or to pursue revenge for past slights. Some past MLAers also used to go for illicit sex, but now academics are older (average age forty-eight), sex can kill, and something's lacking. As one young heterosexual woman complained to Ms. Mentor about MLA: "Where else can you, for three whole days, watch thousands of men trail by—intelligent men with whom you have everything in common—and not feel one sliver of sexual attraction toward any of them?"

Still, it is possible to give oneself a happier MLA. Ms. Mentor offers these hints to Hoarding Prozac and others planning to go to MLA or its counterparts:

- Do not read the program beforehand. The wealth of esoteric knowledge will depress you. Even Ms. Mentor, who knows virtually everything, finds that the program puts her into a blue funk.
- Go only to sessions where you already know something about the subject, so that you'll add to your knowledge—or even know more than the presenters. This is always heartening.
- Go to practical workshops—about the job market, about academic women, about being an independent scholar. At MLA, the Women's Caucus for the Modern Languages sessions are always excellent, and Ms. Mentor would say so even if the Caucus had not also been the first to publish her column in *Concerns,* an extraordinary and meritorious journal.
- Think of the conference as a series of anthropological rituals enacted for your observation, if not your pleasure. Notice body language, fashion, voices, and styles. Is it true that most academics look alike? Discuss.
- Wear comfortable shoes and bring your favorite snacks. Do not share them with anyone.

- Imagine that the presenters are your teachers. How do the good ones do it, and how do the bad ones fail?
- Eschew doom and pessimism, lest you wind up like the unloved dean whose doctor told him he was terminally ill. The dean barked, "I want a second opinion!"—whereupon the doctor added, "You're ugly, too!"
- Treat yourself to the book exhibits, an intellectual feast, and enjoy meeting the editors. They are often the most interesting, knowledgeable people at the conference.
- Be mindful that groaning about MLA is itself a convention, for most MLAers actually do enjoy the meeting. It always provides opportunities for character assassination.
- Enjoy the many brilliant presentations by feminist scholars, and note that the atmosphere is different from that in the combative patriarchal sessions. See how women share ideas and add to each other's knowledge. Be proud of your gender.
- Do not think that MLA, or academia, is all that life offers. There is a real world, too, and you don't even have to pay to attend.

    You can just sneak in.

Educated Sheets

Q: I'm one of those impossibly rare Americans who clawed her way up from poverty to an almost-Ph.D. And so I especially resent the way that some academic people treat "the help" in conference hotels. I've worked as a maid, and I've had to clean up sheets where people not only left blood or semen (these things happen), but also liquor, chewing tobacco, vomit, urine, and feces. How can scholars be so gross?

A: Ms. Mentor has always believed that the sign of a well-bred person is kindness toward those who serve, whether they be student workers, waitresses, porters, cab drivers, or hotel employees. Yet when some academics leave home, they seem to think they should behave like rock stars, trashing hotel rooms and leaving loathesome personal reminders.

It doesn't work. They'll never be mistaken for Motley Crüe.

Moreover, Ms. Mentor agrees that this is no way for educated people—or anyone—to act. She is glad that academic women rarely participate in such shenanigans.

But academics are guilty of another sin: According to hotel staffs consulted by Ms. Mentor, famous scholars are famously stingy. Ms. Mentor reminds her sage readers that the people who clean your rooms have to eat, too, and they don't have tenure. Leave them a generous tip.

Ms. Mentor was most diverted, however, by the reflections of one cleaning woman who had observed the mores and folkways of a contingent of scholars famous for graybearded pomposities.

"I changed their sheets and cleaned out their bathrooms, and except for a few slib-slobs, it was a snap," the cleaning woman reported. "They don't throw food around, they don't smoke, they don't drink, they don't even fuck around.

"Who *are* these people?"

First Year on the Job

"Nova Smith," freshly Ph.D.ed, arrives at her new assistant professor job, nervous and exhilarated. Now—at last—she'll be an academic adult. She'll take her place in a community of scholars where ideas are the currency and the merit dream is the rule. At last, she'll be in a milieu where intelligence and the promotion of knowledge will be amply rewarded and cheered.

Sometimes, indeed, all that does ensue.

But every new faculty member is also part of an academic department. Nova's new department may be an easy-sailing ship, with high morale and warm collegiality, where people take turns hoisting the flag and saluting it. Or her department may be a collection of nasty brutish feuds and fiefdoms (foreigners vs. Americans, theorists vs. practitioners, old vs. young, artists vs. critics, men vs. women) whose warring members are united only in their ferocious opposition to the other side, whoever that may be.

The technical term for such departments is "snakepits."

Ms. Mentor wants new faculty to know that all perfectly running departments are alike: rare. Often they are held together by a charming long-term autocrat who somehow gets "resources" (new hirings, raises, equipment) where other department heads fail. Even in eras of scarcity, when other chairs are reduced to begging for fresh chalk for their faculty, chairs with longevity often retain what they have: photocopying machines, lounges, long-distance phoning, travel money, secretaries, even maintenance people. (Ms. Mentor suspects that long-term chairs know where the bodies are buried.)

Meanwhile, departments that attempt to be democratic sometimes run with great vitality and new ideas. But if the participants are highly verbal or very high-strung, would-be communities of equals usually degenerate—into warring duchies and lethal little municipalities.

Since bad news always travels faster than good, and a colorful story has far more mileage than a depiction of static calm, Ms. Mentor is much more apt to hear about departments full of demons.

In her first year as an assistant professor in a Midwest English department, "Nova" felt baffled, buffeted, and buffaloed.

At first, she was feted and lunched and dined by the younger faculty, most of whom were around her age—mid-thirties. (Nova's partner remained back in Oregon, and Nova's being in a commuter relationship gained her much sympathy.) Her younger colleagues were a jolly, congenial lot, well versed in movies and music and popular culture, and full of clever, witty stories.

But at department meetings, whatever the subject, they turned into raging tigers.

Not that the senior faculty, all but two of them men, were any calmer. "They'd like to rip each others' throats out," a visiting writer once observed.

Indeed, they were vicious. One's ideas were "Procrustean"; others were "asinine" or "soporific" or "preposterous." When one of the "little-boy humanists" rose to speak, half a dozen bass voices from the creative writing section brayed their disapproval, and one roared: "Who elected you Moses among the Hottentots?"

Nova knew, of course, that "vigorous debate" was to be part of academic life. But this wasn't quite what she'd expected among, well, humanists.

Nevertheless, Nova faithfully attended every department meeting, and never uttered a peep throughout her first year, which proved to be the smartest thing she could do. She made no enemies, looked alert, seemed respectful, learned more than she let on, and kept on good terms with all. (Over the long-distance wires, her partner in Oregon consoled, laughed, and wailed with her.)

Meanwhile, in the eyes of the senior faculty, Nova was a fresh slate. Over the first few months, she was summoned to many an individual lunch or office visit, during which each full professor gave what he—always a he—considered "the real lowdown" about the toxic department fights.

All were the results of past feuds, she learned. *A* hated *B* because of an attempted coup several years ago to dethrone the department head *C* and install *D* in his place. *E* still resented losing his sinecure as director of graduate studies, a change he felt *F* and *G* had conspired to manage some six or seven years earlier. *H* and *I*, meanwhile, had been part of a plan with their journalism colleagues (*J* and *K*) to withdraw from English entirely and create a new School of Communications—which plan was thwarted when *L* and *M* ratted to Dean *N* about the conspiracy.

None of it struck Nova as worth the venom, but each of her self-appointed mentors concluded with some version of George Santayana's most famous statement: The fights in academia are so intense because the stakes are so small.

Nova recorded that point in her journal, many times, during her first year.

Nova listened carefully to everything. The senior men in her department, she noticed, loved to have an audience, and no one cared whether she spoke or not. She just needed to look interested (caffeine kept her appropriately wired). She also never voiced that well-known, wayward thought that comes to everyone in a new full-time job: "I'm Surrounded By Idiots!"

She wore conservative clothes; she kept her Queen Latifah and Riot Grrrl posters at home. Her only office decorations were one jade plant and a Mary Cassatt poster of a woman reading.

Nova also made friends with Women's Studies faculty, who were honest, helpful, and sometimes wickedly satirical. She enjoyed their comradeship and their laughter and learned to view her male colleagues' department meeting fights zoologically—as ground-pawing, antler-crashing, grown-up versions of "Whose Is Bigger."

Nova also began her Tenure Diary that year, noting and filing every piece of paper about her work and worth. She put in copies of her contract and contractual agreements; student evaluations; peer reports from colleagues who observed her teaching; and favorable reactions to her publications or research plans. When the university president sent a note of praise for her feature in a magazine, that note went into Nova's Tenure Diary.

If her chair told her she'd be teaching a certain course, Nova wrote him a memo to confirm it and kept a copy in her Diary. She kept copies of her best students' papers, to show what she could motivate them to do.

Periodically, she wrote down her goals for the year or the month and her plans for summer research. She knew she needed to keep focused, lest everything dribble away in daily deadlines.

Nova also studied the university's Policy Statement on Tenure and Promotion ("PS-25," reprinted in the Faculty Handbook), and quietly recorded procedural violations. She was not, for instance, given a copy of her first-year evaluation, although the Policy Statement said she was entitled to get it. Nova said nothing about that. If, later, renewal or tenure went awry, she'd have ammunition for an appeal: the rules hadn't been followed.

Knowing that strange things could happen, Nova kept her Tenure Diary tucked safely at home and wisely devoted her first year to two things: being well liked and setting up a research routine.

One might suppose that Nova would devote herself to teaching, but Nova knew she had been hired, as she wanted to be, in a "research institution," where publication would be most important. She taught adequately, but budgeted an hour a day and three hours each Saturday and Sunday to writing the book she needed to publish to get tenure.

An earlier mentor had advised her not to be a "responsibility magnet," and Nova avoided being on time-consuming committees: "I need to get a head start on my book," she'd say with an apologetic smile. "Maybe next year?"

She also self-promoted, making sure that her colleagues knew her "research agenda" was well underway. She notified the department and faculty-staff newsletters whenever she gave a conference presentation. She sent copies of her publications to her department chair, dean, and interested senior colleagues. She hyped her achievements in her annual report.

In her second year, Nova would give a talk for the faculty, an impeccably organized presentation that she'd practiced many times. That presentation would help determine whether she got a second three-year contract.

(Nova also kept her private life very private: even Ms. Mentor does not know the gender of Nova's long-distance partner.)

Meanwhile, Nova kept up regular lunches with her colleagues, who not only relished department feuds and gossip, but also told her about a few good deals. The bookstore gave a 10 percent discount to faculty; reserved parking spaces often became available mid-year; exams were not to be given during the last week of classes; long-distance calls could be made only from certain department phones; allergy shots were free through the student health center. And the best vanilla ice cream in town was available from the student-run College Creamery.

Her lunch bunch also warned her against one dramatic and terrible danger: being interviewed by the student newspaper, whose fledgling reporters would garble her quotes and infantilize her ideas. (When that happened to "Cecile" in the French department, she wound up spending weeks doing damage control.)

Nova spent her time with people she liked and respected, including the one secretary who'd been there the longest and who appeared to hate everyone. Nova made a point of befriending her—and introducing her to the martial arts.

Nova was smart, committed, and ambitious. And when anything truly flummoxed her, she did the right thing: she wrote to Ms. Mentor.

Hot Air Waves

Q: Only a week into my tenure-track job, in the cold Upper Midwest, a senior male colleague sidled up and breathed into my ear: "I can be in your bedroom every Tuesday night." It turns out that he has a video show, but what should I have said/done? Was it sexual harassment?

A: Ms. Mentor feels that your colleague, call him Dr. Video, should be forced to read feminist literature every Tuesday night—so that he'll learn the difference between collegial pleasantry and, yes, sexual harassment.

Technically, of course, his slithery little comment was not sexual harassment: it was an isolated incident; it was not quid pro quo (such as "lay for an A" or "tail for tenure"). It was not by itself a hostile environment.

But it was rude and crude and very unfair to a newcomer.

Questioned about it, Dr. Video would no doubt claim that he was merely being witty; that his comment was a form of gallantry; and he's sorry that you—and Ms. Mentor—don't share his sense of humor. (Among his buddies, he might also mutter about "humorless bitches" and "damn Affirmative Action" and "no one can take a joke anymore"—all the usual canards brought up when women want to be treated seriously.)

He will also claim that he is merely being himself, the Video Host.

There is no particular way you should have handled the incident: Ms. Mentor hopes that you are not berating yourself. When all else fails, a blank stare can be the best (and most natural) reaction. Trying to educate someone like the Video Host is usually futile, but you can mention the incident to any sympathetic women full professors, who may one day make general hints to him, and other men, about appropriate ways to treat young women as colleagues. Senior men should be welcoming and mentoring the young; they should not be slithering, panting, and making innuendos.

You should also write down the incident, with dates and particulars, in your Tenure Diary. If there seems to be an overall hostile environment in your department, you will have an example. But if it is only an isolated and annoying event, concentrate on the things that you enjoy in academia: teaching, writing, the library or the lab, and comparing ideas with lively and knowledgeable colleagues.

Ms. Mentor also advises you to make a point of not watching videos on Tuesday nights.

Sometimes silence is the best revenge.

They Won't Meet with Me

Q: I wanted to get together a bunch of new assistant professors, like myself, to talk about new, better ways to teach, but no one came to a meeting I called. Then I tried to get together a writing group, so we could share our work and get feedback and encourage each other, but no one came.

What can I do when I call a meeting and no one comes?

A: You can go ahead and imagine that everyone hates you or that you have bad hygiene or bad karma. But Ms. Mentor suspects you're just fine.

Most likely, you've landed in a bed of thorny insecure colleagues who don't want to risk any kind of criticism from their peers. They're almost certainly believers in the Udder Theory, the image of the world as a vast cow with only a few nipples. If you manage to grab onto one, no one else will get fed any of the goodies—such as tenure, raises, grants, research assistants, offices with windows, parking spaces, or whatever other big and little sweetmeats and privileges may be dangled at your university.

But it's also possible that your peers know something you don't know. Is there a tenure quota at your school? How many of the faculty in your department are in tenured ranks (associate or full professor)? What kinds of records did the last people to be tenured have? If four people come up for a tenure decision at the same time, is it routinely understood that at least one will be lopped off?

If that's the case, your colleagues see you, correctly, as their competition for scarce resources: the Udder is not just a Theory. And you can understand why they won't help you out or let you see their weaknesses.

You can still help yourself, though. Seek out like-minded people at conferences or over the Net. If you're in touch with graduate school pals, they can help: do writing and idea exchanges by ground or e-mail. You won't be competing, and you might even find people who'll be strong outside referees for tenure.

But also join women's faculty groups on your campus, as well as local chapters of NOW (National Organization for Women) and AAUW (American Association of University Women), which often enrolls retired faculty women. They'll know many of the truths and secrets from the local university, and they're almost certainly eager to tell you.

As you've found, there are many people who resist sharing their writing. But everyone wants to share good gossip.

Monster of Mean Street

Q: New on the job, I've been assigned an office in the most unpopular part of our building, known as Mean Street because of a savage full professor who, machine-like, cranks out nasty, ranting, belittling memos to his colleagues. What should I do if (when) he starts sending them to me?

A: Ms. Mentor is familiar with Dr. Mean's type, the man who mauls his colleagues with his mighty memos. His type is known in other professions, too: he bawls, he threatens, he sues. He flames hapless e-mail users; he burns up talk show phone lines.

Dr. Mean often flourishes in academia, where it is the job of professors to correct, publicly, the mistakes and misdeeds of others. Some courses—physical education, foreign languages—even consist of students' public fumblings and stumblings. Stung by the humiliation, some of the best students later become professors. They want Revenge.

But before tenure, the wise ones usually confine themselves to mild pranks and critiques. One recovering administrator in a Big Ten school used to dread sending out memos—because he always got back several copies, anonymously corrected for grammar and style, with a bright red "C-minus" at the top.

After tenure, though, the furious can fly out, unfettered. At an elite university in Baltimore, springtime used to be "open season on the assistant professors." Tenured associate and full professors would leave hostile memos in the junior ones' mailboxes and mark up their publications for errors, mistaken inferences, diction and punctuation lapses. Sometimes there'd be an overall comment, such as "You call this scholarship? I call it Podunk."

Few assistant professors ever got tenure at that university, although most went on to become stars at other schools. Many became famous for their extraordinary kindness to students and junior colleagues.

Which is Ms. Mentor's roundabout way of saying that people *can* learn and change—although maybe not Dr. Mean.

Whatever happens, you have not done anything to trigger his wrath. The average Dr. Mean has a predictable past: an angry father; an adolescence as a nerd, rejected by even the so-so girls; a superb senior thesis at a college where no one cared about anything but football. If Dr. Mean is married by now, his wife doesn't meet his loftiest needs (which he would be hard put to describe). He's still mad at his now-dead dad.

But that's not your responsibility. Young women often believe that being unfailingly kind and nurturing to angry men will heal them, but many a battered wife knows better. You should be polite to Dr. Mean, but stay out of his way.

How to do so? Do not pop up and make yourself a target. Do not ask impertinent or ignorant questions in faculty meetings, or say much of anything during meetings, in your first year. Don't take part in any department quarrels: that's suicidal. Even when senior faculty say justly nasty things about your grad school professors ("Old Chauncey as drunk as ever, and still can't keep his pants on?"), let no negative vibes pass your lips.

Being friendly and smiling will show everyone that you're a sweet person—so that if/when Dr. Mean attacks, he'll seem rude and boorish. You can also defang him by asking him inconsequential questions: How can I get a grade book? Where do we pick up our checks?

But if Mean's memos do surface in your mailbox . . . If there's anything resembling a threat, take it immediately to your department chair and to campus security.

If it's just a "C-minus" on something you've written, leave him a bland note, "Thanks for reading my publication; I always appreciate feedback." If he's riled up about something you did, write back, "I'm sorry you were displeased by what I did; I'll try not to offend."

Or you can just ignore his memos—and later deny you ever got any.

But do not write long, reasoned self-defenses. They waste your energy and only make Dr. Mean glad he was able to get you worked up. Too, worrying about him will take away the mental clarity and time you need for your teaching and research.

Ms. Mentor suggests that you imagine Dr. Mean as a Doberman or a Chihuahua: a wild, loud dog with a desperate need for obedience school. The best way to train Dr. Mean is to be firm and fair. If he growls, go to a neutral corner until he calms down. Imagine him inside a dog pound. Imagine yourself with a big stick.

Ms. Mentor knows you feel better already.

Cock of the Walk

Q: I've noticed that whenever there's a public lecture at our university, the first to speak in the question period is always a man. But what's fascinating is that his question hardly ever has anything to do with the subject, yet it's very long and swollen with self-important jargon.

Last week, for instance, a visiting scholar (a woman) gave a fine talk about Jane Austen, and the first question was from a man who droned and harangued about Ethel Mertz and neocolonial literature for fully five minutes. Finally the woman said, "What is your question?"—whereupon the man said, "I've made my point," and sat down.

I was almost the only person who laughed. What does all this mean?

A: You are describing a phenomenon for which there is a proper technical term: it is called "Peacocking." Also known as "Hello! I Have a Penis!" it arises primarily in public areas, and especially when a woman is speaking.

Ms. Mentor believes it is an ancient territorial imperative that impels men to their feet: they must occupy the woman's space, or even dislodge her entirely. Peacocking may take place in legislatures and lodges, churches and chain stores. But it is particularly evident and bizarre in academia, a world where everyone is supposed to produce logically ordered exchanges of ideas. Peacocking does seem to be a strange tangent.

But in reality, it is just another tactic of domination, such as shouting or interrupting. Its not-very-hidden purpose is to divert attention toward the audience member: his erudition, large vocabulary, and deep voice. Since his question is rarely actually a question, it is safely regarded as a form of public display: "Hello! I Have a Penis!"

Ms. Mentor congratulates you for seeing its comical side. Most people are too cowed.

What is the proper response? A woman speaker cannot easily say, "Ah, yes, you have a penis. Let's see if anyone has questions"—although Ms. Mentor thinks it would be very refreshing if someone did just that.

More often the speaker is forced to smile weakly, surrender the line of her argument, and respond to the member's pronouncements, whereupon his agenda, not hers, rules the rest of the discussion. "Hello! I Have a Penis!" can be translated as "Hello! Now the Real Leader's in Charge! I Must Be Heard!"

Ms. Mentor thinks that the best strategy is to interrupt, politely, and then ignore the peacocker. He should not be encouraged in his tedious and silly demonstration. But Ms. Mentor also harbors a fantasy that, someday, women will take it upon themselves to Combat Peacocking, to fight fire with feather.

In Ms. Mentor's vision, every woman going to a lecture will pack a peacock feather (real or fake), then listen and lie in wait. When "Hello! I Have a Penis!" starts his peacocking, suddenly there'll be a whoosh of women, like amber waves of grain, fanning themselves with their peacock feathers. They'll be daintily cooing, smiling with a common understanding—which will encourage the rest of the audience to titter and giggle and guffaw. Word will get around, snickering will spread, and soon a wave of laughter will sweep over audiences from sea to shining sea.

And then, at last, women will get to ask the important, interesting questions. Everyone will listen and think, and public lectures will be for meaning, not for preening.

Outcome

Q: I'm a new faculty member at C.U. Should I come out as a lesbian? And if so, how?

A: Ms. Mentor asks another question first: Why?

If you are teaching queer theory, everyone will assume you're a lesbian anyway. If you teach about lesbian and gay rights, or if you advise the local homophile group, or if you hang out in lesbian/gay bars, or if you speak out against homophobia—or even if you're unmarried with very short hair—many people will assume you're a lesbian.

So what? Your sexuality is your own business. (Ms. Mentor is perhaps old-fashioned: she doesn't think anyone, of any gender or sexual variation, should do it in the road and frighten the horses.) You don't need to apologize for *or* announce your preference/orientation at all, unless you have a compelling reason to do so.

Ms. Mentor can think of some good possible reasons. Coming out may meet your emotional or political needs; it may tell needy students that being a lesbian is OK. Maybe you want to alert your colleagues not to make heterosexist assumptions—or you want to educate them generally. Maybe you prefer to introduce your "roommate" as "my lover." (Ms. Mentor, however, thinks all public displays and proclamations of sexual affection rather lacking in taste. Who needs to be peeking into your bedroom?)

The most dramatic time to come out is, of course, at a public rally, and several entertainment and sports figures have done so. Ms. Mentor sympathizes with the feeling of power and relief that comes from baring one's soul. But she also counsels you to think carefully about consequences.

Most particularly: Will you put your tenure (and therefore your academic career) at risk? If your parents don't already know, will they find out in a roundabout way that will hurt them deeply? Or, when you come out, as often happens with people who Tell All on TV talk shows, will nothing at all happen, leaving you with a thud of disappointment and a great feeling of depression?

Professors as a group are older and more jaded: they like gossip but rarely admit to being shocked. Especially for those already entrenched, the sexuality of their younger colleagues may be of no great interest, unless it turns into a problem (pedophilia, sexual harassment).

If you wish to come out, Ms. Mentor wouldn't dream of discouraging you, although you may find that not enough people really care. That can be disappointing, or pleasing: Ms. Mentor gives advice about what to do, not about what to feel.

Mating Ritual

Q: My officemate is always closing the office door so she can gossip about our colleagues. She tells me which one used to sleep with which one ten years ago; which secretary has the hots for the photocopy repairman; which one she expects to come out of the closet next; and so on.

I was brought up to believe that it's wrong to talk about other people's business, yet I find her fascinating. In just my first year at M University, am I becoming morally perverse?

A: No. You're simply becoming wise in the ways of the working world, where gossip is power as well as entertainment. It *is* important for you to know who's sleeping with whom. You can avoid many a *faux pas*, and your workplace will be far more interesting, if you know you're intercepting Significant Glances Across the Crowded Room.

Be careful with whom you gossip, but treasure your officemate. She is a gem.

Shrinking Violet

Q: Does social life matter when departments decide on promotion and tenure? I hope not, as I'm very shy.

A: In some academic departments, Ms. Mentor is sad to say, social life is not just the main thing in promotion and tenure decisions. It's the only thing. Usually it is called "collegiality," a term which may connote (to the unwary) the qualities needed for a community of scholars. Actually, it means charm and fitting in.

At research universities, of course, publication is officially the major standard for promotion and tenure. Many humanities departments expect a candidate to have a published book by tenure time. Social scientists need to do "major articles." Tenure candidates in science and engineering are also expected to bring in grant money, and sometimes even a minimum dollar amount is specified. Although teaching is always talked about lovingly, often it matters much less than research—unless the candidate's teaching record is extremely poor or the candidate is already unpopular for some other reason.

At smaller universities and liberal arts colleges, teaching is valued more, and faculty are expected to "contribute to the college community." In religiously affiliated schools, churchly work may be expected.

But Ms. Mentor cautions you not to rely solely on written tenure and promotion rules. Some type of faculty social life is always expected—

and that's where a woman can employ the fine intuitions she has honed all her life. (Remember those teenaged phone conversations: "What did she *really* mean?" and "How did he look when he said that?" All good training.)

Use lunch for social and anthropological purposes, Ms. Mentor advises. Even a shy person can leave "let's do lunch" notes in faculty members' mailboxes, but a personal self-introduction, with smile and firm handshake, is even better. If the department is small, you may follow the example of Lynn M., a new sociology professor at a Middle Atlantic university, who, separately but in alphabetical order, invited every professor in her department to lunch with her in the student union.

These lunches were congenial and informative: "What should I know about this department?" and "What do you think I should do first?" and "Who are the really fine teachers and scholars in this department?" (Notice that the questions are all positively phrased, with nary a word about enemies or pitfalls. First-year lunches are for smiling and making friends.) Flattery is also never amiss: "I've heard your work in stratification is really important. What are you most proud of?"

The cynical might call Lynn M. a manipulative, cunning tool of the system—but Ms. Mentor knows that Lynn M. was making herself into a well-informed teacher and scholar. She was charming, and she knew she shouldn't talk about how to teach: that's a taboo subject among many senior professors. They're insecure about how they do it, and very few are willing to be watched in the act.

Some professors are even weirdly reluctant to discuss their own subject matter. Tom, a young turk at a prestigious Southern university, once made an English department mailroom comment about Thomas Hardy's novels, whereupon a senior professor bellowed: "Keep your literary thoughts for your writing or the classroom. They don't belong here." Tom did not get tenure.

Like Lynn M. and Tom, you will have to scope out department ways. In your first months, try to go everywhere you are invited: dinners, dances, birthdays, banquets, bowling parties, Halloween howlfests, sock hops, sports events, roasts, showers, whatever. Claim illness if you must, but never say you're "too busy."

Especially if you're a woman of color or an out lesbian or a woman with a disability, your colleagues will be watching to see if you will "fit in." In some ways, you won't, and you'll need friends outside the university with whom you can be truly candid, vituperative, or satirical. (For really juicy conversations, use the phone: e-mail's not thoroughly private.)

But among your new colleagues, be a cheerful listener: "That's really interesting; tell me more." Resist the temptation to argue: you're not yet in a position to educate. Also, most academics would rather orate: they love an audience. That's where your shyness is a great asset.

Do invite department friends for dinner. Especially if you're single and a not-so-good cook, you'll be lauded for your valiant efforts. But avoid *tête-à-tête* dinners unless you really crave romance (and Ms. Mentor warns that romance within a department is a very bad idea, with a potential for sexual harassment, punishing breakups, and gobs of ill will). If you happen to have a husband who cooks, everyone will be thrilled.

In essence, strive to like and be liked. Then, if your teaching and publications are good, your path to tenure should be fairly smooth. For no matter the written policies, a tenure decision is really a Yes or No answer to one question: Do we, the entrenched faculty members, want this person around for another thirty years or more?

It's up to you to make sure that they do.

But Ms. Mentor adds that it's also up to you not to forget feminist principles. In your soul, while you're smiling and listening, you should distrust hierarchies and slogans, and welcome new ideas, and support other women, and ponder ways to change departmental silliness, fogeyism, or inertia.

While you're learning about your new department, and making yourself liked, you can also be waiting for your chance to make a difference.

Misgivings

Q: Have I committed career suicide by accepting a beginning job at a no-rank college? (No assistant, associate, etc. ranks: everyone's in the same rank.) Am I cutting out any chance to shift to a tenure-track job at a university? After all my hard work, eight years of graduate school, and a commuter marriage, I wonder if I haven't thrown away or somehow devalued myself.

The one bright light is that next year I'm going to be promoted to directing our small graduate program, doing fund-raising as well as administration. That excites me, and makes me think it may be worth staying here.

I went into this appointment pragmatically, so should I just stop whining, build my new career, and bloom where planted?

A: You seem to be asking Ms. Mentor a simple question: "The no-rank college is the only job offer I got. Should I have turned it down and waited for a university job?"

Of course not. In this market, Ms. Mentor shudders at the thought that anyone wishing to remain in academia would turn down any full-time position. There may never be another.

The fact that No-Rank is not a Research I university, with doctoral programs, posh libraries and labs and the like, also doesn't matter. Prestige does not pay the rent.

However, No-Rank College has many a possible weed in its patch. If there are no ranks, there are no promotions. There may not be tenure. How will you be evaluated, and who controls your salary? Can you be fired if financial exigency is declared? (Why will you be fund-raising? Is the school solvent?)

Ms. Mentor feels that you must study your plot of earth. You may ask your boss, with seemingly naive enthusiasm, how you'll be evaluated: "I'd like to know what I'm doing right, and how I can improve." Ask other faculty how they've been evaluated, always inquiring in a cheery, nonconfrontational way. (Some administrators are extraordinarily touchy when employees seem to be rooting about in their plots.)

Yet a hole has been dug for you already. The "directorship of the small graduate program" looks very like what Ms. Mentor calls the Early Administration Trap, or E.A.T., because it eats you up. Junior women (new, young, untenured) are often tapped to run exciting projects, such as Writing Across the Curriculum, Small Business Workshops, Diagnostic Labs, and even Women's Studies Programs. The programs get bright, capable, energetic leadership, but the fledgling administrators have no time to publish. And so they do not get tenure.

(Here Ms. Mentor warns everyone: Do not believe claims that "Teaching is most highly valued at X University." That is rarely true. Publication, which is visible and quantifiable, is a much surer key to tenure and other jobs. As M. W., a wise cynic of Ms. Mentor's acquaintance, says: "A career built on teaching is a career built in sand.")

And so Ms. Mentor implores you to study your situation with passionate self-interest. Women—even hardbitten Ms. Mentor, when she was young and naive—often fall into the compassion trap: doing everything for others, leaving nothing for themselves. What will directing the graduate program do for you? Will you have released time from teaching to be the director, or will you just add it to your other duties? Will you be expected to publish as much as faculty who do not administer? Will being director force you into conflict with administrators who'll be voting on whether you stay?

Ms. Mentor does not sneer at psychic satisfaction, but she also believes in money and power and tenure for women. Although it does not seem to offer permanence, the No-Rank teaching job can be a firm stepping stone while you publish, continue networking, and apply for jobs where your skills and talents and achievements may be more clearly and permanently rewarded.

Ms. Mentor would like you to grow in happiness and security, in the rich red earth of tenure.

Men's Club—Girls Keep Out

Q: The guys in my department have a poker club, which they brag "reeks with testosterone." In my first year, I'm the only woman faculty member in the department, and the only Asian American. Just lately the guys have decided I should be invited to their club. Should I go?

A: No.

New Tenure Line Trauma

Q: I'm in my first year in a tenure-track job, after five years as a healthy-as-a-horse adjunct, instructor, lecturer, etc. And now I've been developing all kinds of health tics I never had before. My hands are numb with carpal tunnel syndrome; I get faint with low blood sugar in the middle of my afternoon class; my jaw aches when I wake up; and I'm full of aches and twitches, urpings and sneezings. I'm chronically worried, anxious, and bilious. I thought finally getting on a tenure track would be heaven—but is it toxic instead?

A: Generations of college students have known about "the freshman ten": the ten pounds that every dorm-fed first-year student puts on. What you are describing now has a name, thanks to Ms. Mentor: New Tenure Line Trauma.

First-year tenure-track faculty almost invariably get sick.

Usually it's sundry small ills: knee and back pain; itches, headaches, pimples, canker sores, miscellaneous queasinesses. But in some new profs, it can escalate to pneumonia, or worse. Ms. Mentor has heard of a world-class hypochondriac who, in his first year at F University, tried to retire on disability. He was convinced that he had brain cancer.

What new tenure line faculty often have is bone-weariness, coupled with an equally strange new freedom. They're no longer teaching five and six courses, with no time to think, but now they have a slew of new duties to juggle.

Now they have to pay attention to who's powerful and who's not in their departments (because now it matters). Instead of the long-anticipated blocks of time for contemplation, there are only tiny wedges eked out between new responsibilities: much more complex class preparations; committees; graduate students; thesis grading; and department meetings, crises, and conspiracies.

By second semester, everyone needs something: student reference letters, annual reports, panel appearances, quotes to the media, wining-and-dining with potential new faculty. October and April are clogged with conferences to attend, papers to write, articles to revise, deans and chairs to placate, and, often, opportunities to hear state legislators yammer that professors "have it so cushy: they only work nine hours a week."

Of course, no one—except Ms. Mentor—talks about the stress of preparing and then performing in front of a live audience for six, nine, or more hours per week. Standup comics rarely do more than two forty-minute shows in a night, but university professors may perform for up to six hours a day, to audiences who often are not lively, well fed, drunk, or eager to impress their dates.

Nor do standup comics also have to give their audiences tests, homework assignments, and grades.

All of which leads Ms. Mentor to opine: if you get sick in your first year, you have a wise body. It's telling you to rest and giving you the chance. If you're home sick, you can put on the answering machine and hide it in another room, cancel everything, snuggle with your cat, and maybe, secretly, do some of the writing and reading you love.

At last.

Your students won't suffer: they'll be pleased to have a day off. Your colleagues may miss you, but they might even remove you from a couple of committees, out of sympathy. Do not allow yourself to feel guilty. Sickness, lingering but neither fatal nor contagious, is a grand escape.

Ms. Mentor's further advice for victims of New Tenure Line Trauma:

• *Home Medical Tips*: A low-salt diet can control carpal tunnel syndrome; Vitamin C helps prevent colds; comfy shoes help combat the blues. Unless they're your own, stay away from little children during the winter: they're like Typhoid Teddy, inveterate spreaders of colds and flu. Take hot baths, and be good to yourself.

• *Good Eating*: Do not diet—starvation will make you grouchy and boring. Buy frozen foods; cherish the microwave; assign housemates and kids to cook for themselves. Or, as Erma Bombeck once suggested, encourage 'em to be the kind who "send Mother's Day cards to Colonel Sanders." Choose and stick to your four favorite food groups, at least one serving a day. For high energy and self-love, Ms. Mentor recommends chocolate, potato chips, and caffeine. The fourth is your free elective.

• *Picking or Pitching Your Worries*: BE ADEQUATE, NOT PERFECT. Tape that motto to your fridge. Hire someone to clean the house, or decide that a dirty, cluttered abode is the sign of a sublime mind, someone who doesn't fuss with the small stuff. Do errands only on Friday afternoon, and if they can't all get done, put them off until next Friday. Routinize: get a haircut every fourth Friday; do all chores at the same shopping center; pay bills while watching MTV (if anyone phones, tell them it's PBS).

• *Simplifying*: If it's around the house and it needs fixing, washing, cleaning, or tending, see if you can get away with throwing it out. Avoid making lists of undone tasks. Don't obsess about the shape and color of your fingernails. Cut 'em short and forget 'em.

• *Teaching Without Trauma*: Reduce your performance anxiety by surrendering the teacher-centered classroom. Students like to work together in small discussion groups, whatever the subject; they like to perform skits and sketches and make each other laugh and groan. They can often use technology better than you can: Louisiana State University Intro to Literature students have, for several years, made hilarious, zany videotaped interpretations of Kate Chopin's *The Awakening*. (In one, the heroine is played by a Barbie doll who swims, endlessly agitated, in a Whirlpool washing machine.)

• *Getting Primed*: Adapt the old trick you learned in grad school, when you had trouble getting started on a project and feared being paralyzed by anxiety and the terror of the blank screen. You learned to tell yourself, "I'm going to write something really terrible," and that made it infinitely easier to get started. Now tell yourself: "I'm going to muddle through, and I refuse to do anything distinguished or competent." Then whatever you do will be a prize and a pleasure and an achievement you can boast about (once your cough stops).

• *Boasting*: Women never boast enough. Write or call three friends and tell them Ms. Mentor insisted you inform them immediately about your greatness. Describe your magnificence in grand and loving detail. Give them the opportunity to worship your accomplishments. Grandiosity is good for the soul.

Marie Curie, Rosalyn Yalow, and Me

Q: I just got my chemistry Ph.D. from a prestigious university and have been hired as an assistant professor at S University, and I'm terribly bewildered. I thought being a Ph.D. scientist meant teaching and mentoring young scientists—which I'm trying to do, with starting a chapter for women chemists—and doing my own lab research. But I'm getting the message that the university just really wants me to get a lot of grant money, hire various assistants, and basically run an empire rather than be a scientist. If I'd wanted to be an administrator, I would have gone for an M.B.A. What gives?

A: What gives is that you're an academic scientist, which means that you've, PRESTO!, metamorphosed from someone who loved the bench work of chemistry to someone who'll rarely, if ever, get to do much of it again.

Such is the melancholy state of scientists today, thanks to the grant-team approach. No more Dr. Faustus toiling away in his lab, dedicated to knowledge and willing to sell his soul for it. What you're expected to do now is a much more prosaic kind of alchemy: turning basic research into gold—into money for your university.

Ms. Mentor thinks you should not despair or even moan. For you are still the visionary, the sorcerer-in-charge who decides what to study. Your little battalions of students and research associates and technicians and sorcerers' apprentices do the rote work, but they can also be comrades and cheerers. Unlike humanities people, whose work requires them to hide in cubbies and libraries and hunch over their computers, you get to be gregarious—to work with and for people.

Best of all, most research associates are women. You get to do science with teams of women.

For Ph.D. women like yourself, many of whom have developed "people skills" in spite of themselves, science can be a world that challenges and uses all their talents, not just the academic ones.

Ms. Mentor also congratulates you on holding an academic job: only 21 percent of Ph.D. chemists do. And if you're a clever networker, you can keep other options open—government labs, industry, smaller colleges where you work more closely with student projects and actually do hands-on lab work.

You are in a position of great opportunity. Ms. Mentor encourages you to boast.

Making the Grade

Q: I just returned the first set of papers in my upper-level class, and two students went to the chair's office to complain about their C's. I realize I'm in a regional state college where most of the majors are in English Education, but I don't think my standards are too high. (After all, I was a T.A. at a similar college when I did my M.A., and I taught a lot of underprepared students while doing my doctorate at a non-elite city university. Also, I did give some A's and B's on the first paper, so my goals for them were not out of reach.)

However, I'm getting really mixed messages from my chair. He says he "always backs faculty" and will support me "all the way." But he also says that he learned when he got to this school that he had to put less emphasis on essays and give more objective tests.

What has me most worried is that I've been told the department really values teaching and puts a lot of weight on student evaluations when it makes decisions about contract renewal and tenure. Should I be worrying?

A: Yes.

Your choice, starkly phrased, may be this: Do you give higher grades and curry student favor, or do you give lower (perhaps more "honest" grades) and suffer negative consequences to your career?

It would be fine, of course, if Ms. Mentor could tell you to follow your loftiest principles and rise above the trifling considerations of money and tenure and the like. But she will not. Ms. Mentor is a realist.

If you were training future physicians, slips in standards could be fatal—to your career or to your patients. But the worst that can happen if you lower your grading standards is that a few more underprepared education majors will be loosed upon the world of teaching. They won't be able to do a great deal to help their own students, but perhaps they'll harm them less than, say, untrained substitute teachers who are hired when there are no permanent faculty available at all (as is sometimes true for math and science in big-city public high schools).

Until schoolteaching pays better—and until public schools are treated as prizes instead of prisons—there will be little incentive to have higher standards for teachers. For over a generation, many of the worst college students have majored in education. That does not seem to be changing.

Ethically, you can persist in your C grades. But as you say, the great sufferer might be yourself, as the one denied tenure.

Ms. Mentor thinks your wisest choice, right now, is to save yourself. Give higher grades (and, indeed, such grades will be "given" instead of "earned"), but to salve your conscience, encourage students to rewrite some of their worst work. If a rewrite will mean a grade change and make you look generous and nurturing, your evaluation scores will also improve.

Post-tenure, of course, you can give honest grades—and scare away the weaker students. (Many a faculty member enjoys post-tenure teaching for particularly that reason.) Post-tenure, too, you'll have more time. You'll have prepared your classes; you won't be frantic to get published within a time limit.

Post-tenure, Ms. Mentor urges you to think about what you can do to improve the state of American education. You may already work with teachers, but you might also visit school board meetings and encourage your students to do so (possibly with extra-credit assignments). Much of what goes on is appalling, full of ignorance and grandstanding. Some students may retreat in horror and switch majors.

But others may dedicate themselves to making social change, to getting the bozos out of office and putting in people with vision, ethics, and knowledge.

You can help. You can even be one of them.

Good Bi

Q: I am beginning a new teaching job. I know that I should self-promote, that I should let my chair, dean, and senior colleagues know what I've done, so they can praise and reward me. But I have a potential problem. In an article that I've written, to be published next year, I mention in passing (several pages into the article) that I am a bisexual woman. And now I'm anxious about whether to give that article to my bosses. I suspect they don't read faculty's writings carefully (if at all). But if they do, would it be unwise of me to let them have that piece?

A: When she first received your query, Ms. Mentor discreetly consulted other experts on Coming Out in Academe—or Coming Half Out. (From her ivory tower, Ms. Mentor does not come out at all.) The experts had many and conflicting ideas, and no one had the definitive word. And in advising you, Ms. Mentor herself also comes down fiercely on all sides of the fence.

What is the issue, and what is at stake? Ms. Mentor and her consultants had many questions—some useful, some pugnacious, and most directed to you. A sampling:

- Isn't everyone, in reality, bisexual (or pansexual)?
- Why should anyone feel threatened (or even enormously interested) if someone comes out as a bisexual? Gay or lesbian, yes—but bisexual?!
- Shouldn't you earn praise for your candor?
- In mentioning your own sexuality in print, are you opening yourself up for sexual harassment from colleagues who can't distinguish theory from practice?
- In coming out as half-lesbian, will you be subjecting yourself to lesbophobia (homophobia)?
- Besides the battles every new woman faculty member faces to be taken seriously, do you also want to take on the task of fighting homophobia when you're not even (thoroughly) lesbian?
- But isn't it simpler to come out deliberately as a lesbian or part-lesbian right away, rather than suddenly coming out later and shocking the pants off everyone?
- Isn't it better to wait after tenure to come out?
- If you don't distribute your article, will your colleagues get copies from

their friends anyway? If they do, they'll certainly read the piece thoroughly and figure you're covering up.

- What is this world coming to, and why is this even an issue? Your sexuality is your own business. You, wily Ms. Mentor, must have made this up. (Ms. Mentor did not.)
- Where do you work? That's a big factor.

Ms. Mentor agrees. At a big state university in a big city, colleagues will have their own lives and friends and not have a prurient interest in your private life. You can be completely open if you want to be. But if you're in a small college in a small town, especially church-related, you may find it simpler to keep your private life under wraps until tenure. Or quietly seek a job in a more congenial place.

For you, and all university faculty, Ms. Mentor recommends developing a community of friends outside one's job. They can be comforts, supports, and lovers. They are also a reality check when one begins to think that academia is the only world, and that committee meetings form the nucleus of the universe.

But, Ms. Mentor, what if you were in the letter writer's shoes?

During her first semester, Ms. Mentor would make herself highly visible as a committed teacher and eager researcher. She would get to know everyone in the department (including secretaries) through lunch, hall, bathroom, or mailroom chats, and outside social activities where possible. She would ask their professional advice on academic matters, and she would strive to appear bright, friendly, and interesting.

When her "I'm a bisexual" article came out during her second semester, Ms. Mentor would forthrightly give copies to everyone in the chain of command: dean, department chair, any mentors she'd acquired. She would attach a cover note saying that she wants to share her latest work with them.

But Ms. Mentor would not do this out of recklessness. Ms. Mentor, a recovering nerd, is never reckless. Rather, Ms. Mentor would distribute her article out of simple expedience. It's easier to get it over with than to worry.

Ms. Mentor is allergic to worrying.

Tough Cookies

Q: In my first year at N University, I'm one of half a dozen young (thirtyish) women faculty, instructors and assistant professors, in a college of mostly over-fifties. The older women are friendly to me and my age co-hort, but we're strong feminists who have nothing in common with them. They thrive on pouring tea and baking cookies and having showers for the secretaries.

We can't stand that stuff, and we've drawn lots as to which of us will make an appearance at such gatherings and then leave quickly. The older women are just from another era and generation, and it might be easiest if we all just left each other alone.

Recently, though, I wrote an article about the generation gap in my col-lege, and it was published in a national journal—whereupon my chair, a man given to rages, duplicated it and distributed it all over campus. Al-though I tried to be kind to the older women, it's being read as if I trashed them. Everyone seems to hate me.

Is my goose cooked?

A: Ms. Mentor wishes you hadn't written the article. Or if you had to write it, that you'd left it in your computer and not sent it out. Or that the journal had refused to publish it, in order to protect you. Or that your chair had been a kind person who bought up the journal's whole press run, and burned it.

Truly, there are very few gracious ways for young people to criticize their elders in public. (There are, of course, countless very old and un-gracious ways, ranging from T-shirts saying, "Don't Trust Anyone Over Thirty" to Oedipus's very crude treatment of his dad.)

But even a much milder young critic can easily come across as a whiner ("my mom makes me SOOOOO mad") or an insensitive boor ("I hate it when she . . .") or an ingrate ("she's always talking about all the sacrifices she made for me, but I didn't ask her to make them").

You'll notice that Ms. Mentor's examples are all from mother-daughter conflicts. Indeed, she suspects that your objections to the older women smack of some *matrophobia*, the fear of becoming like your own mother. The older women are doing the stuff your mom did, but by becoming an academic you've rejected your mom's Sterile, Boring Life as a Housewife. You don't want to be thrown back into that Drivel.

However, the tea-and-cookies-and-whatever events have been, for gen-erations, a form of female bonding, a celebration of achievements that male members rarely note: births, marriages, life changes. Ms. Mentor admits that some shower activities can be silly or boring, such as name games or discussions of infantile diarrhea. But gift exchanges can be fascinating: can you link the gift to the giver? Best of all, you get to see your female co-workers away from the eyes of the patriarchs.

You may hear wildly raunchy stories: once unleashed, women of all ages can be wickedly witty. Showers can be centers of female power, with gossip, networking, and discovering that *everyone* knows that the old goat Professor Hefner never looks at women's faces. You may think you're the only one he's annoyed, but you'll find out that he's already spent umpteen years (as the song goes) trying to "do the breast stroke in the typing pool." No one knows more than the secretaries do, and no wise woman academic skips a chance to get ammunition from them.

That means more than "just putting in an appearance," which strikes Ms. Mentor as a rude gesture. An hour out of one's day is not a great sacrifice. It is a kindness to other women, and a chance to achieve some real female solidarity.

But meanwhile, your raging chair, the distributor of your article, seems to be creating female solidarity of a totally different kind: getting the women you criticized to unite against you. You evidently patronized them, and they feel, perhaps rightly, that you were one step away from outright trashing.

What can you do now?

Ms. Mentor suggests you look quietly for another job: the tempest you've unleashed may not be quellable in time for you to get tenure where you are. In the meantime, try to mend fences. Invite the older women to lunch with you, one or two at a time, and explain to them that you were misunderstood, or you were wrong. Apologize; grovel. You have made a big mistake, and you need to humble yourself.

You might even consider buying—or better yet, baking—cookies to give the older women. If you can pull it off, give each of them a pastry and label it "humble pie."

Forget pride. Forget whether tea and cookies are—to you—stupid. If you're a smart cookie, and a feminist, you'll want to be allies, not enemies, with all the women in your world.

That's what being a feminist means.

The
Perils and Pleasures
of Teaching

In graduate school in her well-spent youth, Ms. Mentor learned all about the famed philosopher Friedrich Nietzsche, an academic whiz who became a full professor at the age of twenty-four. Still discontented—like all academics—Nietzsche had a habit of endlessly kvetching about the burdens of teaching. He wildly resented, he said, the requirement that one must "think in front of other people."

Nietzsche, of course, had many other difficulties. Among them were a repellent personality and a very small penis—problems that do not trouble women who teach in American universities nowadays.

But the core requirement—that one must think in front of other people—remains. Especially for young women teachers, it can be debilitating, as in the following missive to Ms. Mentor:

Q: Because I teach about the Americans with Disabilities Act, I often get interesting and strange questions in class. Here's one a student posed recently.

> I read in a tabloid that on their wedding night, Pamela Anderson (of *Baywatch*) and Tommy Lee (of Motley Crüe, Heather Locklear's ex) had such wild, passionate sex that she bit off his nipple ring. They had to go to a hospital emergency room. Will he now be considered disabled?

Ms. Mentor, how would you answer such an enquiring mind?

I should tell you that the fellow who asked the question is not dull witted. He is a smart, wisecracky fellow who sits in the back, baseball cap on backward, and sees it as his duty to entertain the class, often at my expense.

I'm young, fairly new to teaching, and unsure about my authority, and he picks all of that up, I'm sure. (Where do they get this evil radar?)

How do I establish authority with college students? And *will* Tommy Lee be considered disabled?

A: Ms. Mentor finds it hard to imagine that intact, unpierced nipples are ever a necessity for male employment, or that a damaged nipple could require "reasonable accommodation" (an ADA requirement to allow disabled people to keep working). But perhaps Ms. Mentor's imagination is failing her.

She does rule, however, that both newlyweds lacked common sense, decorum, and discretion. But that is not considered a disability. It is simply bad taste. Ms. Mentor cringes.

Ms. Mentor also cringes at some of the bawdy and peculiar questions young undergraduates ask, although she concedes that they have a right to their ignorance and their tacky wit, just as grownups do. She is glad that the students can also console or distract themselves with sex, drugs, and rock 'n' roll.

Ms. Mentor's larger concern is new faculty, and the savage shoals of teaching.

Few people are natural teachers. If they are, they're more apt to make better nurses or dictators. Academic personalities, in particular, may have trouble with teaching, since it requires skills so different from scholarship.

Ms. Mentor is impressed each year with the schizophrenic ability of academics to juggle two personalities. To be a publishing scholar, one must work well alone, reading and writing and thinking. But to be a teacher, especially in our media-saturated age, one must be able to put on a show— be a standup comedian.

How many bookworms can also act like Whoopi Goldberg or Lily Tomlin? Could Elayne Boosler or Roseanne write a university press book on postmodernism or a grant proposal about nematodes?

Graduate school traditionally nurtures the bookworm/lab pallor side. The would-be academic learns to do research, plan scholarly activities, and write up grant work. On the side—and it's always treated as a diversion—

the student may also have to teach a course or two, or sometimes even a full teaching load, with little or no help or supervision.

Moreover, faculty traditionally act as if anyone can teach. Newly hired young professors are, typically, hurled into teaching, sink or swim: many do not even choose their own reading lists. Most survive, but they also quickly learn not to talk about their terrors. Teaching goes on secretly, behind closed doors.

Meanwhile, whenever a new president or chancellor is installed at a research university, s/he will proclaim a "new emphasis on first-class teaching." That emphasis is too rarely supported with anything tangible, however, except a few teaching awards, usually funded by oil companies. At some universities those awards are consolation prizes for faculty who otherwise won't get raises, because they don't publish.

Still, teaching may be the scariest of all parts of an academic's job. It requires organization and assertion of authority, two qualities discouraged in women. Many men love ditzes and despise assertive women: *I Love Lucy* reruns are always more popular on TV than *Cagney & Lacey*.

Also, as Erica Jong once wrote in a poem called "The Teacher," students often "aren't hungry for Chaucer." They'd much rather devour the teacher: they "are eating her knees, her toes, her breasts." For "What do they want with words? / They want a real lesson!"

Yet teachers *can* push back the frontiers of knowledge, open minds, change lives, and give their students real lessons. Sometimes teachers do it best when no one's particularly looking, as is often the case at American universities.

Teaching is a job for strong and canny women in the same mold as Ms. Mentor, who, in this section, will help others to attain self-confidence, authority, and sterling teaching evaluations.

Elizabeth or the Queen

Q: I'm fairly new to teaching, and I like a casual tone. Is it OK to have students call me by my first name?

A: Ms. Mentor assumes that you are asking a deeper question: Should I be buddies with my students or have them treat me as a pompous professorial heavyweight?

You probably expect Ms. Mentor to say that you may be folksy in your youth, but formal in middle age—the generation gap. But Ms. Mentor, in fact, recommends the opposite: a judicious distance for the young; an informal warmth for the mature.

Most young women have difficulty establishing authority in the class-room. But if you're teaching Women's Studies, French, nursing, or human ecology—subjects primarily taken by women—your students are not apt to challenge your training and credibility. Women students may steam and bubble underneath and whisper about their young professor's fashion sense, but they still tend to be cooperative. They want to learn from you, or at least get good grades. Young women don't like conflict.

But male students, in science, engineering, and general education courses, can be—well, a challenge. Given the fallibilities of the human gene pool, such courses inevitably enroll a certain percentage of boy louts, including class clowns and showoffs and late-adolescent rebels. They'll argue with you; they'll interrupt and bully you and other students. And especially in Gen Ed, some just won't do the reading (perhaps they can't).

To teach them, you will need to show your fortitude.

One way is through tough grading; another is through being icily firm about grades, requirements, and any other bureaucratic rules. Every young faculty member learns to be very specific, covering all contingencies, in the course outline and information sheets. Do not waver, and do not hedge. Deadlines are deadlines; attendance is required; papers must be in dark type; misspellings will not be forgiven; missed work cannot be made up. Some college students, especially in their early years, still need to learn that school is like a job: you have to show up and do the work.

When you're most firm, you may feel that you're a demagogue more than a pedagogue, but you'll be taken more seriously and treated with more respect.

And do not let the male students, however obstreperous, dominate your classes. Speak to the women; make a point of calling on women who raise their hands; give them ownership of their ideas and make their points part of the class knowledge base ("As Victoria said . . ."). Teach to the women. You are their role model as well as their teacher.

Another way to enhance your authority is to appear older. (Ms. Mentor has always been a natural authority figure, but most women need help.) Speak in a lower voice register; frost your hair and cut it short. Wear long skirts in dark or neutral colors; wear glasses; avoid obvious makeup. If your students are obsessed with what you look like, you've lost their academic attention.

And that may happen with first-naming. In some liberal arts colleges, students and faculty are encouraged to be pals and companions. Students drop over for supper; students and profs share wholesome activities such as volleyball, backpacking, chess, and singing "Kumbayah." (Such places are often rife with sexual harassment, too.)

But in standard-issue universities, especially in urban areas, there's little time or motivation for student-faculty friendships. Many students have full-time jobs; most faculty, especially untenured ones, desperately need to work on writing and publishing. To do so, they must lock their office doors, and students must respect their "Do Not Disturb" signs.

All of which is easier for you and your students if they call you "Dr. Cerebral" rather than "Celeste." Dr. Cerebral has earned a Ph.D. in her subject, knows much more than her students, and is entitled to her private time. When students call you "Dr. Cerebral," they'll be showing respect for women's achievements and knowledge.

(Ms. Mentor does allow exceptions for graduate students. If they and you are very close in age, she will permit them to call you Celeste, and you to call them Arthur, Babar, or whatever. You may also socialize with grad students, at parties or bars or in groups. But no romances. That is one of Ms. Mentor's inflexible rules.)

As you age: grad students are less apt to want to hang out with you. But when you're facing undergrads, much of the respect and authority you struggled for as a younger person will come to you naturally. It also helps to be fatter: women of substance take up more space and seem more powerful as well as more engaging. (Oprah Winfrey is always more popular when she's heavier.)

Age, size, and experience will all make you more self-confident. No one will mistake you for some teenager who wandered off the streets and decided it would be a good prank to play the role of professor. And that's when you can let down your guard about first-naming, joking, bantering, and offering advice—even unsolicited. If you don't mumble and seem to descend into hopeless maundering, you can even tell stories about "When I was your age . . ."

In short, middle age is a time when you can relax in front of the student public. Looks and clothes matter much less, and you can become yourself at last—and not worry about whether your students will respect you tomorrow.

Once you're over forty, you can go ahead and tell your classes, "Call me Celeste." But most students, especially the younger ones, won't. After all, you're the age of their parents.

You can continue to have them call you Dr. Cerebral, as they've already been doing for years. Or—in honor of your age, great wisdom, and powerful presence—you can have them call you the title Ms. Mentor most prefers:

YOUR MAJESTY.

Grovelers

Q: I know many women professors have trouble establishing authority. Maybe it's that I'm a large African American woman with a big voice, but I seem to evoke the opposite reaction: terror and cringing. I don't mean that students hide under their desks, but sometimes they stammer in class discussions, and they're forever having anxiety attacks over minutiae. They agonize over how to space the titles of their papers, or how wide their margins should be, or any number of little rituals that don't have anything to do with learning. It's exasperating, and I don't know what to do about it.

A: Ms. Mentor, ever ready with an elegant phrase, calls their behavior "Permission to Pee": it's as if they're begging for an OK to do what they ought to do on their own, naturally.

Of course, you may have a bunch of students who went to very rigid high schools. Or they may have had very strict parents, or authoritarian teachers in your subject. Or maybe they're just a weird crew of anal compulsives and obsessives.

Whatever. Ms. Mentor sympathizes with your annoyance. You want to teach, not issue hall passes or certificates conferring the authority to urinate.

The simplest way is to give 'em what they crave: rigid instructions. On your handouts for course projects, tell them how they should head their papers and what margins they should use. Insist on dark print or type (a good idea, anyway); tell them their papers must be "mechanically perfect" and you won't read any that aren't. You'll return them, unread.

They'll get the margins and the rest right, and that can be good training.

Many grant and job applicants do lose out when they don't follow directions; national grant panels routinely weed out people who fail to sign and date their applications.

But since your students want to follow rules slavishly, you can also assign and require them to be independent thinkers. (This is sly.) Require them to come up with a new idea, or phrase, or number, or process. Require them to do something original. If they moan, tell them those are your inflexible rules.

You don't have to be as wily as Ms. Mentor to figure out ways to channel students' fears into learning—but it helps.

And do give your students permission to pee, whenever they ask. For the mind can absorb only what the kidneys can endure.

Yolk's on Me

Q: They've got me teaching "Biology for Poets," a lecture course with one hundred fifty students—all of whom look like they think I'm a jabbering fool. Sometimes I dream I've been walking around all day with egg on my face. Is this normal?

A: Yes, but Ms. Mentor suspects you may not yet have a tough enough hide. As Anne Sexton once wrote, "A woman who writes feels too much," and it is often true that a woman who teaches feels too much. She worries too much about not knowing everything, about how she's coming across, about whether the students are learning—and whether they are laughing at her.

Lacking other visual stimuli, they will certainly be watching her closely. They'll be scrutinizing her body, grading her wardrobe, noticing runs in her pantyhose, and erupting in hilarity if her shoes don't match. If she should happen to have a sliver of egg in the corner of her mouth or some crumbs on her bodice, their interest will be unbounded.

But all that says more about the boredom and distractability of youth than it says about you.

You do not have to be Superwoman: your job is to communicate in a well-organized and enthusiastic manner. Open each class with a joke or story or news item: that's called the "motivation" (or, among standup comics, the "warmup"). Standardize everything—assignments, grading standards, deadlines, typefaces on transparencies—and list your expectations on the course outline you hand out at the start of the course. That's called C.Y.A. (covering your ass).

Now Ms. Mentor happens to enjoy the theatrical side of teaching, for it makes good use of her native grandiosity (in another life, she was Tina Turner). She can lecture with equal brilliance to one hundred fifty or to one poor advice seeker. But for shrinking-violet teachers who dread unexpected questions and answers, Ms. Mentor advises: use visuals (tapes, slides, and charts), and get thee behind the lectern.

Yes, women are sometimes reluctant to lecture: it *is* bossy and patriarchal. Indeed, declaiming Truth can feel quite fraudulent if one is thirtyish and an expert on toads and little else. Still, someone who's triumphed in grad school knows more than her audience. That is why she's the teacher.

It is far easier to lecture than to try to wrest any kind of discussion from recalcitrant or puzzled or very large audiences. A lecturer can write on the board, or pace, gesture, dramatize, grimace, snicker. She can use her voice as an expressive tool: Ms. Mentor, who possesses a naturally warm and mellow contralto, has sometimes burst into song, providing transcendent moments for her auditors.

But even for the most committed introverts, planning a lecture takes less time than a discussion, and that leaves you more time for your writing and research. (Far be it from Ms. Mentor to hint that some lecture notes can be cribbed from past professors or books, of course.) Lecturing will also get you the good teaching evaluations an untenured person needs: students generally give better ratings to lecturers. (Ms. Mentor, had she space, would here decry the passivity of today's youth—but that rant will have to wait for a later time.)

As for Egg on the Face: that is a common academic dream. So is The Lost Class, in which the student finds, to her horror, that she's registered for a class she's never attended. At the next level is The Lost Course: the professor finds, to her horror, that she's supposed to have taught a course she knew nothing about. She's never even met the class.

Eventually, though, all those dreams will stop disrupting your slumbers. Instead, like Ms. Mentor, you will dream of grandeur and glory and Margaret Fuller, the sage of nineteenth-century Concord and the patron saint of wise women who reject all pretense of humility. Margaret Fuller once said: "I now know all the people worth knowing in America and I find no intellect comparable to my own." She also wrote to Ralph Waldo Emerson: "I myself am more divine than any I see."

Ms. Mentor often feels that way, and hopes that someday you, too, will feel equal confidence in your own perfection.

Crisis in Counseling

Q: A student recently told me she'd been raped by her stepfather. What can I do to help her?

A: Ms. Mentor assumes that you want to offer comfort, as we should to all suffering fellow creatures. "I'm very sorry" is always the right thing to say. And so is the offer of a name of someone in the counseling center who can listen and help. Or failing that, someone in the local Rape Crisis Center, or Women's Center. Or if you don't have a name, offer to call around and find one. The local Battered Women's Program should have a name and number to call.

Ms. Mentor advises you not to become the student's freelance therapist or counselor (unless you have some background and experience in the field). The risk of saying the wrong thing is enormous. For instance, you may think the student should report the rapist to legal authorities, but the student may be terrified at the thought. You may think the student should seek revenge, or an abortion, or public confrontation, but the student may be thinking more about suicide.

If you give inappropriate advice, you may also leave yourself open to lawsuits, which, besides damaging you, may destroy the student's privacy forever.

Many teachers like to believe that by being nurturing and compassionate listeners they can truly turn a student's life around. The idea is appealing and seductive and central to many movies and TV shows. The endlessly patient teacher says all the right things, devotes selfless hours to the troubled but gifted underachieving student, and saves that student's soul.

"TEACHER SAVES THE DAY" is a fantasy that draws many people into being educators. But in real life, a professor rarely possesses the skill, the time, or the power to be such a savior. Ms. Mentor wishes we could all save one another, but we are fallible.

And so she advises you to offer your suffering student sympathy, and tea, and tissues, and a listening ear if you're the only one available on the spot. But resist, gently, any pressures to be a long-term adviser or counselor.

Ms. Mentor also commends you for being an approachable teacher, the kind of woman students want to confide in. You are probably a warm and likable person, and a wise one. And sometimes the wisest thing you can do is to say as little as possible—but with kindness.

Grade Not Appealing

Q: All semester I had an obnoxious student, "Sid," who constantly challenged me. He'd claim I misspelled words on the board (I didn't); he'd interrupt and "reinterpret" what I said for the class; he'd emit a continuous stream of objections and irrelevant questions, all designed to embarrass me and derail my lectures. I didn't see any reason for his conduct except an animosity toward women—both me and women students. I was desperately relieved when the semester was over.

Now, though, he's filed a grade appeal over his B. (He deserved a C, but I thought a higher grade would shut him up.) My department seems to take grade appeals very seriously, and I've been told to schedule a mediation meeting. I'm untenured, and this is my first grade appeal ever. How do I prepare?

A: Ms. Mentor assumes you are in the humanities. Most grade appeals are in first-year composition, in fact, and most (according to composition directors) are frivolous. Most are based on the appealers' belief that "grading on writing is totally subjective" and "if I appeal, maybe they'll give me a better grade."

In general, few grades are ever changed, and faculty are almost always upheld. But you can protect yourself against any painful confrontations by documenting, documenting, documenting.

When "Sid" first started acting up, it would have been wise to write down what he did, very specifically. That would also be a good time to ask your department chair, or the composition director, about your alternatives: Do you have the power to remove a student from your class? Can you require a student to take a course via independent study and not attend class? At minimum, you should write a letter to Sid's academic counselor about his behavior.

Then if Sid continues acting up, you can call him into your office for a conference and ply him with sweetly reasonable questions: Does he have some sort of attention deficit or other problem that is keeping him from concentrating on the course work? Does he need tutoring or extra reading? Is he having trouble hearing you or seeing what's on the board? (It will not be amiss to record this conversation, via your phone machine.)

It can be very effective to tell Sid that other students have complained about his behavior. He's still, after all, a teenager, and teenagers are terrified at being thought uncool by their peers.

If Sid persists in his rude ways, you may suggest that he drop the course, get advice about his attitude, switch to independent study, or take whatever other alternatives your research has turned up. (Ms. Mentor knows it is no ideal solution, but some departments do harbor a resident bully, a large male faculty member who'll tell Sid to settle down, or else.)

If Sid persists, that's when you consult your composition director and/or department chair again and write Sid a letter, setting forth the case: he was disruptive on September 15, September 22, and October 4, and he is hereby warned that his behavior may result in his removal from, or failure in, the course. Copies of the letter should be filed with your director and chair, his academic counselor, and anyone else who should be notified.

At this point the Sids of the world usually do settle down, although they sometimes wage a guerrilla war, urging other students to rebel, write letters, interrupt, or be uncooperative. Usually they meet with only moderate success: most students just want to get their grades and degrees and get on with their lives. Some students, especially women, may decide they hate Sid, but few will actively confront him.

(Sometimes, though, the women will conduct a lively and highly effective whispering campaign. "Cheryl" once spread the word that "John," the class loudmouth, had made some sexual oinkings in her direction, but that she had told him to "get out of my face." From her friends, Cheryl knew— and told everyone, including her professor—that John "has a needle dick and no idea what to do with it.")

All this can, of course, poison a classroom atmosphere, and sometimes you can't recover from it. Do not blame yourself: life is short, and no one's ruined by a bad or awkward course. But it's worthwhile to put an explanatory note in your department dossier in case your evaluation scores are lower than usual.

Back to the grade appeal meeting: Sid may be snarly, but he hasn't a case. You can come armed with a typed description of his transgressions (even if you don't have exact dates); a typed statement that his behavior was detrimental to the education of other members of the class, with specific examples; and a record of his grades. If his final grade was higher than he deserved, you can point that out—and offer to give him the truly fair grade, the C.

(This technique also works with the Comparative Complainer: "You gave me a C on my exam, and my buddy Joey got a B. That's not fair!" Your answer: "I'll look over both your exams, and grade them both again, but you'll have to tell Joey that *his* grade may be lowered in the process.")

Ms. Mentor knows that grade appeals can be particularly distressing for women faculty, who are more apt to dread confrontations and bullying. Even winning such an appeal is no great pleasure.

She urges you to schedule the grade-appeal meeting as soon as possible, to get it out of your life. Otherwise it will fester in your psyche and destroy your rest.

And once it's over, go home. Take a long, hot shower and settle down with some bonbons, and a good book. Ms. Mentor especially recommends a Jane Austen novel.

You've earned an appealing reward.

Grading the Teaching

Q: How can I get good student evaluations when students value cold, pompous male lecturers much more than warm, lively female discussion leaders?

Q: I won a teaching award, and a colleague (we're at a major research university) told me that's the kiss of death: I won't get tenure. Can that be true?

A: These two queries illustrate the peculiar views held by some academics about teaching: it's valuable, but not entirely; it's valued most when it's done the way men do it.

At research universities, teaching awards are indeed sometimes sops to faculty who won't get tenure. Women faculty can be stereotyped as "teachers first," meaning that their research and publication won't be taken seriously. Rhetoric and composition, a dynamic field in which women have made extraordinary and original discoveries, is sometimes dismissed as "the kitchen." At truly mean schools, popular teachers (of any sex) are known as "popularizers" and "whores."

Yet at the same research universities, there are sometimes, alas, untenured faculty who haven't listened to Ms. Mentor: women who brag that they "always keep my door open for students." As a result, they don't have time to publish. They haven't met the university criteria—and out they go.

It is also a melancholy truth that students can be snowed by the appearance of authority. As Susan Basow and other researchers have shown, students often enjoy small discussion classes with a vital, nurturing female teacher. Sometimes they even say they learned more ("it was eye-opening") in such a class. But when it comes to rating their instructors, numerically . . . the male profs, pacing at the podium and lecturing to multitudes, get the higher scores.

A loud voice also pays off: it promotes confidence in listeners as well as speakers.

What's a woman to do?

Ms. Mentor decrees: If teaching counts and the wise assistant professor does not have tenure, she must figure out what "sells" in teaching evaluations. She can lecture, striving to be audible and self-confident. She can be entertaining: students enjoy humor and illustrative stories, especially in technical fields such as agriculture, biochemistry, and engineering. Whatever the subject, adolescents adore gory stories.

In the humanities and social sciences, pointed anecdotes are often the best teaching devices. (Jesus used parables; Ms. Mentor shares stories from real life.) Tale-telling teachers need to avoid bizarre fixations, however: one semester, an obscure Colorado linguistics professor created a workbook in which every single sentence dealt with Jeffrey Dahmer, the notorious multiple murderer and cannibal. ("Too creepy," said one student who dropped the course and enrolled in "The Literature of Horror" instead.)

Realists do, of course, know the single thing that does the most to improve a teacher's evaluations: giving high grades. Occasionally a researcher in the *Chronicle of Higher Education* will claim there is no correlation between students' grades and their evaluations of their teachers. Perhaps the researchers are not deliberate liars, says Ms. Mentor, but they are surely wrong.

The truly self-protective, or cynical, teacher will pay special attention to what she does just before the course evaluation forms are distributed. Some prepare lively jokes or stories or handouts; some sing and dance; some show videos. One untenured Penn State professor used to be famous for throwing a wine and cheese party for his students on the last day of class, evaluation day. (He stopped the parties once he got tenure—about the time there was one of those periodic crackdowns on underaged drinking.)

Once tenured, of course, women faculty can work to create evaluation forms that reflect and value women's teaching styles. "Mastery of subject matter" can be changed to "Communication of subject matter," for instance; mutuality can be stressed. "Encouragement of student participation" can be emphasized, and "Presentation of essential facts through lectures" downplayed.

Many evaluation forms now assume the Banking Model of Education: the pouring of knowledge from one head into another, via lecturing. But evaluations could be based on the Midwife Model: the teacher brings out what the learner already knows while adding new information, more complex approaches and paradigms, and a greater depth and richness to the mix.

Ms. Mentor, ever the pragmatist, recommends that women do what they must to get tenure, and then change the recipe. Only the permanent chefs, after all, ever get to tinker with the sauce.

Teaching About Disability

Q: Because I'm teaching at a newly built campus that prides itself on being accessible to people with disabilities, I have students in my classes with serious physical problems. One carts around an oxygen tank, for instance, and another has a special gadget that seems to enable her to see sideways. But the "able-bodied" young undergraduate teenagers seem pretty insensitive and giggly, and I'd like to teach them a thing or two about disability. Does Ms. Mentor have some suggestions, both for my Women's Studies and non-Women's Studies classes?

A: Ms. Mentor is never without suggestions. Herewith, she offers some essay questions that you may use for discussion.

SOME QUESTIONS ABOUT DISABILITY

1. When did you first see someone who had a disability? Were you trained to look away from people with disabilities? What were you told NOT to say?

2. What hidden disabilities do you have?

3. If you have a hidden disability, do you think it's a good idea to come out as a person with disabilities or stay in the closet?

4. Would people you know go to a panel discussion on "Women with Disabilities," or be afraid to go?

5. Do women who work outside the home try too hard to be Super-women, ignoring all possible "weaknesses"?

6. In your observation, are mothers mostly blamed for children's disabilities? If so, why?

7. Young women suffer through street sexual harassment, constant judging of their clothes and looks, and worries about their worth as possible sexual partners—besides trying to establish themselves as professionals and perhaps as mothers. Older women, and disabled women, are liberated from much of that. Conclusion?

8. Do "professionals" such as doctors listen to the experiences and observations of mothers and caregivers, or do doctors pursue their own, more "objective" theories?

9. Wheelchair users need wide paths, but wide paths can be confusing for blind people who must navigate with canes. What would you do to make your place friendlier for disabled people?

10. If you're talking with a blind person, do you find yourself tempted to shout?

11. Is it better for families to treat disabled people the same ways they treat non-disabled people, or should people with disabilities receive different and special treatment?

12. If you were living in Baton Rouge and in love with a person in a wheelchair, would you tell your parents in Seattle about your lover's wheelchair? What about being in love with someone who's blind, or has had a leg amputated?

13. If you're having a meeting and a woman says she can't come if anyone wears perfume because she's allergic, do you ask everyone not to wear perfume or treat the woman as a neurotic complainer?

14. In a group, do you notice who may not be hearing what's said? Do you try to get others to speak louder or sit closer to her?

15. If you see someone park in a "Handicapped" spot with no evidence (special sticker, license plate) that the person is handicapped, do you ask that person to move?

16. Some feminists argue that oppression, not disability, is what causes pain. True?

Mommy Track

Q: I've never had a sunny disposition. By nature I'm a loner and often a grouch, especially in the morning. I do my lab work and interact pleasantly with colleagues, but then I want to go home, kick off my shoes, make myself a drink or three, and watch mindless TV or play with my cats or just veg out. But my department keeps trying to push me into "mommy track" jobs: supervising labs, handholding students through orals and job hunting.

Meanwhile, the men in the department never get pushed to do that stuff: their research is taken far more seriously as the best use of their time. Plus, anytime I've been coerced into doing the mommy stuff, it's meant frantic calls at home and earfuls of student problems (bad boyfriends, sexual abuse, and who knows what-all else). I'm not by temperament suited to any of that. Like Greta Garbo, my all-time favorite actress, "I vant to be alone."

A: Ms. Mentor, who treasures the solitude of her ivory tower, sympathizes with you, but also suggests that glamorous Greta Garbo is not the best image for what you want. Scientists do have to work in groups, after all, and slinking away—slouch-hatted, sloe-eyed—will make your team members, well, unappreciative.

They *will* appreciate, of course, your doing the "mommy jobs": everyone loves a comforter and problem solver, an earth mother who brings pies to work and cheerfully cooks huge, multicourse dinners every weekend for everyone who looks the slightest bit hangdoggish—all the things you must not do if you want a serious scientific career.

You want to be treated as a scientist, not a mom.

If you have tenure, you *can* just snarl, "Lemme alone!" But it's infinitely more gracious to educate your colleagues in an activity stressed by moms, but important to all: taking turns.

If you're asked to supervise a lab, agree to do it *this semester* (or even better, *this week*) "but the job should rotate to Bill next week." If you're asked to help a particular student, you may agree "this time—but the next case should be George's to handle." Given the way you describe yourself, you're no better suited to playing mom than any of the men, and there's no reason—except sexism—that you should do so. The men have shoulders that can be cried upon, too.

Ms. Mentor congratulates you for not suffering from the chronic female ailment: guilt. You are not responsible for everyone's happiness; you don't have to listen to everyone's problems, bandage knees, heal hurts, kiss bruises, and make everyone well. Your responsibility is to be the best scientist you can be, and it's up to others to help you achieve that goal.

It's OK with Ms. Mentor if you're not a mom. But she hopes that sometime, somewhere, you will be, now and then—a mentor.

Mentoring the Maladjusted

Q: As the lone woman faculty member in our science department, I've been fastened upon by a woman graduate student who continually appears in my office with complaints of unfair treatment by several professors—involving (variously) her gender, sexual orientation, race, or immigrant status. Many of the complaints are believable, but it has also become apparent that the student is (not to put too fine a point on it) nutty. Maybe because of her mental problems, she's now screwing up course work, losing lab notes, accumulating Incompletes, and threatening to sue everyone in sight. How can I get out of this mess?

A: As quickly as possible, and preferably with outside advice. You cannot help a student who is "nutty," and some nuts are indeed harmful. You must tell her that she is no longer on your research team, while making sure that you have her lab notes, that she has a duplicate copy, and that any research you publish with her work includes her name (even if someone else has to check and redo her experimental work).

You should also get advice from the student counseling center, and from campus security if she seems at all dangerous. And from your department chair—to cover yourself legally.

Here Ms. Mentor knows many readers will object: if you turn in Ms. Nut, her problems will be used against all women. ("We used to have women graduate students in this unit, but they didn't work out.") But if you *don't* separate yourself, then all women will surely be lumped together, and dumped upon. You can't be a role model if you're a victim.

Women often nurture beyond the point when nurturing is even safe, never mind useful. ("Show me a woman who doesn't feel guilty, and I'll show you a man," Erica Jong wrote two decades ago in *Fear of Flying*.) If you need an extreme example: think of the Tejano singer Selena, shot and killed by a fan she could not help.

Just help yourself out of the situation, and preserve your energies for your colleagues, your work, and those students you can raise to be your colleagues. Sometimes you need to run away, to mentor again another day.

Evening Wood

Q: I'm in forestry, which involves field trips into rough country. But I never wanted to be waving the feminist banner, too. Three months after I was hired, as the first woman on the department faculty, three undergraduate girls—OK, young women—showed up in my office complaining that the prof running the field trip for their required freshman course had announced to the whole bus that the motel they were staying in had pornographic movies on its cable system. (His pretense was warning the guys not to stay up all night, since they had a 6 A.M. start.)

The female students didn't object to the motel's policy, but to the professor's announcement. And, of course, they expect me to *do* something. But I am not their mom, or their elected representative. I think it was up to them to speak up when it happened. As Rick says in *Casablanca*, my favorite movie, "I stick my neck out for nobody."

A: Ms. Mentor, also a *Casablanca* fan, notes that Ingrid Bergman's character had an easier time than you do: she didn't have to represent all women. You, unfortunately, have been cast in a role for which you never auditioned.

Ms. Mentor agrees with you that women should fight their own battles. The students are asking you to tangle with a senior professor who controls your future as well as theirs. And they want you to do so based on hearsay: their version of events.

They're expecting you to say to your boss "I heard you said something sexist on your trip. That's not nice"—to which your boss might rightly retort: "Since when is it your business?"

In this case, truthfully, it is not your business. And if you become a buttinski, you'll do nothing but make enemies. But there are other ways to handle such situations if, as is almost certain, you wind up on such a field trip yourself.

Suppose Dr. Porno makes his announcement. That's your chance to say to the women: "Well, the women will be meeting in my room to talk over the project." That's neat, firm, and businesslike, and it lets the women students exit gracefully from the macho scene. (You may not be a mother hen by nature, but you don't have to be: they'll appreciate the gesture.)

Inviting the women to your room also forces Dr. Porno to notice that there *are* women. He may blush at what he's just said; he may writhe with terror at the thought of women's meeting by themselves. Once "the chicks" are all together in one room (he may be thinking), what's to prevent them from making up stories about the men and their tiny penises?

In reality, while you're having a good, professional natter with the women, the men will be rooming together in pairs—and few things make men more nervous than watching sex together, two by two. (In porno movie theaters, men rarely sit together: see the beginning of John Grisham's *The Pelican Brief*.) The next day, if you or the women students are feeling frisky, you can ask the men, sweetly and conversationally, if they watched any TV movies. If they flush . . . you can smirk to yourselves.

Ms. Mentor knows that you don't want to be a feminist champion. But since you'll be cast in that role anyway, you may find that the women students are superb supporting players and networkers: they can tell you what your male colleagues are up to. The students, like the department secretaries, can be your allies and comrades.

Sisterhood is very powerful, and you shouldn't miss the forest for the trees.

Chilly Classroom Climate

Q: I consider myself a strong, committed feminist, but—Goddess help me—I truly prefer teaching men. (I teach American history.) Male students are more energetic and responsive in class. They argue, they throw ideas back and forth, and they work at proving and winning their points. My women students are much more quiet and passive. Sometimes they make me feel guilty that I'm not doing enough to draw them out in discussion.

Should I wallow in guilt, or go with the flow?

A: It is a far, far better thing to do what you have done: to write to Ms. Mentor. She will straighten you out—after telling you that guilt is a useless emotion. No feminist should submit to it.

You should be aware, though, that you are part of the problem, not the solution, to the "chilly classroom climate" originally described nearly two decades ago by Roberta A. Hall and Bernice Sandler. Teachers of both sexes are more apt to call on men, ask them more thought-provoking questions, give them more conversational space, and encourage them to develop ideas. Women students get less time and attention; they're asked rote questions; and are even deprived of eye contact with teachers.

Moreover, many of the questions and assumptions in standard classes are male-oriented. Algebra problems ask about dumping sand or gravel, but why can't they ask about recipes? (Nowadays, everyone cooks, or should.) Children's books still show many more boys than girls, and textbook examples of activity, adventure, and valor are too often still male ("The pioneers and their wives went West . . ."). Football may be talked about as a universal language and source of idioms, examples, and emotional sustenance. But in fact many more students grow up watching sitcoms, in which women and family life are featured.

(Ms. Mentor herself recommends soap operas, the only TV genre in which women's concerns are central. College men especially like soaps as a way of learning about emotions.)

But back to the classroom. As youngsters, boys may have been more active and demanding, but by the time they reach college, they don't have to be. They've been rewarded again and again, and the curriculum and standard teaching methods have been honed to meet their needs. A classroom where argumentation is stressed, and where the combatants aggressively interrupt each other, and where winning points is the goal—that rewards men.

Such an atmosphere also, too often, silences women.

Throughout their lives, young women have been learning that they should value connection, caring, listening, and sharing. They've also learned not to fight or confront over ideas (some researchers call this young women's "loss of voice"). Ms. Mentor believes that feminist teachers—indeed, all teachers—should have as their main goal: getting women's voices back.

How to do it?

There are many ways to make people share in class. Some are mechanical: at the start of discussion, give everyone a green card. Once a student speaks, she writes her name on the card and puts it down on her desk. She's not allowed to speak again until everyone else has spoken. (Ms. Mentor has witnessed one or two greedy students stealing other people's cards, but that is rare.)

In lecture classes, everyone can be assigned to contribute by writing and turning in a daily comment or question on a card. Some cards will be read and responded to during the next class, and the teacher can particularly choose to react to the women's comments.

(Ms. Mentor also recommends comparing women's and men's cards. Women will usually add to what's been said, with examples and amplifications: "What you said reminded me of . . ." Men, though, will almost invariably object, and begin their comments with "But," as in "But you failed to mention . . ." Women try to extend the discussion; men try to control it.)

But suppose you want a simple, free-flowing discussion. You can encourage women's contributions by the kinds of questions you ask. Men respond eagerly to polarizing questions: "Was Abraham Lincoln or Robert E. Lee right?" Men like to take sides and yell at each other, even over very-long-settled feuds. They like to choose their team, and vilify its opponents.

Women tend to be more thoughtful about competition, and not because it's unladylike: women can be very tough sports competitors. But women have a more complex relationship to loud, aggressive arguments. By the time they reach age eighteen, a quarter of American young women will have been sexually molested, and one out of ten has been an incest victim. Women know all kinds of domestic violence; they know that out-of-control arguments can escalate into something fearsome. Women often prefer not to get involved.

Ms. Mentor recommends that you ask different kinds of questions, to get women involved: "Suppose you're Abraham Lincoln. Knowing you have some serious problems down South, what are some of the goals you might have for your presidency?" Or, "Suppose you're Robert E. Lee, and you're ambivalent about slavery. Why are you ambivalent? What will it take to make up your mind?"

This kind of questioning elicits a list of possibilities, which you can write on the board, thereby giving everyone something satisfying to write in their notebooks. These questions also encourage all students to think about human choices and needs, the stuff that women already know best: *why* people do what they do.

From there you can go on to another list: "Once you, as Robert E. Lee, have decided to cast your lot with the South"—a tragic and melancholy choice, full of human interest that emotionally engages students—"what will you need to do first? What will you lose and gain?"

The list-evoking question can get even the shyest of women to respond, because there's no risk. And once she's spoken, and the teacher's said "Good," and reinforced her by listing her contribution on the board, a young woman's intellectual life can be changed around.

Ms. Mentor knows of many such cases.

She also knows that you may be an impatient, energetic teacher, one eager to "get on with the lesson" and "cover the material." In that case, you may think that orienting the class toward women's interests and styles of thinking takes longer—but it may not. If you listen closely to the arguments propounded by polarizing men, you may hear a good deal of dross: posturing, insulting, filling up space with sound and fury.

With the quieter consideration of women, you teach people to ponder before they open their mouths, and to listen to others—and to raise their hands when they want to speak (a good lesson for all). By concentrating on women, you can teach that thoughtful is better than glib, and that thinking about human motives is as valuable as dryly reciting data.

History is dynamic—but so is herstory. Ms. Mentor hopes you'll devote yourself to teaching that.

Learners Laugh

Q: Last week, a senior colleague asked me why there was so much laughter in my classroom. He seemed suspicious that we were having too much fun. I know from students that he's a dour sour puss. What should I say or do?

A: Just close your classroom door. Then you and the students lucky enough to be in your classes can chuckle, snort, guffaw, chortle, giggle, hurl, titter, and roar all you like.

When Cultures Collide

"Nobody like me has ever been an academic."

Ms. Mentor has often heard this said by academic women. Indeed, it is mostly true. Although we are told that the professoriate is now open to all comers, it still remains mostly white, heterosexual, middle class, Christian, and male.

Despite more than two decades of feminist activism—and the existence of over six hundred Women's Studies programs around the nation—women are still just 10 percent of the full professors, the top rank in academia. In fact, most of women's increase in numbers is at the bottom: the instructors, with few benefits and less security.

The situation for women of color is no better than that of white women. Although right-wingers continually claim that "unqualified" people of color are getting all the good jobs (and why are white men automatically assumed to be "qualified"?), in fact most of the tenurable slots go to—the people they've always gone to.

Pale and male.

It is true that only 43 percent of U.S. faculty hired between 1986 and 1992 were native-born white males, but men were two-thirds of those hired at research universities, the most prestigious and best-paying. Men were much more apt to have tenure-track slots, while women toiled as instructors and lecturers. Asian American men made the greatest gains; African Americans fell behind.

What has changed dramatically, however, is the composition of the paying customers. In some of the best California state universities, whites are now a student minority. Throughout the U.S., graduate programs in engineering and math, and many in the sciences, are now kept afloat by foreign students—not all of whom get along smoothly.

American universities today are full of cultural collisions, and not just over multiculturalism. Ms. Mentor's correspondents worry about cultural abysses: not only the old boys' network arrayed against the younger girls, but the WASPS against the "ethnics," the quiche-eaters against the hamburger-chompers, the straights against the gays, and—as always in American life—brash, rude New Yorkers against everyone else.

Like her counterpart Miss Manners, Ms. Mentor thinks everyone could be more civil, more tolerant, and generally nicer.

She is not holding her breath.

Interracial Deportment

Q: I'm an African American woman teaching in a predominantly white college. I'm also in my mid-twenties, which makes me one of the school's youngest teachers (I'm a mere instructor, with an M.A.) A lot of the male students seem to think I'm here for one purpose, which one of them summed up for me just after he made an indecent proposal during my office hours: "You want white dick." That's not why: I'm here because I want a job teaching. But what can I possibly say that doesn't sound dumb, racist, or foolish?

A: You and Ms. Mentor both know that the comment made to you is dumb, racist, and foolish. But she agrees that there are few ways to answer such comments except by stooping to the other's level—by appearing dumb, racist, and foolish.

She proposes that you try a Miss Manners technique instead: be condescending, even haughty, in the guise of being slightly dullwitted.

If such an offer or comment is made again, look at the speaker and ask, "What did you say?"

He will repeat it.

And then you say, "Again—what?"

He will repeat it again.

And then you say, "What do you mean by that? I don't understand."

Or even, "Why are you saying that to your instructor?" or "to someone who'll be grading you?"

Continue to quiz the individual in that vein, until he gives up in embarrassment or exasperation. Most likely, if he's in your office, he'll get up and walk out—whistling to cover his exit.

It is tempting, of course, to engage in a verbal duel. But in a confrontation, someone loses, and in this case you don't want to win anything. You just want the overtures to stop.

Ms. Mentor also suggests that you make sure nothing you do can be misinterpreted as a sexual invitation. Ms. Mentor is not blaming the victim, but pointing out a fact about racism: that many white men, especially adolescent ones, regard young women of color as potential sexual prey. Ms. Mentor assumes you do not wear any kind of short, tight clothes, no matter how chic: they will be misinterpreted. If your students are admiring your body instead of listening to you, you are not an effective teacher. You need authority, not compliments.

You should also keep a precise record of the overtures: names, times, dates, places, exactly what was said. Keep that diary at home. If the offender returns to your office, do not hesitate to tape his remarks. Spurned suitors can turn into stalkers, and you need to protect yourself.

Unfortunately, you cannot always rely on those in power, such as department chairs, to help you. But if you have a sympathetic chair, keep her/him informed. Let any sympathetic tenured women know. Also contact the Affirmative Action/Equal Employment Opportunity Office, or Women's Studies, or African American Studies. At minimum, someone besides you—maybe the Director of Women's Studies—should also have a record of what happened.

Most likely, though, you have just encountered an overheated adolescent with a fantasy life that includes you. And your best chance to escape is to appear dense, dullwitted, and boring.

Luckily, that is one of the easiest poses to adopt. For models, there's always TV.

Principal Investigator or Principal Tool?

Q: My department (Social Work) used to give undergraduates purely practical training. But now (due to changes in the field) we're developing master's programs, which means tenured faculty are for the first time being pressured to do research.

I duly spent nearly a year developing a proposal, finding out how to do the project, getting advice from colleagues elsewhere, and writing up a request for funding from a federal agency. After I turned it in, it had to go to my dean's office for documentation of budget support, through a university human subjects committee, and so forth.

I got back a copy with all the signatures in place, stamped and dated, so I know it got to the federal agency in time. But on the cover sheet, an assistant dean of my college appears as "Principal Investigator" with my name as "Associate." What's going on here? *Maybe* this is legitimate and helpful. She has a doctorate and I don't; perhaps the feds won't look at funding requests from non-doctoral researchers. But nothing was said to me, and my history with this assistant dean is not good. Should I do something?

This case is even more complicated by race and class. I am African American and from the inner city, while the assistant dean is a Virginia lady with a Junior League (matronizing) attitude, especially toward most faculty women who are not married to high-status men. Like most black professional women, I am not married, but thanks to a wide network of friends, sisters, moms, and aunts, I'm hardly lonely. I'm actually much happier in my personal life right now than in my professional.

From this dean, I just want appreciation for my work, and I don't want to be ripped off. But I also don't want to seem like I have a chip on my shoulder—which is, of course, one of the destructive images of African American women.

What can I do to get over with this Miss Anne?

A: Ms. Mentor sees two problems in your letter: you and your research, and you and the assistant dean, whom you unfortunately call "Miss Anne." Ms. Mentor will call her Dr. Dean.

Research first: It's easy to find out if the grant agency prefers Ph.D. researchers. If that's not on the grant instructions, you can call the agency and ask. "Ph.D. or equivalent" is often a requirement for principal investigators, and Dr. Dean may have been doing you a favor, lending you her name and degree to make you fundable. (Ms. Mentor agrees that someone should have told you that.)

If you discover it is a favor, Ms. Mentor recommends that you write Dr.

Dean a warm note of thanks for making your proposal competitive, so that you can contribute to the college's new "research thrust." (Ms. Mentor knows that sage readers giggle at the obviousness when they hear about new "thrusts" and "seminal" and "penetrating" research and "hard" science. Ms. Mentor has been known to titter into her handkerchief as well.)

But to return to business. If the grant is funded, another note of thanks and a phone call or office visit to Dr. Dean will be most appreciated. You might even send her flowers. What could be better, or more gracious, for a Virginia lady dean?

As to Dr. Dean's matronizing attitude: whether she likes you is not really important. Nor is her social outlook, even if it makes you bristle. Yours is just a professional relationship, in which you both need to interact courteously. Too, she may be as ill at ease as you are about class and race differences, and you have the knowledge edge: you've been observing and studying white middle-class people all your life. You know their ways; she doesn't necessarily know yours.

Moreover, women are sometimes reluctant to separate the professional from the personal: we would like our colleagues to be friends, and our friends to be colleagues. But you can think of your relationship with Dr. Dean as a coalition. You're together because you have a common goal (research and buck$), not because you're boon buddies. Keep your eyes on the prize.

And remember what civil rights and arts activist Bernice Johnson Reagon of Sweet Honey in the Rock said long ago about coalitions: "Most of the time you feel threatened to the core and if you don't, you're not really doing no coalescing. . . . And if you feel the strain, you may be doing some good work."

Tower of Babble

Q: I am in a mathematics department where most of the other faculty are male and Asian. I am a Greek woman. Most of my colleagues are East Indian or Chinese, and they are always feuding. Often the North Indians and South Indians are fighting each other. When they're not, the mainland Chinese and the Taiwanese seem to be having at each other. (It's all verbal, but includes sulking and scheming about how to control department meetings.) The few white Americans in the department usually have coffee with each other, and they pretend nothing's happening (although last week, one of them threw a half-full coffee cup at one of the Chinese).

No one's in my category, and I'm coming up for tenure soon. My research record is pretty good, as are my teaching evaluations, but I'm worried that all the warring men in my department might unite in one cause: getting rid of me.

What can I do?

A: Ms. Mentor is puzzled. As far as she can tell, no one's even trying to get rid of you. You don't mention enemies or feuds or vendettas that involve you, and no one's been losing your data or disparaging your publications. You don't mention any negative annual performance reviews along the way. No one's harassing you or even looking at you sideways.

If They were out to get you, They would have given you broad hints by now.

Meanwhile, your being a token woman may give you a cultural advantage in your department's sorry squabbles. While you're above the fray, you also have potential ties to everyone. You work with the men and think mathematically; you live as a woman, and know about women's lives—not only the secretaries and graduate students, but the wives of your colleagues. Many of them are undoubtedly foreign, ill at ease with the language, horrified at the sexual and other freedoms of American women, and desperately lonely. As a European woman, you're nowhere near as foreign, yet you're also not native.

You may be the only one who can unite the various factions—at least long enough to vote overwhelmingly for your tenure.

How to cement your tenure? Have a dinner party for all your colleagues.

Ms. Mentor is not surprised if you recoil at the thought: how unprofessional! Ms. Mentor wants me to be a cook, not a mathematician!

No, not really—because Ms. Mentor has in mind that you host a potluck, at your home. (Use a holiday as a pretext, or someone's birthday.) Everyone will bring something, preferably a United Nations of food. You need to provide only the beverages, tables and chairs, and paper plates and plastic utensils and cups. You are the hostess—the administrator.

Few people are churlish enough to say no to an invitation with food. And after they're well fed, most people become better disposed toward one another. There are small, noncompetitive games you can play (the director of your university's international students program may have ideas). Especially find ways to get the wives interested and involved; make sure they meet each other.

Energizing Greek music will also provide a lively background. If you happen to have charming, outgoing Greek friends, they should come, too. Get people to be sociable, and make sure they appreciate the role you've played in putting them together.

There are no guarantees, of course. Your guests could, in their wild joy, decide to follow the old Greek custom of breaking plates—in which case you'd have a true mess on your hands (that's why Ms. Mentor recommends paper plates). Or you could wind up having sour, mumbling people all standing around in your house or yard, which is why it's good to bring some outsiders, especially Greeks, to be the social glue.

Mathematicians are famous for their (alleged) lack of social skills and their disconnection from the real world. But even they need food, and sociability, and pleasure.

Eventually, too, once you have tenure, you can make your parties a department institution: one for Halloween, for instance, and one for Mardi Gras (especially if that's not regularly celebrated in your part of the country). Thanksgiving and Christmas get-togethers, for those far away from home, are the most appreciated.

If you make these social gestures, any new women in the department will be endlessly grateful to you. Not everyone knows how to evaluate candidates for tenure, but food is a universal language. And few do it better than Greeks, and women.

Hairy Adventures with Harry

Q: I happened to knock on a young male colleague's office door, a little early for a meeting. When no one answered, I foolishly popped in—only to discover one of our grad students (male) sitting on Harry's lap, affectionately nibbling at his ear. "Oops!" I said. "I'll come back later." Since then Harry and I, who used to be among each other's best on-campus friends, haven't been able to look each other in the eye.

Further complications: until the scene I've described, I'd assumed Harry was heterosexual. He'd talked about past girlfriends, and seemed to have a lively social life.

I, however, am a closeted lesbian—mainly because I don't want to deal with homophobia in my career yet. I plan to come out after I have tenure.

Yet now I'm torn. Would it help Harry if I came out to him? Should I warn Harry about the dangers of consorting in any sexual way with graduate students—the possibility of being charged with sexual harassment, or worse? Or should I just steer Harry to some of my gay male friends?

A: Ms. Mentor thinks your generous impulses may be leading you to risky behavior. Your first duty is to yourself, not to Harry, who sounds like a rather reckless fellow. If you were able to walk in on him, anyone could: the department chair, other students, the head of the local antigay Christian right-wing sect, his own mom . . .

Harry's not protecting himself should not rub off on you.

You've chosen to be closeted for your own reasons, and you certainly don't owe it to Harry to come out, or to matchmake for him. You should remember what mothers say when the little ones whine that some other child is allowed to do something dangerous: "If Harry jumped off a bridge, would you do it, too?"

If you want to hand Harry a copy of the university's sexual harassment policies, you can do that without implicating yourself. But not much more.

Ms. Mentor feels sorry that you've rather lost a friend, but she—and you—know that you're not Harry's keeper. You're your own.

Racing Colors

Q: I've spent all my life in the Upper Midwest—the Dakotas, Minnesota— and my world's been pretty much white bread, white people. But now, with a new Ph.D., I've taken the only teaching job offered to me, at a big-city community college in, roughly, the Northeast (I don't want to mention the name, because I'm afraid they'll find out I'm so lacking in self-confidence).

Anyway, for the first time in my thirty-five years I'll be among people of other races. Are there things I should know and do, or not do? I should mention that there's no way I'll blend in. I'm Norwegian by ancestry, six feet tall and gawky, blonde and blue-eyed, and look like I'd be more at home wearing a Viking helmet and singing a Norse opera.

A: Ms. Mentor agrees that you won't ever pass as a woman of color. But she can help you feel less uncomfortable with your suddenly high visibility.

She can assure you that everyone will instantly know who you are. You'll encounter jovial inquiries you've rarely heard before ("How's the weather up there?") and field odd queries ("Are you a guard or a forward?"). If there's another tall blonde, you'll be instantly and forever confused with her. If she teaches German, people will forever be jabbering in German at you.

All of which should sensitize you to a world of rainbow students in which people often see race or color first and only afterward move on to the content of a person's character. You're also living in a time of great, often unspoken, racial tension, in which any classroom discussion of race is apt to generate a vast, brooding, hostile silence. Everyone's afraid to be called a racist; everyone's afraid to be attacked; and you, by yourself, can't handle, soothe, or solve problems that have festered for hundreds of years.

But depending on your subject matter, there are some things you can do to be a good teacher, and to encourage your students (and yourself) to relax.

• Read *Essence* and *Ebony* and learn about middle-class African Americans. Study (white-created) mass media images: Why are African Americans hardly ever shown except as athletes, entertainers, criminals, or crime victims? Why do they appear mostly in comedies or violent action flicks? Why doesn't Whoopi Goldberg have on-screen romances?

• Alternate between saying "black" and "African American" at first. But once you get to know your students, ask the blacks/African Americans what they'd like to be called. In the late 1960s, the changeover from "Negro" to "black" was almost instantaneous, because the people themselves chose "black" as a sign of pride ("Negro" was a white folks' invention). But there's no such unanimity about "African American": some consider it more accurate; others, cumbersome. Encourage a discussion of possibilities, and then have the people themselves vote on their choice. (As a consciousness-raiser, whites may not vote in this election: they'll have their own.)

• Poll all your students about what words they'd use to describe their ethnicities: "Hispanic" or "Latina/Latino?" "Native American" or "Indian?" "British" or "English?" "Oriental" or "Asian American" or "Vietnamese American?" "Scotch" or "Scottish?" "White" or "Caucasian?" Keep reminding white people that they do belong to a "race."

• Use examples that aren't white males—especially in an apparently neutral subject like science. Don't always state white male characteristics or results first: that fosters the idea that white male is the norm and everyone else a deviation. When you're discussing studies, state whether they were done on white males (in the past, even breast cancer was studied in white men), and whether they're generalizable to everyone. Check Sue V. Rosser's *Female-Friendly Science* for other ideas.

• Don't assume that your non-Caucasian students are revolutionaries or more politically aware than white students. Most college students care most about degrees, good jobs, and happy home lives.

• Don't assume you know about the backgrounds of your students who aren't white middle class. You don't, nor do you know what stresses they may endure regularly (such as shouts of "Nigger!" outside frat houses). Don't make the error called *epistemological solipsism*: "If I haven't heard of it, it doesn't exist."

• If you talk about racially charged topics, such as slavery or civil rights, be calm but explicit about what you think. Don't assume students will know you believe in equal opportunity. Unless you say otherwise, many black students will figure you think racism's a good thing, because it benefits whites like you. If you're describing racist ideas, be sure to say whose ideas they are, and give the person's name. Otherwise, your audience may think you're describing your own ideas. Irony can also be misunderstood. Come right out and say, "Slavery was wrong" and "Affirmative Action allows people who grew up poor or discriminated against to have opportunities they wouldn't otherwise have. That way we all get the benefits of their talents and skills."

• Make comparisons, if they're useful, between being a white woman and being a person of color. Women and people of color of both sexes are stereotyped, underpaid, assumed to be less intelligent, sexually exploited, and subjected to many more indignities and inequities than middle-class white men. Until the late 1960s, after all, the Supreme Court had always been all pale males. African American men have been legally equal to white men by federal law since 1868. Women never have been.

• Note how language discriminates: "black" as evil and "white" as good; "devil's food" vs. "angel's food"; "darkening the picture" vs. "lightening up." Compare language used for women: Why are female animals called "bitches?" Why does "pussy" have various meanings?

• When you imagine blacks, do you think of men only? When you imagine women, do you think of white women only?

• Get to know the African American/Africana and ethnic studies professors. Tell them you don't know much. They'll look at you and believe you and probably laugh—and then help you out.

• Tell a few Norwegian jokes. Imitate a Norwegian accent and teach your students to say, "Uff da!" The silly stories of Ole and Lena's moronic behavior are exactly the same as "moron jokes" or "Polish jokes" or "Cajun jokes" or "Cork and Kerry man jokes" in Ireland. There are few things more ice-breaking or hilarious than discovering that all men are sometimes recognized as fools.

Finally, Ms. Mentor knows you'll feel tense and self-conscious, especially at first, but that should give you empathy with your students. The best teachers are those with imagination and compassion as well as book knowledge. Be humble. You're entering a new, marvelous, rainbow-colored world.

No Fur Peace

Q: I wore my mother's old fur coat on one of our coldest days, and some animal rights students threw ketchup on it and me. (They said they wished they'd had blood handy.) Now they're writing letters to the editor, damning me as an "animal killer." What can I possibly do? On top of all this, I'm a vegetarian.

A: Ms. Mentor presumes you're a vegetarian because you don't believe in killing animals. And yet you're not queasy about wearing the skins of dead creatures? Ms. Mentor marvels.

She also believes you were unwise to wear the fur coat, no matter the rationalizations ("the coat's so old, the animals would be dead by now, anyhow"). That won't convince animal rights people, nor does it persuade Ms. Mentor.

What to do? Ms. Mentor advises you to give the coat to a homeless person or a battered women's program. Then write a letter to the newspaper, explaining your coat wearing any way you can. The truly mendacious might claim they thought it was fake fur, but Ms. Mentor hopes you're not so unprincipled. You might say you've seen the light, and apologize.

But whatever you do, since it's a student protest, it will almost certainly blow over, and everyone will forget your sin. Because there's virtually a complete student turnover every four years, few campus events are remembered for long. Nor do faculty often recall the details of student uproars, unless there are perpetual students hanging about who can prod or threaten their profs ("Remember what we did in 1972? If you don't want that done to you now . . .").

Fortunately for you, the customary student amnesia will enable you to put your past, and your fur, behind you. Resolve to wear only cloth; scarf up your broccoli and sprouts; and avoid leather. As an academic, you're one of those rare individuals who actually has a chance to forget her past and rework her image.

This time, do right.

Token Jew

Q: In the small college town where I've just taken a position, I feel like a freak. Not only am I from the Northeast, but I also seem to be the only Jew in town. Help!

A: First of all, Ms. Mentor thinks it unlikely that you are "the only Jew in town," although you may not have seen any synagogues or community centers yet. The college may not attend to Rosh Hashana or Hanukkah, and crèches and Jesus may be commonplace, along with Christmas and Easter—but there are almost certainly Jews in the area.

You can seek them through social justice groups (such as the National Organization for Women or the American Association of University Professors), through the Unitarian Church (often the home of disaffiliated Jews), and through the Internet. College Democrats, courses on the Old Testament or literature of the Holocaust, and Women's Studies are also likely sites.

What's in store for you?

If you announce that you're Jewish, you may have a few odd encounters. Ms. Mentor doubts that many Americans still believe Jews sprout horns (a belief still current in some parts of Delaware in the 1960s). Nor will you be considered a "Christ-killer": it was thirty years ago that Pope John XXIII stated unequivocally that the Romans, not the Jews, killed Jesus. You may, though, be asked about Jewish-Arab relations, or Jewish-African American relations. Earnest students may ask if you think Barbra Streisand should have had a nose job, and what happens if Jews marry Gentiles.

You may encounter a few stereotypers who believe Jewish women must be smart, aggressive, and rich, if not overly intellectual, bitchy, and money-grubbing. A few of the really provincial may think you harbor weird beliefs in place of "regular ones," like the Virgin Birth.

You may also be considered exotic, and even unique—which opens a cornucopia of new opportunities.

You may find yourself wanting to know more about your Jewish heritage. Maybe, in your exile, you'll get curious about Jewish women, or the Holocaust, or Jewish voting patterns, or Yiddish humor, or Jewish genetic quirks. Almost every field—except maybe physics or engineering—can have a Jewish component, questions that may never have been asked before, in your new community.

For instance, why has most of Western thought been shaped by four Jewish men (Jesus, Marx, Freud, Einstein)? Why is it that despite generations of black-Jewish animosity, so many African American activists have Jewish mothers? Why, unlike Gentiles, do virtually all Jewish women go to college? Why, among all the world's religious groups, were Jews the *only* ones to protest against the anti-Muslim genocide in Bosnia?

Ms. Mentor especially encourages you to celebrate Jewish mothers, and the much-maligned Jewish American princesses, and the brilliant and marvelous achievements of Jewish women over thousands of years. Volunteer for speakers committees, and invite Jewish writers and thinkers and activists to campus: it's often easy to get grants from your state humanities council. Ruth Bader Ginsburg would be a fine campus speaker to invite—as would Gloria Steinem, Betty Friedan, Barbara Boxer, Dianne Feinstein, Bette Midler, Roseanne, Adrienne Rich, Ellen Goodman, and countless others—including, for the younger generation, *Clueless* actress Alicia Silverstone and her director, Amy Heckerling.

"But I don't want to change my whole academic career," Ms. Mentor hears you saying, angrily. "I'm a—" musicologist, or French professor, or botanist. "Suddenly doing Jewish studies won't do anything for my career."

But it will.

Doing Jewish studies—and being by default the only "expert" on the subject—can truly benefit your career, and your life, in a small college. Once it's known that you can talk knowledgeably about Hanukkah or Yom Kippur, you may be greatly in demand as a guest lecturer in classes. That's how you get to meet the powerful professors: let them observe the excellence of your teaching.

If you can work up a mini-lecture on Jewish humor (using the writings of E. M. Broner, Nora Ephron, Dorothy Parker, Cynthia Heimel, and Sarah Blacher Cohen, for instance), you will be particularly cherished. Everyone loves an entertaining speaker.

Being the Jewish speaker also gives you a "unique niche," a crucial argument for tenure. You do something no one else does; you cover a subject that every school knows must be covered. Also, you needn't publish widely to develop your niche. Just be the local authority.

From the local historical society, you may discover considerable Jewish history and lore. Natchitoches, Louisiana, for instance, has several prominent families originally descended from wandering Jewish peddlers; Grand Forks, North Dakota, has a group of originally Jewish fur traders. Numerous small towns around the nation, including Aaronsburg in central Pennsylvania, have been named for their Jewish founders.

Still, you may encounter annoyances, such as campus-wide celebrations of Christmas and Easter. If the local American Civil Liberties Union hasn't pointed out that Christian symbols and celebrations are not universal, you may have to bide your time and resist the temptation to pick some fights.

Ms. Mentor cautions you not to go stomping into your chair's office railing about "anti-Semites" if you see secretaries decorating a Christmas tree or bringing goodies for the department's Christmas party. For them, it's a welcome break from truly monotonous work. Better to ask them, in your usual friendly and polite way: "Do you mind if we call this a holiday party, so everyone feels included?"

Meanwhile, you may comment discreetly to the local African American or Black Studies Program about the December celebrations. "Christmas" shindigs do ignore the importance of Kwanzaa, and sometimes complaints from African Americans get more immediate attention. Make this your chance to find allies in Black Studies.

Still, Ms. Mentor agrees that being "the only known Jew in town" is a lonely niche. If you do not find other Jews, you'll need to broaden your community. Travel more; join the National Women's Studies Association's Jewish caucus; read the Jewish women's journal *Lilith*. The Internet and networking may also get you a job in a larger city, if your college town proves truly intolerable.

Jews have always been citizens of the world, but you *can* create your own world.

Baby or Bathwater?

Q: Last week I brought my new baby to campus and to my classes, but a senior woman colleague advised me not to do it again, that I'm giving the wrong impression. What does she mean?

I should add that I'm an assistant professor in a sociology department, and that I won't be coming up for tenure for another two years. I adore my little daughter, and hate to be away from her, ever.

A: Let it not be said that Ms. Mentor is unsympathetic with mothering. Bearing, nursing, and raising children is difficult in the best of times, and hiding the fact that one is doing so is even harder, if not downright peculiar. Yet that is exactly what Ms. Mentor must advise you to do.

You are in the immemorial bind between being a woman and—gasp—being a person in the eyes of your male academic colleagues. Having a baby, and showing the baby about, will not help you toward tenure, and may actively damage your chances.

For academia is still run according to unspoken male norms, according to the traditional clockwork of male careers. In his twenties, the academic male is supposed to be getting his degree; in his thirties, he gets tenure; in his forties, he starts becoming distinguished in his field. Along the way, his time and energies go to research, while his wife deals with the everyday stuff, including children and home and food and clothing and keeping body and soul together (and never letting the children disturb Daddy's rest or writing).

Scarcely any family actually fits that model anymore, but men can still come much closer than women do. A man who is married is viewed as settled, an admirable adult; a woman who is married may be considered a "hiring problem." But children, their care and feeding, are the great separator. People who are most often seen as mothers are not considered "professional."

In recent years, some universities have made it easier. Most will "stop the tenure clock" so that a woman who has children can have more than the traditional six years before a tenure decision is made. Many schools have day-care centers, and some men have opted for what Ms. Mentor calls "ostentatious fatherhood": trundling about their children and getting praise and oohs from admiring women. (One professor Ms. Mentor knows in a Southwestern university used to proposition, or sexually harass, virtually every woman who complimented him on having "his" baby with him.)

Nevertheless, a woman seen with a baby is believed to be "un-serious." Viewing herself as a mom first, she's thought likely to drop her career at any moment. This unfair characterization is almost universal, and neither you nor Ms. Mentor can do much to change it. Nor can most academic women, since only half of them even have children.

Especially when you do not have tenure, you must "fit in," and children simply don't. Bringing a child to work, even if the child naps quietly most of the time, stamps you as unprofessional.

Ms. Mentor agrees that it is indeed strange that motherhood, like homosexuality, has to remain in the closet until tenure. But such is the strange world of academia, and only those who somehow get tenure can ever change it and make it more friendly to mothers, children, and the next generation.

When in Lesbos

Q: I come from a very butch lesbian community on the Coast, but am now in a small town where most of the lesbians appear to be of the lipstick-femme variety. Should I change my stripes?

A: Ms. Mentor agrees that choosing a butch or femme identity and appearance can often determine, irrevocably, the tone of your life in a new town.

If you're thoroughly out of the closet to those who hired you, presumably they saw you in whatever mode you chose. Whatever eccentricities of dress or appearance you may sport are seemingly OK with your faculty colleagues. (Students, though, often react with distaste and horror at women faculty's unshaven armpits, for instance. If you're furry on principle but don't want to distract the students, Ms. Mentor suggests you invest in long sleeves.)

Your issue, though, is neither colleagues nor students, but the friends you can make in your new town. For Americans have always dreamed of junking it all and starting a whole new life. That's what still propels Hoosiers to California and malcontents to Nevada. Schoolchildren, too, still dream that over the summer they'll grow tall, gain breasts, lose zits, and somehow become popular.

Moving to a new town, you have the opportunity to remake yourself. Will you choose to fit in, by changing your stripes? Or stand on the identity that you chose, and felt comfortable with, in the past?

If there's no difference in your career, Ms. Mentor throws up her hands (inside her long sleeves). It's up to you.

Costumed for Success?

Q: Just before Christmas, my family's ethnic celebrations fall on the same night as a big department party. I don't have tenure, so must attend it. I know my colleagues will consider my ethnic costume in poor taste or laughable, but I'm proud of my heritage (Eastern European). Should I wear the costume to both gatherings anyway?

A: Ms. Mentor was pleased to hear from you, for too many white people deny their heritages and act as if only people of color are truly "foreign" or "different" or "special."

However, Ms. Mentor does not mean to be smarmy, as in "we're all so special, and we all have our special talents and backgrounds to share, and isn't the melting pot wonderful?" Ms. Mentor knows as well as anyone—knows better, in fact, because she knows everything—that the United States is not a melting pot but a rather unstable gumbo in which pieces of okra sometimes rise up, onions shift to the bottom, sausage bits hover at the middle . . . well, most metaphors do wear out.

Your question is simpler: Should you wear your costume to the department party?

Luckily for you, many holiday parties are more festive than formal, and a bright red and green costume will suit the season. If it's odd but attractive, especially on you, Ms. Mentor sees no problem with wearing it.

But what if the costume is very peculiar, or lowcut, or has an elaborate headdress, and your colleagues are formal, stuffy Anglophiles? (Some Ivy League departments consider themselves colonial outposts of Oxford and everyone's favorite color is tweed—though there's some fussing over harris vs. herringbone.)

In that case, Ms. Mentor regrets to say that you should consider changing your clothes. For although many a department will say that "anything goes" at a Halloween or New Year's Eve gathering—at which some boorish full professors will inevitably become drunk, loud, garrulous, and boring—anything doesn't go for untenured women. Everything they do is remembered, especially anything that seems strange.

And so, if the ethnic costume is truly strange and not adaptable (with a different blouse, for instance), you may have to resort to a clothes change on the run. Hotels and fast-food places usually have large public bathrooms, and Ms. Mentor especially recommends the handicapped stall.

But she also hopes that your costume is wearable to the party, for then you can be that rare individual whose roots and professional world fit together harmoniously. Henry David Thoreau, that odd New Englander who warned us all to "Beware of all enterprises that require new clothes," would be so pleased.

Easy Biker

Q: I'm a first-year faculty member at Backwater Community College, a traditionally minded two-year college in a modest agricultural community. I often wonder why I was hired: intellectually and professionally, I don't fit. But I'll stick to a more limited problem: fashion. Backwater is a flat town with a year-round mild climate. I live only a half-mile from campus, so I bike to work. I like the exercise and peace of mind on my short rides each day, and it's good for the environment.

But what do I do about my dresses? Full skirts threaten to get caught in the spokes. In the past, I've just tied these pesky skirts up and pedaled away, but here that attracts the disapproving stares of colleagues. In this community, I think it's important for me to wear dresses or skirts some days, so going with an all-pants wardrobe would not be the solution. If I change from pants to a dress in the bathroom, I have to carry all those undergarments (slips, stockings) around in a bag.

What's a girl to do?

A: As faithful readers know, Ms. Mentor is a maven on all matters sartorial, but before she rules on what you should wear, she wants to pose a different question:

Should you ride your bike to work?

The pluses are obvious: exercise, fast movement, fresh air.

But so are the minuses: disapproving glances from colleagues; an academic culture in which you're expected to wear skirts or dresses some of the time; and the folderol with extra underwear. (Ms. Mentor is relieved that you, unlike so many in your generation, know that underwear is to be worn *beneath* one's clothes, not over them.)

Still, you may be committing a *faux pas* far beyond fashion, which Ms. Mentor will now—after straightening her own hose, patting her hair, and plumping her lap pillow—explain.

You do not seem to have asked the essential questions for traveling on any road (to life, to hell, to tenure): Where do I really want to go? And what's the best route?

Here Ms. Mentor recalls a fluty-voice professor of Old English who, in a college town in the Great Plains, used to ride her bike to work in all weather. Seated prim and high in the saddle, her braids tucked under a saffron stocking cap, this professor became the target of considerable ridicule from undergraduate louts. "Mary Poppins!" they would hoot as she pedaled by. "Lookee! The Wicked Witch of the West!"

But she ignored them, serene in her eccentricities and her long, long tenure (she was said to have given Beowulf his first draught of mead). She cared not a fig what others thought, and much later in life, women who'd snickered when they were teens came to revere her memory. She was that rare miracle: a woman who actually did just what she chose.

You, however, do not have that option. The young are always judged more harshly, as are the female and the powerless—the untenured. There is also a long and deplorable history of college teachers who've been denied contract renewals, tenure, or promotions for what can only be called "lifestyle violations." Ms. Mentor recalls some of the victims:

- The man denied tenure in a West Virginia department because he disliked Mexican food and so "didn't fit in";
- The woman not recommended for a contract renewal at her Ozark university because she'd stowed her bicycle in the department's mailroom (that was truly the only criticism she ever received);
- The long-haired woman in Pennsylvania who was "too sloppy" for her colleagues at third-year review time;
- The unmarried assistant professors pushed out of departments where perky, up-with-people nuclear families are considered the norm;
- The teetotalers in stag drinking departments;
- The chic faculty in very cold climates where professors dress like lumberjacks;
- Occasionally: working-class people, racial and sexual minorities, or the very religious or irreligious.

Ms. Mentor does not mean that all academic units want clones. Many, especially in large cities, do value diversity and artistic temperament. But many small colleges truly prefer faculty who are youngish, hardy, and approachable—the casually dressed kind who'll backpack, bike, and tree-hug with their students.

Unfortunately, Backwater does not quite sound like such a place. Ms. Mentor advises you to trust your intuitions. Having noted the "disapproving stares of colleagues," you know you need to wear dresses and skirts. Biking is therefore undignified, and hiking up one's skirts to do so is even worse . . . and carting one's underthings around in a paper bag courts disaster, if not truly low comedy.

None of these things keeps you rolling on the road to tenure.

Ms. Mentor reminds her sage readers that all jobs require some conformity in dress. (Even 1960s hippies wanting to "do their own thing" expressed their individuality by all looking alike.) Today, except in really cold climates, dresses and skirts (knee-length or longer) are a woman's professional uniform. Ms. Mentor also recommends jackets or vests, which connote authority. Young women should not model themselves on fashion magazines, movies, or TV. Rather, they should observe how the highest-ranking women in their institutions dress. Solemnity and somber colors sell. Classic outranks chic. Tailored is far better than trendy. Black is beautiful.

As for your half-mile journey to campus: Ms. Mentor advises you to take a car, or walk. No biking.

But hark! Ms. Mentor hears you and your contemporaries wailing: "Why work in such an oppressive place as Backwater? Why let yourself be restricted by antiquated customs and reactionary expectations? Why not be Free, Free!"

Because, sage ones, there are very few jobs in academia. Bike-riding and fashion are trivial—but they are ways in which women are inevitably judged, and often found wanting. In Ms. Mentor's calculation, it is not worth stirring up the lifestyle disapproval that can lead to nonrenewal or tenure denial, and thus to the end of one's career . . . in order to bike to work.

If, of course, you decide that you cannot thrive, or even exist, in a place so unsuited to your intellectual and professional concerns as Backwater is, then you should consider whether you want to be an academic. Perhaps you do not. That is a perfectly rational choice (and certainly there are senior men in every department who should have made that choice, long ago).

But Ms. Mentor does wish you well, for it is hard to be without congenial peers. Ms. Mentor hopes that you have phone and e-mail friends, and that you'll seek out non-faculty friends who like to bike. Sierra Clubs and environmental groups are good places to meet interesting civilians. Such clubs also attract more than their share of recovering academics.

At least with them, you won't have to soft-pedal.

Strangers in Strange Lands

Q: I'm a Southerner who's just been hired at one of the SUNY branches. I have just one question: Why are New Yorkers so rude?

Q: I'm a Yankee in my first year of teaching in the South, and I can't get my students to argue over issues or even to say what they really mean. Are Southerners mostly hypocrites, or am I doing something wrong?

Q: I'm admittedly a short-tempered, pushy New Yorker, but I'm completely befuddled by my Midwestern students, who seem dull, earnest, and totally humorless. Is this a regional trait, or a characteristic of Generation X that I've never noticed before?

A: These queries were so similar that Ms. Mentor, who believes the Civil War is over, decided to combine them.

She resists the temptation to scold all the authors for their reliance on really old regional stereotypes. The nasty New Yorker, the steel magnolia Southerner, and the nice but dull Midwesterner have all been showcased by, among others, Woody Allen, Tennessee Williams, and Sinclair Lewis. (Women writers are sometimes kinder.) But movies, plays, and novels are not Life, which is much messier and often far more entertaining.

Ms. Mentor will admit that some individual women do conform to their stereotypes—often out of nervousness or distress. In crisis moments, Manhattanites may act out their hysteria by becoming louder, as if they're desperate to be heard above midtown traffic. Southerners do retreat into well-worn patterns of behavior: do not offend; do not argue; and always smile. And Midwesterners, having no native tradition of humor except what the rest of the country considers either wholesome or hickish, prudently choose to come across as ploddingly literal rather than risk the slings and arrows of irony.

Ms. Mentor observes, moreover, that academic folk, like her correspondents, are themselves aliens who rarely share the values of general Americans. People who were popular in high school don't grow up to be professors; the honors students were socially inept bookworms and computer nerds.

As grownups, academics stay in school longer and often sport library/ lab pallor rather than golden tans. Male academics, in particular, are odd-balls, because they read books. In the general public, women buy 70 per-cent of U.S. books sold—but only a handful of women ever curl up with a university press book.

By tastes, too, academic people are aliens. Except in the clean-air en-claves of such places as Minnesota, Colorado, and Oregon, academics' pre-ferences for tahini and tofu, no smoking, Volvos, SAS and Rockport shoes, and frayed clothes mark them as cautious and dull, unlike their more col-orful civilian contemporaries.

Yet the academics' task, wherever they are, is to inspire their students with a love of learning and to pass on whatever wisdom they themselves possess. Which means training young people not to judge books by their covers, nor people by their accents or clothes or regional traits.

And so Ms. Mentor suggests that her correspondents do what few aca-demics do successfully: listen closely to their students. Most of them are natives of the region in which they attend school. The students know how they're supposed to behave, locally. Sometimes they have no idea that anyone behaves differently anywhere else. (Some Southern students of Ms. Mentor's acquaintance were shocked to learn that New Yorkers rou-tinely say, "Yeah," rather than "Yes, ma'am." "That's so rude!" said the Southerners.)

Indeed, what's different may seem either rude, dishonest, or baffling. But, Ms. Mentor proclaims, anyone who is a teacher needs to figure out how best to reach her audience without insulting, patronizing, or confusing them.

Her sage readers need to know, for instance, about regional differences in storytelling. New Yorkers and Southerners do it for entertainment value; Midwesterners characteristically don't. In Minnesota, natives mostly talk to communicate facts; in Manhattan or Miami, they may also want to make each other laugh, cry, or wince.

And so a colorful anecdote or parable can be used to illustrate a point much more easily in Brooklyn or Baton Rouge than in, say, Bismarck. In Bismarck, the conscientious teacher will have to state, specifically, what the story means. Likewise, a Flannery O'Connor-ish tale of gory dismem-berment, one that Baton Rougeans or Brooklynites might consider a hilari-ous display of narrative skill, might, to Bismarckers, seem perverse and somehow wrong.

Another difference is timing and manners. In the Upper Midwest, people are by necessity abrupt: one can't stand about schmoozing in a Montana blizzard. In New York City, the pace of life makes people brusque, but often pithy and crude at the same time. In the South, though, the rhythm is slower: when the weather is almost always warm, no one races. "Passing the time of day" in leisurely conversations, even a few sentences with the cashier at the grocery store, is part of Southern manners. To state your business, grab your sack, and stride out is considered deeply rude.

Finally, the alert amateur anthropologist—the teacher who wants to teach well—will watch how people handle disagreements. Midwesterners are most apt to state, literally, what they believe and think. They are also the best listeners, and the most honest workers ("They lack the cunning to lie," a Virginian once said about them, with mixed admiration and snideness.)

Others disagree in their own styles. New Yorkers may add an insult or twist, an extra fillip that will be either convincing or entertaining. New Yorkers love one-line putdowns. But Southerners may appear to an undiscerning observer to have no opinions. They seem reluctant to risk alienating anyone by stating, strongly, a point of view.

What they do have, though, are certain circumlocutions, evolved over generations to let people disagree without insulting one another or making enemies of those who must remain in the same town. (Among Americans, Southerners are the least likely to move elsewhere, and the most likely to come back to where they were born.)

Southern women, for instance, may start out, "I don't want to say anything ugly, but . . ." or "I just love her to death, but . . . ," and then make a rather straightforward criticism of the absent woman, just as a New Yorker or North Dakotan might. But then a Southerner will conclude with a self-deprecating laugh, as if to ward off the evil eye.

Knowing how the various regionals communicate, the astute teacher will ask questions differently—allowing New Yorkers to argue, Midwesterners to pursue earnest possibilities, and Southerners to come around to saying, like a mantra, that "it's up to the individual" (which they know it isn't at all).

Conversation everywhere is a kind of code, and respect for students requires understanding and respecting their codes. Ms. Mentor hopes that all her readers will endeavor to do so, so that the academic world will be a place where cultures truly meet, rather than just colliding and smashing against each other.

Muddles and Puzzles

Ms. Mentor prides herself on being able to help with virtually any problem, however peculiar. Academic matters are her speciality, but she rarely hesitates to give advice on anything at all. (She prefers Thai food to British, for instance—as anyone with a palate should.)

In this section, she presents a stew, miscellany, gumbo, casserole, potpourri, or what-have-you. Oddments, in short, for the cogitation and delectation of learned sages and gentle readers.

Ms. Mentor hopes they will provoke debate and study.

She does not recommend the appointment of committees.

Notorious Woman of Letters

Q: I happen to have the same name as a very famous woman professor. She's also quite notorious for, it's said, sleeping with big names of all sexes to get where she is now. (I *am* skeptical about that. As Ellen Goodman says, "If women can sleep their way to the top, how come there are so few of us there?")

But that's not my problem. My problem is that I sometimes get mail intended for this famous woman. And sometimes, especially when it's from foreigners, it's very spicy and salacious and detailed. Yes, I know I should just send it off to her, but of course it *is* addressed to me (sort of), so I always read and photocopy it.

But that's not my question, either. I know what I'm doing is wrong, and that's one of the pleasures.

My question is this: I recently got several letters addressed to her in a language I can't read (I think it's Arabic). I'd like to get one of the Arabic scholars at my university to translate the letters for me, except that I'm afraid of what they might say to this famous woman, or about her (and, by implication, me).

How do I cover my privacy—and hers?

A: Ms. Mentor is intrigued by the niceties of your personal ethics. And she agrees that it is unwise to share gossipy and delightfully wicked letters that are *très amusant* with just anyone, such as whichever professor of Arabic happens to be around. And, of course, what if the letters in Arabic are actually to *you* and not to the famous woman whose name you're lucky enough to bear?

What if the letters contain illicit or explicit suggestions, or sordid and kinky revelations about widely known individuals whose reputations have hitherto been unstained? What if the letters are nothing but lurid, irresponsible gossip, full of imagination and far-reaching innuendos?

The more she thinks about the possibilities, the more Ms. Mentor feels she has come up with the perfect solution.

You should send the letters, unopened, to Ms. Mentor, immediately.

She will handle them.

A Cosmic Question

Q: Among male academics, which discipline has the sexiest guys, and which one has the most sexist? Please hurry your reply. I need to know at once.

A: Ms. Mentor will pass along some of the conventional wisdom that she has gathered over the last half-century. She does not vouch for its veracity.

- Engineers make faithful husbands: they are plodders who lack imagination.
- Political scientists are the best dressed at their annual conferences (say publishers' representatives).

- Psychologists have the highest rate of sexual harassment of graduate students.
- Sociologists think they have marvelous senses of humor.
- Psychologists and sociologists are most apt to have beards. Next likely: men in English departments. Least likely: men in business or military science.
- Physical education (kinesiology) professors have the best-toned bodies.
- Men in agriculture have a peculiar habit of referring to women as "females," never as "women" (or even "ladies" or "girls").
- Veterinary men have gentle hands, and can treat your cats.
- Mathematicians are most likely to button their shirts wrong, letting their belly buttons show.
- Men in theater or dramatic arts have the best hair.
- If you want someone to hum "Some Enchanted Evening" romantically in your ear, on key, try a professor of music.
- Men in the humanities are unsure about their masculinities, because they cannot fix their own cars.
- Men in Spanish have macho ideas.
- There are scarcely any men in French, human ecology (home economics), or nursing.
- Men in art or interior design are not necessarily gay.
- Historians sometimes smell musty.
- Archaeologists always do.

Overall, however, Ms. Mentor thinks the question both too deep and too silly to dignify with a reply. She exits, harrumphing.

Once His Auditor, Always His Audience

Q: My husband was my professor. (Yes, yes, I know: well, they didn't have rules about sexual harassment when we got together.) Now, years later, he still can't stop pontificating at me. Recently, sarcastically, I suggested installing a podium in our living room. He was genuinely thrilled with the idea. How can I get him to stop being such a pompous ass?

A: Your query reminded Ms. Mentor of a much-married professor she once knew in the Far West, who won the heart of a young lady from a tiny town who worshiped his mind. And so they were wed, but the professor had many a child support and alimony payment to make from his past lives, and the newlyweds were quite poor, especially when the new wife (his fifth) immediately became pregnant. "I want to bear Roger's child," she said, radiant.

But her glow faded when she found herself living in a trailer, which was all they could afford on the remnants of her salary. And her beautiful and brilliant Roger now spent his off days in front of the TV, hairy in his undershirt, scratching his testicles with a fork.

(Yes, dear hearts, a fork. Ms. Mentor and Miss Manners would both have preferred a spoon.)

Your problem is simpler, Ms. Mentor feels. You're just a captive audience for a man who expects to be worshiped. Unlike doctors and judges, who may be merely experts on spleens and writs, university professors are permitted to pontificate everywhere on everything (they're on TV every night). Academic men can get enormously inflated views of their own worth and interest. (This is rarely a problem with women: most women are not appreciated enough.)

But now that Ms. Mentor has pontificated a bit herself: What should you do?

The usual marital solutions include therapy; encounter groups; church or synagogue counseling; or immersion in mindless television, including talk shows and psychic friends and home-shopping networks. Ms. Mentor recommends some kind of intervention, so you don't seem to be the only spoilsport who fails to recognize his greatness. He may think about trading you in for a younger, more worshipful model.

Assuming you want to keep him, then, you need to get him to pay more attention to you—or at least less to himself.

At home, tickling or flailing at him with a loofah bat can be good starters. Another waker-upper: insist that he give you a long essay test and grade it immediately. Or you give him a test. Or ply him with heavy doses of carbohydrates—fettucine Alfredo is especially good—so that he stretches out snoring after dinner and never launches into his lecture at all.

Or you can enroll in medical school and threaten to dissect him.

He'll have to notice that.

So Young, So Flatulent

Q: Under stress, I tend to have intestinal troubles, which result in (how can I say it) gas. I don't have tenure. What if I fart at a bad moment?

A: Ms. Mentor knows that there are few situations more embarrassing for the young. That may be why there is no juvenile equivalent for the term Old Fart.

Moreover, the social edginess accompanying flatulence appears to cross all classes and cultures. Consider, for instance, the famous time that Queen Elizabeth's horse (to be frank about it) farted during an official military ceremony.

The Queen apologized to the nearest soldier, who responded, gallantly, "If you hadn't spoken, Your Majesty, I would have thought it was the horse."

For the nonroyal, one of the best coverups is to imply—by facial expressions and nose-twitching—that the gas was leaked by someone else. Polite people will ignore it, and you're beyond the prankish undergrads who store the expelled gases under their coats and then flap them at unsuspecting strangers.

There are medical products and antacids; calcium sometimes helps. In social situations, avoid such "fart foods" as carbonated drinks, broccoli, cauliflower, cabbage, onions, pretzels, nuts, and dried fruits. And, of course, eschew anything with beans ("Beans, beans, that terrible fruit / The more you eat, the more you t——").

If all else fails, and you are socially embarrassed, just smile weakly. Most adults are forgiving, especially if what you emit is not loud. Even if it is the toxic silent-but-deadly variety, most people would rather pretend it did not happen.

After all, the next eruption could be their own.

What the Ladies Think

Q: I have a colleague (male) who persists in asking me for "the woman's point of view" on almost everything: curriculum, nuclear arms, language requirements, dirty rock lyrics, baseball. He's persistent and shallow. What should I do?

A: Ms. Mentor senses a maladroit form of gallantry. Your colleague wants to include you in conversations but also note your "femininity" (whatever that may mean). He does not realize that the best way to welcome women as colleagues is to be inclusive—asking *everyone* for opinions on nuclear arms—rather than singling out women as a "special" instance of expertise.

Some people would confront your colleague ("Whaddya mean, women's point of view?") and lecture him on some of the subtler forms of sex discrimination. Ms. Mentor, however, would smile serenely and say, "Women have varying points of view on everything, just as men do," and ask him his opinion.

Ms. Mentor believes that serenity, charm, and mild condescension will do much to make academia a less snarly and more pleasant workplace.

Mentor or Malice?

Q: An older female colleague, something of a mentor, recently proposed a departmental course of action with which I strongly disagreed. The other members of our small department, all male, sided with me. I don't wish to alienate this woman, whom I admire for what she's done for me and other women (she is the only woman full professor in our college unit). To make things even dicier, I have now been elected department chair, although I am an untenured assistant professor. I believe my female colleague helped engineer my election (which I did not seek), perhaps to give herself further power within the department. Do you have any suggestions as to how I may navigate the deep waters I see ahead?

A: Ms. Mentor does indeed see sharks lying in wait—as well as icebergs, sandbars, and knife-wielding pirates. Ms. Mentor is appalled that a department would elect an untenured person, with no job security, as chair. In that role, you will

- have to struggle with the dean for department resources—and then hope that the dean will favor your tenure;
- have to say no to faculty members who want money, released time, computers, and the like—and then hope that those disgruntled colleagues will vote to give you tenure;
- have little or no time to publish—and then have to argue that you've published enough to receive tenure anyway.

You will also, inevitably, make enemies among students, secretaries, maintenance staffs, and faculty you don't even know, for real or imagined slights.

Ms. Mentor wonders why your colleagues have elected you chair. Perhaps they're fond of you; perhaps they feel that the leadership experience will be good for you. You may indeed be the brightest, most capable person in the department. (You did, after all, write to Ms. Mentor.)

But too often such a peculiar election suggests deep discord. Possibly there's chronic feuding, and no one else would take the job. Possibly not enough people know or care that academia is deeply hierarchical, and that an untenured, low-on-the-totem-pole person will have no clout. Such a chair cannot be effective in getting respect or resources for the department.

Or maybe somebody just dislikes you and wants to make you squirm.

You need friends and supporters, and your mentor, Professor Senior Sister, is the key. Forget your recent disagreement; shrewd people don't take professional tiffs personally. Invite Professor Sister to lunch, where you'll make a point of praising her: for a recent publication, or a teaching achievement, or for spectacular mentoring. This praise is sincere, but also useful.

For Professor Senior Sister knows the department lore and history that you need to know. Ask about feuds and factions, triumphs and terrors, and how Prof. Sister handled them. There is nothing so flattering, or so wise, as a request for advice. Prof. Sister can be (has to be) your best source and ally.

Will the men in the department resent this alliance? Probably—but every department has soreheads who hate the boss on principle. (They probably have unresolved conflicts with their fathers.) You'll do best by forming connections with everyone through regular meetings, lunches, and social events. Try to appear open-minded, candid, and honest, while being attuned to mutinies, conspiracies, and backbitings.

You may also comfort yourself by reading academic novels: Alison Lurie's *The War Between the Tates* is a particularly good satirical window on faculty meetings.

Finally, though, Ms. Mentor advises you to quietly consult job lists and put out networking feelers. A department that would choose an untenured assistant professor as chair has troubles, and you may prefer to spend your academic life elsewhere.

But having been an administrator may turn out to be your ticket to ride.

Plagiarism

Q: I suspect one of my colleagues is plagiarizing from my research and publishing it under his own name. How can I rescue my good name—and my research?

A: Ms. Mentor regrets that plagiarism seems to be a more and more common offense in academia—along with scientific fraud of all kinds. When Congressman John Dingell (D., Mich.) investigated the field, he found a snake pit of cases, including one that seemed to involve Nobel laureate David Baltimore. With the vital, committed Dingell no longer chairing the Energy and Commerce Committee after the 1994 elections, Ms. Mentor suspects that all kinds of despicable and new shenanigans have ensued.

Researchers do know that "who discovered what" can be murky. In science, recently, as many as one hundred or more authors have been listed on papers: one notorious paper credited over eight hundred "authors." Yet in other instances, there have been grievances and suits from researchers whose names have been left off published reports. In one Research I university alone, there were recently four cases of faculty and graduate students filing grievances and suits against each other—all claiming plagiarism ("theft of intellectual property").

In the humanities, plagiarism can be messy to prove. If a Harvard professor publishes under her own name part of a student's interpretation of a Shakespeare sonnet, is the professor guilty of plagiarism? (Ms. Mentor thinks yes; many academicians would say no.) If a Pennsylvania student writes the first draft of her professor's book on contraception and it is eventually published under his name only, is the professor guilty of plagiarism? (Ms. Mentor thinks yes; many academicians would say no.)

And what of the Southwestern university professor who suddenly begins writing and publishing about feminism—just at the time he begins directing the first student who's dealt with feminism in a dissertation he supervises? Is it a case of student teaching professor, or of professor stealing from student?

In matters of credit, Ms. Mentor is a stickler, a pedant: she thinks everyone should get an acknowledgment. (Emily Toth omitted a few names in the acknowledgments to this book, but they were people who preferred not to be mentioned, for their own self-protective or sinister reasons.)

Ms. Mentor has, however, strayed far from the original letter writer—to whom she returns now, a bit weary and travel-stained, but ready to settle down to business:

Ms. Mentor advises you to document, document, document what you have done. Keep copies of your work at home, and even in a bank vault if you have doubts. Send your lab results to researchers you trust. Publish what you've done as soon as you possibly can. Even before publication, unless it's material that can be "scooped" or stolen, publicize it over the Internet and in conference presentations.

In short, make it your own as publicly as possible. Attach it to your name. Talk about it, obsessively. For in recent years there have been truly vicious, even unbelievable, thefts.

Ms. Mentor finds most astonishing the case of Heidi Weissmann, a world-renowned, extremely successful professor and researcher in nuclear medicine and radiology. Several years ago Dr. Weissmann found that her department chief at Albert Einstein College of Medicine, Leonard M. Freeman, was taking her work, even already-published work, and republishing it under his own name, with her name whited out. In at least two other incidents, he had secretaries retype her work, and then he sent it out under his name, as sole author.

Freeman's plagiarism was so egregious that his name is now the official unit of measure of plagiarism, named by plagiarism detectors Walter Stewart and Ned Feder of the National Institutes of Health. A completely plagiarized text equals one Freeman unit; lesser offenses are measured in "millifreemans."

Weissmann sued and was awarded the largest settlement an academic has ever won: $900,000. She has used it to set up the Center for Women in Medicine and the Health Sciences (P.O. Box 191, Paramus, NJ 07693-0191; phone 201-825-9747), which can also be reached c/o the Feminist Majority Foundation, 1600 Wilson Blvd. No. 801, Arlington, VA 22209 (phone 703-522-2214).

Ms. Mentor wishes, though, that there were an academic version of the Competitive Cook's Trick. Whenever the Cook was asked for her favorite cake recipe, she gave her admirer a copy, but left out one ingredient so the admirer's would never taste quite right. Ms. Mentor likes to imagine a heroine's fabricating a research report, with fake data and made-up procedures, and leaving it around temptingly for Professor Plagiarist to publish—and get caught.

For Ms. Mentor knows that women have always been ripped off. A century ago, the suffragist Matilda Joslyn Gage called human history a continuous tale of "theft" of women's resources, talents, energies, and discoveries, by men. Even until the last two decades or so, wives were routinely thanked in acknowledgments for "typing and editing" their husbands' books, when too often, as in the case of Jane and Dr. Benjamin Spock, the woman had actually written the book.

Ms. Mentor therefore would like the world to know that she has written her own book, but only thanks to Emily Toth.

Crock or Spade?

Q: Why all this fuss about words like "differently abled" and "physically challenged?" Crippled is crippled. Let's call a spade a spade. This politically correct language is a crock.

A: All right, Ms. Mentor will call it as she sees it: your note is foolish, ignorant, and irritating. And now she'll control her indignation, and correct your vacuities.

Some history first: In the early 1990s, the term "politically correct," long used for ironic humor by feminists and leftists, was seized upon by right-wingers, many of them funded by the Heritage or Olin Foundations.

There's a war on! claimed the right-wingers. Feminists! African Americans! Gays! Bad Leftist People! are attacking our sacred institutions and calling them Politically Incorrect! These "doctrinaire" feminists-and-their-fellow-dupes are out to muzzle or destroy (among other things) the universities, American society, free speech, heterosexuality, the universe as we know it, et cetera! Argh!

Ms. Mentor hopes you realize that their campaign was and is a true crock—a defense of white men's right to be bigots.

In reality, the terms that right-wingers (and others) now deride as "silly" and "hyper-politically correct" are almost always awkward attempts to be kind, polite, fair, and generous. "Crippled," "deaf and dumb," and "handicapped" (not to mention "geeky," "gimpy," and "fatso") are rude and insulting. They also reduce a person to a label.

"Physically challenged" and "person with disabilities" are dignified terms that are neutral or even honorable. They acknowledge that someone may *have* a disability, yet that's not the person's sole definition.

After all, you would not want everything you do to be judged and labeled ("Stupid Fool!") on the basis of this rather juvenile epistle that you've sent to Ms. Mentor. We all have the right to rise above, or regret, our weaknesses and sillinesses.

Ms. Mentor hopes that you will learn to do so.

Honor or Insult?

Q: The local right-wingers have targeted me, because I'm the only untenured faculty member in psychology/Women's Studies. In their newspaper,
which is full of attacks on professors and ideas they loathe as "P.C.,"
they've given me a sarcastic "P.C. Teacher of the Month Award," with a
"special citation" for my teaching about Freud's phallic symbols. (I hardly
think that's a radical act, but who knows how they think?)

What should I do?

A: Ms. Mentor can think of three possibilities:

1. Ignore it, and let it blow over.
2. File a grievance against their "noncollegial" behavior. But you may
    lose, since they can argue for "free speech" and "freedom of the
    press."
3. Celebrate the award.

Ms. Mentor finds (3) the best alternative. You can list the award on your
vita, and write up a press release in this format:

Dr. Anna Howard Shaw, assistant professor of Psychology & Women's
Studies at Woodhull-Sojourner University, was recently named "Teacher
of the Month" by *Folderol*, a monthly newspaper covering trends in academia. Dr. Shaw, cited for her teaching of Sigmund Freud's theories, will
be honored at a banquet at the Centreville Marriott on April 12. For
further information, contact *Folderol*: 555-555-5555.

Send the press release, with your photo, to every venue that might use it:
university and town newspapers, TV, and radio; your hometown media;
your alumni magazines. Act as if it's a great honor. If you're asked how you
feel about it, give gushy sound bites.

You'll probably get congratulatory notes from the president of your university, from some members of your university's board of trustees, and from
people who are running for political office. (In Cleveland, one perpetual
office seeker still writes notes congratulating anyone who gets in the *Plain
Dealer* without committing a crime.)

With your picture everywhere, you've made it impossible for *Folderol* to howl: "No! No! It's not an honor! We meant it as an insult!" Any requests for banquet tickets will throw them into a total tizzy.

But will there be a banquet? But of course. On April 12, Dr. Shaw and her half-dozen best friends will gather at the Centreville Marriott and treat themselves to a lovely dinner. A highlight will be the many toasts to Dr. Shaw, for all her talents and all her successes.

To her friends (and to Ms. Mentor), she will always be Teacher of the Month.

Healthy, Fine, and Dandy Me

Q: I'm youngish (under thirty-five) and healthy. My parents are in good health, and I chose my ancestors wisely. Why should I care about disability right now?

A: Americans are often into deep denial about a fact that other cultures readily admit: we all die. By the time you are eighty, you will almost certainly be either partly disabled or, gasp, *dead*. Therefore, unless you die in your prime at the height of your fame (which can guarantee immortality— cf. Janis Joplin), it behooves you to plan for the years in which you will not be so healthy, rugged, and self-satisfied as you are now.

Of course, you can opt out of disability entirely, via The Harold Washington Approach. The late mayor of Chicago reportedly spent the last year of his life as a total glutton who devoured industrial-sized pizzas for lunch. Then one day he had a massive heart attack, essentially exploded, and died. It was a sad day for Chicago, but perhaps not for Harold Washington. (He reportedly died with the taste of anchovies on his lips.)

He also evaded disability altogether, but most women will not. Women live longer than men and suffer much more from disabling-but-not-killing conditions: women are 75 percent of the sufferers from rheumatoid arthritis, for instance. Women are also less apt to have family members taking full-time care of them (men often have wives as caregivers). Women without daughters will probably spend their last months or years in nursing homes, cared for by paid professionals.

Ms. Mentor believes that everyone who's healthy ought to put in some screaming time for old-timers. Now-healthy people can write letters, lobby, call representatives, drive to meetings, and campaign for health care reform, accessible bathrooms and staircases, easier travel for people in wheel-chairs, parking spaces truly reserved for those who need them, motorized carts in shopping malls, no smoking everywhere, and other services and gadgets to enable people with disabilities to enjoy life and contribute to a better world for all.

Ms. Mentor adds that academic women should be thinking about how to teach students with disabilities, including hidden ones. Since at least 10 percent of adults have hearing impairments, soft-voiced women teachers should learn to speak clearly and loudly, and face the class. All faculty should write legibly on blackboards and demand clean, mold-free class-rooms. They should promote and demonstrate generous and compassionate attitudes toward anyone with disabilities—including characters in books or movies.

Faculty can also ask for classroom chairs without constricting writing arms—since larger-than-average students (women of substance, pregnant women, and football players) often have trouble fitting into standard desks. If a call to the Disabilities Office won't do it, getting bigger chairs can become an informative class campaign for a composition or rhetoric course. How many letters will it take?

Ms. Mentor exhorts you to think in more than individualistic terms, for "I'm fine, what's wrong with you?" is ultimately self-defeating. Feminism means working for a better world for all—for a Healthy, Fine, and Dandy Us.

The Late Professor Octopus

Q: One of the elderly professors in my department died suddenly of a heart attack. Many people have been talking in glowing terms about what a wonderful, kind, honest, loving man he was—but I knew him as a vicious sexual harasser, who couldn't keep his hands off me and other young women. It's because of him that our department has very few women faculty: by himself he retarded the progress of women, by driving us away. When I hear him praised to the woodwork, I want to barf. What should I do?

A: The young, Ms. Mentor responds with a sigh, often feel that to be honest—i.e., brutally and crudely frank—is a virtue. But exhortations to be "open," or to "share your real feelings," are often invitations to be boorish and cruel.

Ms. Mentor exhorts you to avoid the temptation.

Certainly you would be setting the historical record straight if you stood up at the memorial service for Professor Octopus and said, "Stuff it, earthlings! You know what a philandering, evil monster he was! Why are you lying?"

But you know Why. There is no point, now, in speaking ill of the late Professor Octopus, for attacking his memory will only prolong the pain of his survivors. Too often Professor Octopuses do leave long-suffering, heavy-drinking wives. The widow of Professor Octopus may be glad, in her heart, that he's gone. But to suggest publicly that her years with him were wasted makes her seem like a victim or a fool.

Best to let sleeping Octopuses lie, but invite the Widow Octopus to tea, or lunch, or dinner. Widows often need befriending. The best way to combat Professor Octopus is to support and comfort women.

And who knows? Perhaps you'll find her a very merry widow indeed. That will be both a vindication and a pleasure.

Disability Power!

Q: I have a colleague who's never cut her long braids and never gotten over being a 1960s revolutionary (she still brags about when they took over five buildings at Columbia in 1968). She just joined the American Association of Retired Persons, which she claims is an ass-kicking group that welcomes people fifty and over, and says I should join when my time comes (I'm 48). But what really got me is that she's hooting and raving over the Americans with Disabilities Act, which she says is a GREAT READ. Is it?

A: Indeed it is, says Ms. Mentor: it should gladden the heart of every baby boomer who ever yearned to change the world.

The "ADA," passed in 1990, is called "the civil rights bill for the disabled," and it's a detailed, sweeping statement about what's needed for the 43 million Americans who have physical or mental disabilities (as Americans age, there are more every day).

The ADA is written in ringing language: it calls unequivocally for "the elimination of discrimination against individuals with disabilities." (Ms.

Mentor likes to imagine a law requiring "the elimination of discrimination against women." It would never pass.)

For 1960s rebels who fondly remember lists of "non-negotiable demands," the ADA has great ones: "clear, strong, consistent, enforceable standards" to eliminate "isolation, segregation, and discrimination against individuals with disabilities" in jobs, housing, public accommodations, education, health, and recreation. Some of the problems it targets sound very familiar to women, including "overprotective rules and policies, failure to modify facilities and practices, and relegation to lesser or no opportunities, which include purposely unequal treatment, stereotyped characterizations, and political powerlessness."

Disabled women, Ms. Mentor notes with awe, may have legal rights that abled women don't have. Employers also cannot

- refuse to hire an individual just because s/he has a disability, as long as the individual can perform the job;
- refuse to make reasonable accommodations to an employee's disability;
- demand medical examinations or information about medical conditions that do not affect job performance.

Hurrah! says Ms. Mentor: women who've spent their lives pushing for social change can crow with pleasure over the ADA. It is making a difference everywhere, not only with "No Smoking" and "Handicapped" places and spaces, but with elevators, ramps, public toilets that flush automatically, faucets that turn themselves on and off, and many and varied grocery carts.

Many college campuses lag, though: at one major university in the Southeast, the Affirmative Action office can't be reached except by climbing a steep staircase. Ms. Mentor also wonders if all those snappy young rebels who took over the buildings at Columbia University in 1968 could race up those five flights now, if they needed to. Now they need to agitate for elevators.

Still, the ADA does represent "Power to the People," for everyone can do a little bit to enforce it. Ms. Mentor nudges: the next time you see a car without a "Handicapped" permit occupying a "Handicapped" parking spot, leave a nasty note. Or surround the car, pretending it's Columbia. Or at least shriek as loudly as you can. That always gets attention, even in the 1990s.

(If you want a copy of the ADA [1990], your Congressional representative should be able to get you one. You can also find it in most university libraries. It's Public Law 101-336, available in the book entitled *United States Statutes at Large, 101st Congress—2nd Session—1990, Vol. 104—Part I, Public Laws 101-241 through 101-440*. The ADA begins on the page numbered 104 Stat. 327, and its essence appears through 104 Stat. 334, although there's much more.)

Planning to be Spontaneous

Q: Your column is wonderful! I am a doctoral student at Y University. . . . There are a few women project leaders, and your column is circulating among them at this very moment! It's so nice to feel like a member of a team (women) and to have fun laughing at our position, while learning to empower ourselves. We are eager to learn subtle ways to orchestrate meetings!

A: Ms. Mentor thanks you for your good words: no woman is ever appreciated enough. Ms. Mentor hopes that your mother is proud of having raised such a splendid daughter, and that your colleagues also regard you as a sensational role model.

Now, to answer your request, Ms. Mentor begins with a truth rarely acknowledged: that the most dramatic meetings in academia are often rehearsed.

She hastens to add that orchestrating a meeting is not a thoroughly sinister activity. Often when the issue is small and the stakes insignificant, a preplanned meeting saves time. Sometimes it is understood that meetings will consist of "discussion" (posturing) followed by "voting" (ratification of whatever has already been decided). In departments where meetings are routinely orchestrated, only the truly naive and unmentored believe all meetings are "real."

The interest comes when not everyone knows, or agrees, that a meeting is orchestrated. Or, even livelier, a new (undisciplined, strident, and self-righteous) faction decides to orchestrate the meeting for *its* purposes. The old orchestra is aghast, the combatants pummel each other with impromptu scurrilities, and everyone is vastly entertained.

Yet Ms. Mentor advises her sage readers to stay out of department fights unless two conditions obtain: (1) the issue is very important, involving money or power or personnel or (sometimes) curriculum; and (2) the reader has tenure. Those new to academia should know that the truly significant decisions are not made in public. Hiring choices sometimes are, but tenure and promotion are usually handled by secret ballot. Some departments discuss salaries openly, but in most, salaries are decided by the department chair/czar, who may or may not communicate the criteria to the faculty.

But for readers who want to be armchair anthropologists, and for those who want to wade in, Ms. Mentor herewith offers a primer on orchestrating, or choreographing, a meeting.

Why orchestrate? To get a favorable outcome, without the messiness and spontaneity of true democracy. One's colleagues, orchestrators believe, cannot be trusted to judge an idea on its merits. They need to be nudged, bullied, and led.

A meeting might be orchestrated to get a particular change ratified, such as new courses, requirements, or curricula. Or the meeting might be used to reject changes. But the more voluminous the work already done, and the more paperwork generated, the more likely it is that the change will pass (regardless of its merits). The most orchestrated meetings are the "frank discussions" (or "forensic sessions") that precede voting.

How to orchestrate. One person cannot do it alone: that is why orchestration is performed by orchestras. Typically, a group of faculty members, often with something else in common (tenure status, children, critical or sexual orientation, or office proximity) discover that they agree about an issue. They have a common agenda.

They also have the first prerequisite: allies. (Given the rampant paranoia among pale males in academia, a conspiracy of women and/or people of color should recruit at least one white man. Tokenism, yes, but politically useful. At one small Midwestern college, the women faculty and students once created a Feminist Forum, whereupon the male faculty retorted with a Balls and Beards Club. One man attended both, as a double agent.)

But to return to the scenario. The allies may, in planned or random fashion, lobby fence-sitters by visiting their offices, buttonholing them in the mailroom, or even sidling up to them in bathrooms, theaters, laundromats, or supermarkets. This may suffice. If not, the allies may call a secret pre-meeting meeting, usually at a neutral site, off-campus.

Much lore circulates about pre-meeting meetings. Ms. Mentor recalls the chair in a Southern university, for instance, who invited colleagues to his home allegedly to taste some fine wines, but really to lobby them to reelect him. The wines were fine, many a hangover was initiated, and in the next meeting, the host was re-acclaimed as chair by unanimous vote.

Other pre-meeting meetings (call them "conspiracies") have been less successful. For one in the Upper Midwest, the professor presiding at his house wore a peculiar Middle Eastern nightgown, which proved so diverting that many attendees never got whatever message he had in mind. In another university, on the East Coast, the planned bloc-voting of certain faculty became so widely known that one's office was dubbed "Election Central." Lampoons circulated.

Successful conspiracies are dignified, not overt, and well disciplined. Conspirators sometimes decide who will sit where, who will object, and who will propose the ideas scripted by the conspirators. The conspirators may even designate someone to yell, "Call the question!" after a while, so that the winning vote can be taken.

If the meeting's chair is part of the conspiracy, s/he can refuse to call on those who do not have scripted parts (this is dirty, but not uncommon). Another tipoff that a meeting is orchestrated: some statements get no response, while others are cheered or vilified. The statements evoking no response are those that are not part of the plan.

Does orchestration work? Yes, most of the time. Unless the issue is salaries, most departments—like most of the world—have a solid corps of middle-of-the-road people who will go along with anything. Of the others, the voluble ones will silence themselves if they scent the possibility of public humiliation. Unless their mission is illegal or completely ridiculous, a well-disciplined cadre can usually put through whatever agenda they want.

Will orchestrated changes be lasting ones? As lasting as any others (although animosities stirred up may last even longer). But decisions made by departments are sometimes not implemented anyway. At one Pennsylvania university, for instance, a master's degree in creative writing was voted in annually for five years, but no one ever did the paperwork to make it a live entity. Other decisions may be quashed by the dean, or forgotten.

Are sexual favors ever involved in orchestrating a meeting? Probably, although Ms. Mentor knows of no such cases. She does have an opinion, nevertheless: sleeping with someone in order to promote curricular change strikes her as a gross malappropriation of one's genitals. They were made for finer things.

The Hair, the Hair Is Everywhere

Q: I'm mid-career, an associate professor in a social sciences department in a Far West university, but I'm not writing about myself. I know that "I have this friend who has this problem" is a cliché, and in this case she's not even a friend.

"Leslie" is a woman I don't particularly get along with and don't particularly like. But I'm truly dazzled by her energy, dedication, and organizational ability. I know that she likes the small administrative jobs she's done, such as chairing a curriculum committee, being an acting assistant dean, and filling in for our department chair when he's been out of town. She's also been excellent in all those positions.

I think she could go far as an administrator—if she'd cut her hair. Leslie has long, 1960s-ish hair, which she rarely trims or evens out. It hangs limp and messy and bedraggled, and now it's turning gray and grizzled. Leslie dresses acceptably (though slightly frumpily) for her jobs. But even when she pins her hair up, it falls down and looks sloppier than ever, with tails and horns sticking out. It's ugly, and terribly unprofessional, and it's holding her back.

How can we (the women in her university) tell her, "Get a haircut if you want to get anywhere?"

A: Ms. Mentor, who goes back a long way, recalls what an issue "HAIR" was in the 1960s. You and your colleagues are trying to give Leslie the same message that grownups were giving the young ones in those rebellious years: cut your hair and conform, or you can't have the goodies in our system.

Well, Ms. Mentor has since discovered that many of the goodies in the academic system are worth having after all ("Time to grow up and sell out," as Lenny Bruce used to say). Leslie needs to get the goodies to share them with other women. You, rightly, don't want her to sabotage her own chances.

Among academic women, it's hard to get caught "accidentally" reading *Glamour* magazine, which just happens to have a picture of the right hairdo for Leslie. Ambitious professional women do not (and should not) routinely chew over questions of fashion and beauty: they have power secrets to share.

Ms. Mentor proposes a different ploy. For Leslie's birthday, buy her a day of pampering/makeover at the best local salon. Unless she absolutely refuses to go, the employees should be able to persuade her to have a haircut "just as an experiment."

If that does not work, you're left with the bedrock strategy: tell Leslie what you told Ms. Mentor. It'd be difficult if you were close friends (she might hate you). But since you're not, and your only interest is that she be a successful administrator, why not just tell her one thing that's clearly holding her back? The cure is so easy, and so painless.

Still, if you cannot bring yourself to give Leslie totally unsolicited advice, you can always start out with: "Leslie, Ms. Mentor answered a question from a woman who has a friend who has this problem. . . . And Ms. Mentor says . . ."

Properly Clad

Q: Is it ever proper to wear a hat and gloves in academia?

A: In matters of social usage, Ms. Mentor defers to Miss Manners's rules: a lady may wear a hat indoors only in the afternoon and may wear gloves indoors only in the evening (after 6 P.M.).

You could, of course, properly wear both hat and gloves to an outdoor garden party, but then you might appear to be crossing the invisible line between the properly professional woman and the frilly lady. Flowery frocks, little white gloves, and oversized picture hats do not become a professor who wants to be most remembered for her mind.

However, there is one season and one region during which it is always appropriate, and indeed recommended, for a woman to wear a hat and gloves.

In the North, that season is called winter.

Rotten Referee

Q: I sent an article to an academic journal, which rejected it with a referee's letter calling it "simply too jejune"—which my dictionary says means "barren . . . not interesting or satisfying; dull or empty; not mature; childish."

Why would anyone say such an ugly thing to a complete stranger? And why should I be in a profession where people do that?

A: Ms. Mentor reminds you that many academics like to inflate their own egos at the expense of those who are professionally weaker than they are. These academics are usually "powerful senior professors" and sometimes "stars" or "major figures in the profession." You and Ms. Mentor know what they really are.

Bullies.

She advises you to ignore their crude power plays and refusals to mentor the young. Do not buy or teach their books. If you're in literature, take pride in the instructions that *PMLA*, your field's major journal, gives its article readers: that they must offer useful suggestions and not make harsh, insulting judgments, such as "This belongs in freshman comp."

But whatever your field, concentrate on the work and research that brought you to your profession in the first place. Do the things that give you intellectual pleasure. Also rethink and rework your article if any of the criticisms seem valid, and consult your writing group if you have one. Do not wait or stew. Do not respond to scurrility. Send the article out again, to another journal.

There are buzz-saw people in every profession. Ms. Mentor exhorts you not to let them grind you down.

Junior Miss

Q: The older women faculty in my department keep wanting to mother me and give me advice. I feel like Esther Greenwood in Plath's *The Bell Jar*, constantly attracting crazy old ladies. What should I do?

A: The above query, first printed in *Concerns*, attracted criticism from a senior professor in Minnesota:

> My dismay comes from the ageism contained within this request, e. g.,
> "crazy old ladies." . . . I have tried to assist younger female colleagues.
> Being met with strangely mixed responses, I have analyzed the situation
> and decided not to continue unasked. I think it's time to open the ques-
> tion of female-to-female mentoring in academe . . .

My other dismay at the item stems from the equation of "older women faculty" and mothers. If older male colleagues tried to speak to this woman, would she think of them as "fathers," I wonder? . . .

Ms. Mentor agrees with the Minnesotan: the question shows age prejudice and role confusion. Motherhood is a sociobiological role, not a professional one, and many academic women have happily chosen *not* to be mothers. They certainly have not chosen to be the mothers of disagreeable newer colleagues.

But addressing herself, now, to the original letter writer:

Ms. Mentor might call you an ungrateful and ungracious child, but more politely, she will inform you that older women are repositories of wisdom. They have already planned, felt, and done what you've done. No younger generation ever invents anything truly new (although students sometimes harbor the delusion that they have invented sex).

You haven't understood that your older colleagues' attempts to "mother" you are really attempts to mentor you. They are teaching you survival skills. They can warn you, for instance, about rhetorical veneers—"we consider only excellence" or "we like to think of ourselves as a family"—that mask many a hidden agenda, unacknowledged prejudice, or tawdry conspiracy.

Older female colleagues can also alert you to departmental feuds and alliances; they can steer you away from known sexual harassers. They can tell you what to notice at department meetings: for instance, do male colleagues listen and respond to female ones, or are women interrupted or ignored?

They can share the past. Have there been horror stories, like that of the female assistant professor in California who tangled publicly with a senior male colleague, only to get, the next day in campus mail, a package of human feces? Or the Pennsylvania dean whose house was torched?

Rather than adopting Esther Greenwood's skewed view of what older women can do, Ms. Mentor recommends that you read more positive literary models: the female communities in Sarah Orne Jewett's stories or May Sarton's novels, for instance, or the stories in Susan Koppelman's anthology *Women's Friendships*.

As for the Minnesotan: Ms. Mentor lauds her efforts to mentor her younger colleagues and hopes that they will learn to value the advice of their foresisters. There is a pleasure in mentoring, too, in passing on hard-won and useful knowledge that can improve the lives of women. Mentoring should not be greeted with some variety of "Please, Mother, I'd rather do it myself!" for it is *not* mothering.

It is feminism.

Secret . . . Admirer

Q: A colleague has decided he adores me. I know I am intelligent and OK-looking, but I am neither gorgeous nor irresistible. Thanks to this colleague, though, I am becoming very worried.

He (a tenured, quite-a-bit-older man) frequently appears at my desk during office hours. But he has little to say and I'm forced to make empty chitchat and play conversational games. After teaching for several hours, this is exhausting.

When I go to the parking lot, Mr. G often appears suddenly and walks me to my car, where he makes a point of standing very close to me, touching my elbow, stroking my face. He has not attempted to kiss me, but that may be because I draw away from him. I've also considered chewing garlic cloves.

His attentions go beyond touching and talking, however. Sometimes there are little poems in my mailbox, in his undisguised handwriting, alleging that my eyes are like stars and my teeth are like pearls—awful clichés, really unworthy of a literature teacher. Sometimes small boxes of candy are awaiting me in the mailroom with notes like, "I'm thinking of you."

Meanwhile, as an untenured assistant professor, I've been assigned a mentor, a male full professor whom I've told about Mr. G's pursuit. My mentor just chuckles and says, "Why, the old goat's in love with you," and "You should be very flattered. After all, his wife's in a nursing home, you know . . ."

Well, I am not flattered, and the fact that Mrs. G is permanently ailing (Alzheimer's is the rumor) makes the pursuit even sadder. I don't want to be Mr. G's plaything; I don't even like him very much. But mostly I feel smothered and coerced, and not the slightest bit honored by his many attentions.

How do I get him to stay away from my office, my car, my mailbox, and my life?

A: Ms. Mentor knows that many "gentlemen of the old school" would call Mr. G's conduct charming. How divine, they might say, to get notes, gifts, and warm little touches—without any expectation of a return! Shouldn't you be blushing with pride?

In a word (Ms. Mentor's one word): NO.

What Mr. G is doing is not flattery. It's closer to stalking.

Much mutual flirtation may go on in any profession, even academia. Smiles, winks, and small nudges, if reciprocal, can please even such a curmudgeon as Ms. Mentor. But Mr. G is not laughing pleasantly or exchanging jokes and banter. Ms. Mentor's infallible test is this: Would Mr. G (presumably heterosexual) be doing to a man what he's doing to you?

Of course not. His is a cloddish sexual pursuit, not a campaign of collegial appreciation. If Mr. G wanted to help you professionally, he'd discuss your research, give you teaching tips, get you on important committees, introduce you to powerful people, and encourage your articles, books, and grant proposals. He would not be fondling your cheek, or sending bonbons.

Ms. Mentor regrets that no legal or moral term exactly covers Mr. G's transgressions. They are not really sexual harassment, since he is not asking for quid pro quo sexual favors. And while what he's doing feels like a "hostile environment," it would be hard to win a legal case, and professionally suicidal to pursue one. To a lot of your colleagues, Mr. G would seem to be the victim, "just a lonely old guy."

Ms. Mentor does not—*does not*—recommend that you present yourself to older male colleagues as a young damsel desperately fleeing the foul clutches of Mr. G. One or two champions may indeed leap to your defense, dump on Mr. G verbally and perhaps physically, and be extremely proud that they have proven they are on top. But you will thereby make a permanent enemy out of Mr. G, who can make your life, and your academic future, unpleasant.

What to do?

You can stay out of private meetings with Mr. G. You can claim that a boyfriend (whether he exists or not) requires your presence—all the little evasions and pretenses that women know.

You can say, or write, to Mr. G, "Your behavior is making me uncomfortable. Please do not send me chocolates or pursue me during office hours." This may work, and it can document a sexual harassment case. But it can lead to deep mutual embarrassment.

Ms. Mentor proposes a different kind of a diplomacy: find a female ally, preferably an associate or full professor who has already been friendly and generous with professional advice. A dean, a librarian, or a Director of Women's Studies may help.

Ask the Senior Ally's advice on an awkward professional problem: Mr. G is a very sweet person, but terribly unhappy and obviously very lonesome. He often comes to your office, but you know you cannot be the friend he needs. Can the Senior Ally communicate to Mr. G, nicely, that he needs other pursuits?

This way, you have not trashed Mr. G; nor have you presented yourself as unkind or wimpy. You've also asked for something that the Senior Ally can easily accomplish.

Ms. Mentor knows of a similar case in New Jersey: a Senior Ally, prompted by a young colleague, told one Mr. H the story of "my friend, who doesn't have tenure," who was being "pursued, almost sexually harassed, by an older man who doesn't seem to know that he's doing wrong." When Mr. H (who was, of course, her target) murmured his sympathy for young ladies, the Ally knew she had him. Mr. H stayed friendly to the young woman he'd pursued, but all other attentions stopped completely.

Ms. Mentor prefers this most roundabout of all tactics, because it teaches in the women's preferred way—through stories—and it lets everyone save face. Ms. Mentor reminds readers who crave certain savage satisfactions that shouting matches, grievances, and lawsuits are the court of last resort, in which women often do not win. It is much better if Mr. G's transformation from goat to gentleman occurs off-stage, leaving you, Ms. Mentor's correspondent, to pursue your own dreams, and consume your own chocolates.

Only the Teeth are Bared

Q: I have a colleague who undresses me with his eyes and then snarls. Shall I charge him with sexual harassment?

A: Raw teeth do evoke atavistic fears, and Ms. Mentor is not surprised that you want to retaliate savagely. But she cautions you to back off (and keep away, in case your colleague bites).

"Undressing with the eyes" usually means up-and-down scoping and judging. The Snarler is probably the sort of fellow who habitually talks to a woman's breast rather than looking her in the eye. (Ms. Mentor once knew a director of undergraduate studies in an East Coast university who could not identify his own female faculty members in a group photo. He never looked at their faces.)

This behavior is more than impolite: it also creates a "hostile environment," one form of gender harassment. Yet Ms. Mentor hesitates to advise you to charge The Snarler with anything unless other conditions are met.

Does The Snarler supervise you? Has he prevented you from achieving your goals, such as tenure or promotion or a higher salary or computer time or lab equipment? Has his scoping kept you from entering facilities you must use, such as the mailroom or a department common room? Has he commented about your anatomy to students or other faculty who have been influenced by his unprofessional behavior?

In other words, you must be able to show that you've been professionally damaged by The Snarler. If you've just been disgusted or grossed out, you're unlikely to win with a sexual harassment charge. You also might be stigmatized as (Ms. Mentor shudders) "that bitch"—and that hurts when you need lab space, raises, promotion, or tenure.

If The Snarler is a senior professor with power, he could just gobble you up, career and all.

But what if—rare, delightful case—you are the senior full professor and The Snarler is a lowly assistant professor, untenured but full of himself? This sort of fellow, with smirk, loosened tie, and strut, seems to be saying with his eyes: "Grrr, I'll show this boss woman what a Real Man is . . ."

In that case, with nothing to lose, you may have the rare pleasure of tormenting a sexist—punishing a phallocrat. You can charge him with creating a "hostile environment"; you can tell him publicly that he needs to govern his eyes. If he does not mend his ways, you can vote against him for tenure. A man who does not treat women as people is a bad colleague.

Ms. Mentor rules: such a man does not belong in a university.

Not Olive Drab

Q: I have a peculiar problem that many people will find laughable. I am an untenured assistant professor in a department with many alcoholic full professors ("the Revelers"). At our department's December party, Reveler I dropped an olive down my new silk blouse. Within seconds, his colleague (Reveler II) had reached down, fumbled around the front of my underwear, and extricated the olive. Both of them laughed a lot, and Reveler II ate the olive with great relish. I ran to the bathroom, where I could not get the alcohol stains off my blouse.

Then it was vacation, so the Revelers presumably have forgotten or re-pressed the incident, but I haven't. Should I send Reveler I the bill for cleaning my new silk blouse? Should I charge them both with sexual ha-rassment? Should I try to ignore the fact that I'll feel slimed when I see either of them? Call me NP: there's No Pimento for me.

A: Your story does indeed have slapstick elements. Reveler II's eating the errant olive reminds Ms. Mentor of a gentleman's famous query to etiquette maven Amy Vanderbilt, sometime in the 1950s (Ms. Mentor is rephrasing from memory): "At an elegant dinner party, I was served a soup with an insect in it. What should I have done?"

Vanderbilt's response: "You may properly remove the insect with your spoon and quietly place it on your soup plate, to be whisked away unob-trusively by the serving staff." But Vanderbilt added that if her correspon-dent were an extremely self-confident gentleman, and the hostess meant the world to him, he could enthusiastically eat the insect, and exclaim, "Delicious!"

Ms. Mentor does not think you should have seized the olive yourself and crowed, "Delicious!" It would have been better to flee the room immedi-ately—though you could hardly have expected Reveler II's rescue mission. You were a rose among buffoons.

But now what?

Some would tell you to file a complaint with your Affirmative Action/ Equal Opportunity/Sexual Harassment office. Others would point you to-ward a lawyer, to file a civil suit. Still others would insist that you write harsh letters to Revelers I and II, threatening to expose them to the univer-sity's chancellor or president or Faculty Senate or Commission on the Status of Women.

Ms. Mentor, however, advises you to do nothing.

If you filed a complaint, wrote a harsh letter, or initiated a lawsuit, what would it get you? Since the incident happened only once, you would get a reputation with the men in your department for overreaction and holding grudges. You would be (at minimum) "that humorless feminist."

Legally, you have no case. An olive down the blouse, and a grope in pursuit of the olive, could be regarded as negligent or hostile acts, but they do not form a "hostile environment" limiting your ability or anyone else's to work. Isolated moments of meanness and rudeness, while deplorable, are not illegal.

You should, of course, record everything in your Tenure Diary: date, place, who said and did what, who else was there. But since you're untenured, the Revelers will be voting on your future in academia. Will you make lasting enemies over an olive and a rude hand?

It is far classier for you to act as if the incident never happened. Just as you would avert your eyes if one of the Revelers had vomited on the floor, you will pretend to have forgotten it all. If you are really good at rising above, you may later claim that you were not even at the party. (That level of tact is really prime: Ms. Mentor doubts that she could manage it. By never leaving her ivory tower, though, Ms. Mentor keeps her silk blouses pristine.)

Your silence will have another benefit if Revelers I and II do remember the incident. They will be grateful that you covered up their clownishness—and prevented their wives from finding out. (Does that make you a "codependent" or an "enabler"? Ms. Mentor, who has no patience with psychobabble, does not care.)

But what about the dry-cleaning bill?

Ms. Mentor thinks that you should pay it yourself, as a business expense. A silk blouse is not worth making enemies or risking tenure. And in the future, since the old-but-serviceable look is always fashionable among academics, you should attend department parties wearing old, high-necked polyester.

The first law of academia is survival.

A Reader Retorts

After the above question and answer were published in *Concerns*, a reader wrote in to disagree with Ms. Mentor. The original correspondent is referred to by her pseudonym: "NP," for "No Pimento for me."

The Reader's Reaction

Q: Having just joined the Women's Caucus, I eagerly turned to your column for exemplary advice. I read first your letter, then your response to it. Both have infuriated me!

I have trouble understanding why you too do not feel outrage toward the two bozo boozers in her department. The sum of your advice seems to be:

forget it! In order to argue a different method, let me try deconstructing your business-as-usual approach. You assume that, since the two drunks will be voting on NP's tenure, she must not risk making enemies of them. But, gentle Ms. M., that is automated thinking, based on old premises we women must change.

In fact, NP has quite a range of choices for action. You cite (and reject) only three: file a complaint with Affirmative Action, sue for assault, or write directly to the offenders, threatening exposure in high places. I agree that all three of these routes could endanger NP's tenure—but only if the two drunks are necessarily involved in it. You don't seem to consider the possibility of NP's letting the facts be known now AND making sure those two are eliminated from voting on her tenure.

Obviously NP needs a wedge, and several are available. First of all, the Chair is NP's ally of choice. (I assume neither of the drunks is he, as she doesn't say so.) Any chair of average intelligence will want to contain the mess within the department, which is NP's main wedge. Why would he/she not grant her immunity from the two jerks, in exchange for settling NP's feelings—and her cleaning bill, too? Perhaps you reply: "Because he/she will want to protect the offenders, i.e., protect power."

OK, then NP can tell the Chair she is going to the Dean, whereupon Chair might change the royal position. (Why wash your dirty linen in the Dean's office?) If this ploy does not work, Dean (again, assuming a brain) will WANT to know of such behavior among his tenured flock. He/she too will want the matter contained in the college. And Dean can also bar Chair from voting on her tenure (with a documented explanation) if he seems angry enough at NP for going to the Dean. Ditto for Provost or other superior officer.

Other strategies could develop through Affirmative Action. As a staff member of same, I could brainstorm several methods with NP: much depends on how SHE wants the case settled. At my university, we are starting a mediation program for just such cases that lack a clear legal definition of sexual harassment. Ideally, if NP liked the possibility, a mediator could meet with her, the Chair, and the two creeps to find a solution agreeable to all of them. Another, less public action is to simply make a statement, not a formal complaint, for Affirmative Action's files on the two men. If NP wanted to pursue the matter after tenure, then she would have the original evidence handy.

Moreover, such a statement might join others from women whom these two had abused similarly. This aspect of the case seems crucial to me, for we must consolidate efforts to stop habitual offenders. I believe that, to most of us, the bottom line here is: such "alcoholic" behavior is intolerable for anyone anywhere, not to mention among the best educated people in our society. Whatever happened to "noblesse oblige"?

If I were the Chair or Dean involved, I would gladly inform the drunks: "Tenure is a privilege granted with the expectation that you behave at all times with professorial dignity. Now that you have failed to do so, I hereby revoke your voting status on NP's tenure. Repeated such incidents may well result in revocation of your tenure itself."

Another item bothers me: Why our "genteel" acceptance of alcoholics? Of course academia (especially the Anglo branch?) has long protected this supposed occupational hazard—of solitude? of Mallarmé's terror of the blank page? I agree with you that women do not inhabit the academy in order to cure its ills; but while we are humanizing it anyway, inevitably, by our intelligent, ethical behavior, why not try to rout this vestige of old-boy compensation for personal deficiencies? I may sound intolerant. But how can we change the institution without ostracizing unacceptable behavior? Consider the current social status of smokers: only the intolerance of non-smokers could have created the rapid change.

Finally, your closing line takes my proverbial breath away. "The first law of academia is survival" bespeaks:

A. Hobbes (or Gingrich, take your pick);
B. Go-along to get-along;
C. An attitude of blindered obedience (cf. Eichmann and co.).

Even if you (think you) are advising only the powerless untenured, you are still stating your woeful general view of the academy. The tenured must JOIN the untenured to improve this workplace. We cannot allow our home to remain a jungle! Yet the more we hear advice like yours, the less willing people will be to do the hard job of civilizing it. If I were NP's colleague, I would not rest until SOMETHING DRASTIC had happened to change the behavior of the two drinkers.

If you are unwilling to print this diatribe, please at least forward it to NP, encouraging her to contact me directly. However, printing this letter might start a forum of sorts. In any case, I hope my anger does not obscure my deep appreciation of what you are doing generally. Your column will prob-

ably be the first item I turn to. You may take my dissent as a compliment:
How many of us gentle readers take your advice as seriously as I do?

Radical Ruth

A: Ms. Mentor does appreciate Radical Ruth's "diatribe." Like the stars
who know that the only bad publicity is no publicity, Ms. Mentor has always felt that the only bad response is no response. She is grateful for the
impassioned retort from Radical Ruth.

But Radical Ruth is far more optimistic than Ms. Mentor about entrenched academics' support of justice and comfort for junior faculty.
Would that it were so—that the untenured were always welcomed warmly,
treated with respect and dignity, mentored ably and encouraged to be the
superb teachers, researchers, writers, and colleagues that most are capable
of being.

Ms. Mentor would delight in being a member of such a department. Indeed, she would love to live in such a world. (Perhaps she might even step
down from her ivory tower to share the wonder.) However, Ms. Mentor
knows that in these deplorable days of downsizing, de-tracking, and dis-
appearance of positions, collegiality is often tossed aside. Some departments are genuinely, even openly, looking for ways to replace assistant
professors with instructors, who can be paid much less.

All of which makes Ms. Mentor much less confident that those running
the show at NP's university—the Chair, the Dean, the Provost—would automatically side with NP against entrenched senior professors. Ms. Mentor
thinks it more likely that the top brass, who automatically have access to
the university lawyer, would feel they had nothing to fear from NP. Should
she file any kind of complaint, they could wait her out, squelch her, punish
her. And then could fire her for being a troublemaker.

They could also send her from one office to another, as Radical Ruth
suggests, which would consume her in meetings, memos, and painfully
retelling her story. The cure, if there was one, might be worse than the
disease.

Yet Ms. Mentor does not want to be misconstrued: she does consider
the original olive event an assault—embarrassing, sexual, insulting, and
vicious. It made Ms. Mentor yearn for the heady early 1970s, when every
well-dressed feminist carried a pack of cards to hand out at appropriate
moments: "You Have Just Insulted a Woman. This card has been chemically
treated. In 20 minutes your prick will fall off."

But now, in the mid-1990s, Ms. Mentor does not want NP to suffer further or waste her time on bureaucratic maneuvers. She does agree with one of Radical Ruth's points: NP should lodge a confidential complaint in the Affirmative Action office. That will start a paper trail, or add to one.

As for the acceptance of alcoholism in academia: Ms. Mentor finds it odd that Radical Ruth calls overindulgence an "Anglo" excess. Ms. Mentor thinks it a male excess, and directs interested theorists to June Stephenson's 1995 book, *Men Are Not Cost-Effective.*

Ms. Mentor does like to imagine the return of chemically treated cards, slyly slipped into strategic pockets when no one is looking: "You Have Just Drunk Too Much. In 20 minutes . . ."

But NP's best revenge is to get tenure, for that is the only way she can begin improving the manners of her colleagues. Her silence now, and her quietly cleaning her silk blouse herself, are but a means to a greater end: to give her the chance to create the kind of world that Radical Ruth and Ms. Mentor will both be pleased to inhabit.

Slouching
Toward Tenure

What does it *really* take to get tenure? the young always want to know. Ms. Mentor is sometimes reminded of the old, and yes, very tacky, Borscht Belt joke about the three Hollywood moguls choosing the female star for their next major motion picture.

One of the possible stars has an Academy Award; the second has an Emmy; the third has a Tony. All have done Shakespeare in England; all have studied with the Actors' Studio or its equivalent; all of them do comedy, tragedy, musicals, and serious drama, with equal deftness and flair. All are truly distinguished, international performers.

But the moguls have no trouble deciding which one will get the part: "The one with the biggest tits."

In academia, there are officially three criteria for tenure: excellence in research, teaching, and service. But the biggest thing to have, especially for women, is—

CHARM.

(Ms. Mentor knows what you were thinking. Now go be ashamed of yourself.)

Virtually every university and college has some kind of written tenure and promotion policies. (If the job market were not so terrible, Ms. Mentor would warn academics away from places without such policies. They're often run on a wing and a prayer by small religious denominations, or are the fiefdoms of a few bizarre and cranky billionaires. They can be mercurial, dictatorial, crazy-making.)

Virtually all tenure policies say that a candidate needs some kind of excellence in all three areas (research, teaching, service), although the wording varies: "satisfactory," "notable," "original achievement." Some also include "creativity" or "graceful, elegant writing." Some policies are vague ("notable performance," "scholarly potential," "evidence of promise"). Others may amount to small tomes, often the residue of a string of lawsuits. (PS-23, the tenure and promotion policy statement at Penn State, is over a hundred pages long.)

But often what matters most is "collegiality"—a mine field for women.

From the time she is hired, "Sophia" (an assistant professor who wisely follows Ms. Mentor's advice in all things) will have been keeping her Tenure Diary, filed safely at home. Sophia's Diary includes her university's written tenure and promotion policies and copies of all letters and memos about her responsibilities, salary, department expectations, and any other professional agreements or understandings. She includes all written communications about her performance, together with notes about any encounters indicating praise or disdain for what she's doing and, of course, any instances of sexual harassment. All these materials are neatly filed and dated.

Meanwhile, Sophia will have been self-promoting since the moment she arrived, ingratiating herself with her new colleagues. ("How crass!" say Ms. Mentor's newer readers. "How wise!" say her older ones.)

Sophia may turn out to be a superb teacher, as measured by student evaluations. She may be an outstanding researcher and published writer. She may win Ford Foundation Fellowships, National Science Foundation grants, Nobel prizes, Guggenheim Fellowships, Pulitzer prizes, and even an Emily Toth Award (a Popular and American Culture Association prize given annually since 1986 to the year's best single-author book in women's studies and popular culture). Sophia may also have served ably on half a dozen university committees, arguing nobly and vociferously for students' rights to choose their own courses, untrammeled by overbearing faculty's traditionalist preconceptions of what a truly educated person should study.

And Sophia, as thus described, may very well not get tenure.

To put it crudely but succinctly (Ms. Mentor being no mincer of words), Sophia's committee performance will have pissed people off.

For a tenure decision, Ms. Mentor reminds her sage readers, is the entrenched faculty's shouting, as one: *We do (or don't) want Sophia around for the rest of her academic life!*

Universities do like researchers who bring eminence and worldwide fame. Sometimes, in fact, such stars will be honored with endowed chairs—meaning they'll make piles of money while they continue to write their books and amass their data. Some "chaired professors" do not teach much or interact with other faculty, but they're often trotted out like jewels or trained puppies whenever rich donors need to be impressed.

Fame also inevitably brings envy. Rare is the well-published academic who has not been called a "trashmeister" or "sloppy scholar" by snippy colleagues. (Dedicated researchers ignore such gibes: "Consider the source," Ms. Mentor or your mother will tell you.)

Universities also like good teachers. Students flock to them, while parents and alumni adore them. No one, of course, agrees on what makes a good teacher, except that enthusiasm ranks very high. (In a famous experiment, two performers gave virtually the same lecture, except that one was a workaday academic who delivered his lecture as a sober research report. The other was a professional actor who knew nothing about the subject but was grandly flamboyant and theatrical. Students rated the actor as a much more effective, and better-informed, teacher.)

Finally, universities also want "service." Sophia must attend faculty meetings, work amiably on committees, and possibly give community talks bringing the department or university's "message" to the public. Often service—what is it? how much is expected?—is ill-defined. But serving on two or three committees, preferably low-profile ones that rarely meet, is usually more than enough for someone like Sophia, untenured. (Small liberal arts colleges usually require more service: Sophia must ask what's expected of her.)

Meanwhile, Sophia will be reviewed and reviewed, but only a few things really matter.

Some departments have annual reviews; some do annual evaluations, with "full reviews" in the faculty member's third year, and a "review for tenure" in the fifth and/or sixth year. For all of these, Sophia must have her paperwork in order: copies of all her publications and student evaluations; lists of her service work; and testimonials to her excellence (including any fan mail she's gotten from students, other professors, journal editors, granting agencies, or people who've heard her give conference papers).

The dossier must be complete and in order, following whatever format the university requires. Neatness counts.

But what really counts for tenure, Ms. Mentor?

Service, in fact, is usually unimportant, except in small liberal arts colleges—or if Sophia is well liked but without a distinguished record in anything else. One assistant professor with mediocre teaching and publications was given a "service award" at a Far West university because her colleagues wanted to tenure her anyway. That happens.

Teaching is often not counted very heavily, except sometimes in small liberal arts colleges. But if Sophia's teaching is horrendous, with terrible evaluations and constant student complaints, those will be used against her, if her colleagues want to get rid of her.

Research and publication are important: they are measurable, public achievements. If Sophia gets major grants, or publishes a university press book, plus articles in the best refereed journals in her field, usually her tenure will be assured . . .

. . . If she doesn't piss someone off.

Here Ms. Mentor must break in to stress a point: "collegiality" is hardly ever part of the *written policies* for tenure or promotion. If someone is denied tenure for "lack of collegiality," and a university says so *in writing*, that person almost invariably has grounds for a grievance, or possibly even a lawsuit. But it is much easier to be collegial in the first place and get tenure, than to have to go through years of grievances and legal procedures.

Ms. Mentor exhorts her readers to Make Nice. It saves time.

But to return to Ms. Mentor's examples:

Some years ago, "Lawrence," an associate professor at a Middle Atlantic university, was denied promotion to full professor, despite a very strong record of publication and teaching and service. Lawrence was also, however, a self-consciously "hip" fellow who prided himself on being "cool" about drugs and "un-hung-up" about bourgeois propriety. His office was decorated with very large nude photos of women, one of them his wife.

"Why the fuck didn't I get promoted?" he demanded of his department chair.

"Because you're a social misfit," said the chair, and hung up.

Eventually Lawrence was promoted, but "Laura"—his mythical female counterpart—would never have gotten as far as he did.

For the rules for women are more stringent. Nowadays a male professor displaying female nudes might be accused of producing a "hostile environment" for women students. But a woman professor displaying male nudes would still be considered a "hussy" or a "slut" or both. It's a rare place that would tenure her.

To get tenure, Laura—and Sophia—must "fit in." They must be liked and respected. They must meet everyone and be seen at every faculty occasion, including visitors' talks. They must "do lunch," have dinner parties, go to all social occasions. They must exchange chitchat, be considerate and friendly, listen carefully, look alert, and smile. These are all qualities that pass for "charm" in academia. (They're also, Ms. Mentor opines, not difficult for any woman to manage. Women grow up learning the basics of social hypocrisy, or good manners.)

Especially in mostly pale-male fields, though, women and people of color face special challenges when entrenched faculty are deciding whether they "fit in." Women don't fit in when the guys play squash; African American men may not be welcome on the golf courses. Women faculty in commuter marriages must somehow arrange to seem, socially, part of the community where they teach. (One way is to have the main residence where the wife lives, and have the husband do the trekking.) Commuting faculty must never appear to be Stars, jetting in and out, waving to the peasants from their L.A.-bound planes.

Although it can sometimes be painful (or boring), faculty who are racial minorities must somehow swallow their discomfort and get together socially with white folks. At least the ones voting on tenure and promotion. Someone who seems standoffish, for whatever reason, will be considered one who doesn't "fit in"—someone who won't wear well in the community for the next thirty years or so.

Ms. Mentor wishes she could say that merit will always be rewarded in academia, but such is not the case. What *is* rewarded is likability, followed by publication. And then teaching.

And patience, for there is one other little hurdle that only women face on the path to tenure: what Ms. Mentor calls the Sexist Stutter Step.

For too many Sophias, assistant professors who seem to be doing fine at everything, a funny thing happens on the road to tenure. Some little thing unexpectedly goes awry, such as:

- A very favorable supporting letter, from a recommender at Excellent University, somehow isn't filed in Sophia's dossier. Yet Sophia knows the letter was sent: Professor Recommender e-mailed her a private copy.

- Professor Recommender was given the wrong directions, or the wrong publications, and so wrote a report that minimizes Sophia's most recent accomplishments.
- Professor Recommender is a close friend of someone in the department who, for some reason, does not like Sophia. Professor Recommender has therefore been coached to write some negative things.
- Someone, somewhere decides that Sophia should come up for a tenure decision a semester or a year earlier than she'd thought. Somehow the stopped tenure clock (for her baby) or the leave without pay (for her research) was forgotten. And so Sophia's fate is being decided before her book has actually been accepted for publication, or before her research is in print.
- Sophia's book has been accepted, but it's not yet in page proofs. "How can we know it'll come through?" Sophia is suddenly asked.
- Or the book's in page proofs, "but how will we know whether it will be well received?"
- Or the department's promotion and tenure committee has some doubts: *Is* Sophia's research on women's popular culture really "substantial," or might it, perhaps, be a little "thin"?

Other questions, suddenly posed at the last minute, are also part of the Sexist Stutter Step:

- Does Sophia have enough conference presentations?
- Has she taught enough upper- (or lower-) level courses?
- Has she directed enough graduate students?
- Does she perhaps publish too much?
- Are her teaching scores too high? Does she pander to students?
- Is she too tough a grader, leading students to drop her courses?
- Is she too popular a teacher, meaning she's not "rigorous" enough?

And then the doubters begin wondering: Maybe Sophia should be tenured but not promoted to associate professor yet? (The two usually go together.)

And more, and more. Ms. Mentor's files bulge with examples—of women whose tenure was somehow delayed, or even denied, under very odd circumstances.

What happens?

Ms. Mentor, who of course holds tenure in her ivory tower, sees the Sexist Stutter Step as a last assertion of patriarchy, a last effort to show a woman who is really in charge. Once Sophia gets to prance across the bridge that tenure represents, and barring extraordinary disasters such as financial exigency, she is genuinely, intellectually Free.

Once tenured, Sophia has the liberty to say what she wishes, in her writing and her teaching. She can call a colleague a dupe, a wuss, or a knave. She can speak out at department meetings. She can tell risqué jokes to her dean or stick her tongue out at the university president (although far too few faculty ever do so).

And so, many academic units charge Sophia a toll at the last exit: a last driblet of anxiety, stress, or aggravation before she reaches the other side (where she is still, most likely, earning less money than comparable men).

But tenure, lifetime job security, is the golden goal that most Sophias can reach, despite that last Sexist Stutter Step.

If, of course, they have followed Ms. Mentor's advice.

I Don't Know If This Is Right, But . . .

Q: My mentor, a nice old man who's decided I need help negotiating my way in academia, says I come across as lacking self-confidence. Whenever I write professional communications, such as annual reports or applications for research grants, I always describe my work with scrupulous accuracy—telling what I've done in the past, and also what I haven't managed to do yet ("I have not been able to finish my work because of the heavy teaching load . . ." "I have decided that my original research plans were not practical . . ." "I am disappointed that my queries received so few responses . . .")

My mentor says that I am selling myself short and that my honesty is "disabling." He says I should keep my self-doubts and losses to myself, or share them with a women's support group (I have to say that he is willing to listen, too). He says that I should instead promote, even inflate, what I've accomplished: "I've done X, Y, and Z in spite of my heavy teaching load . . ." "I've refocused my project to make it even better . . ." "I'm pleased that my queries got so many responses from readers around the U.S."

Ms. Mentor, is he right?

A: Yes.

Hiding My Light Under a Bushel

Q: After spending three years in nonrenewable and temporary jobs writing like crazy to make myself more marketable, I have a number of articles, a book coming out, and a job I love in a small private college that is trying to improve its reputation. The dean says research really matters and has funded me to give papers at three conferences (one international) this year.

It is beginning to dawn on me, however, that I've already got a stronger c.v. (more pubs) than any of the senior people. If they publish at all, it's in the state's tourist magazine or the local historical society newsletter. Should I stop talking to my colleagues about my research? Keep my mouth shut about the international conference this winter? Are they going to be jealous?

I'm especially anxious because my partner, passing as my "roommate," has just found a job she adores at a hospital about forty miles away, and both of us really like the locale. I even like my colleagues, even if they are all heterosexual men over the age of forty-five! On the other hand, I need to keep my research heated up in case they DO let me go.

A: You haven't asked Ms. Mentor a question, perhaps because you already know the answers: keep writing, and keep your options open. As you've already shown, writing is the key to tenure-track jobs, and publishing is the only way you can move if you need to.

Ah, your nonpublishing colleagues: that's stickier. You may indeed have to muffle your enthusiasm and downplay your research. Most schools have not adopted, and never will adopt, the wise policy initiated by Dean Annette Kolodny at the University of Arizona: that only people with strong publishing records can vote on tenure for newer colleagues.

Your best strategy, since you won't have a jury of your publishing peers, is to be charming and well liked by all. Have lunch and coffee with those straight old guys; have 'em over for dinner if your living/bed arrangements aren't awkward.

Many a fellow can resist a strong publishing record. But especially in small private college communities, a good meal with lots of wine is an irresistible crowd pleaser.

Strange but true counsel from Ms. Mentor: The way to a man's tenure vote is often through his tummy.

A Wife or a Life?

Q: I have three small children, one born in my second year on the job at D University. I'm now in my fourth year, and my department says I must have a book under contract to get tenure.

What with child care, housework, and keeping home and soul together, I don't have time to write at night—even if I could get out from under all the student papers, independent studies, and everything else I'm asked to do (and I've been criticized for doing very little "department service," or committee work).

Meanwhile my husband says, "We need to have a *life*," which to him means candlelight dinners, watching videos, smoking, and chatting, not lonely nights with me glued to the computer. What can I do? Should I give up on academia altogether?

A: Your missive makes Ms. Mentor think she's stumbled into a time warp. She wonders: Where have you been in the last twenty-five years?

Clearly, you need a wife, as in Judy Syfers's classic article, "Why I Want a Wife." For those too young to recall the piece (first published in 1970 and reprinted in *Radical Feminism*), Syfers wrote that "I want a wife" who takes excellent care of the children, the home, the vacation, the clothes, the sex, the emotional needs, the pets and plants, plus: "I want a wife who will type my papers for me when I have written them . . . I want a wife who will have the house clean, will prepare a special meal, serve it to me and my friends, and not interrupt when I talk about the things that interest me and my friends . . ." and so on, and so on.

You cannot, unfortunately, get yourself any kind of "Wife" (women aren't permitted to, except in Hawaii: more's the pity). But sage readers will have noticed that you write: "I have three small children."

Who is the father of these children? Is it the husband, the pipe-and-slippers fellow who wants you to spend your evenings catering to his comfort instead of crafting your career? Who is this hostile being in your household, and what is his function?

But Ms. Mentor senses herself beginning a rant, and so she will struggle to give a calmer presentation of the issues as she, in her impeccable wisdom, sees them:

You have embarked on a difficult but potentially very rewarding career. As with most professions, being an academic means being a workaholic. Rare is the lawyer, doctor, clergyperson, politician, or full-time mentor who can confine her labors to forty hours per week. Ideally, a profession is a "calling": something you love to do.

Professionals are also people who've known early, and intuitively, what their callings are. As children, good doctors were curious about human anatomy (and liked to "play doctor" behind the garage). Most football stars were high school All-Americans by the end of tenth grade. Most professional singers were making money singing by the time they were ten years old; gymnasts are washed up by the time they're twenty. Most academics were children who loved to write, or dissect things, or build science equipment, or boss around and hector younger kids.

All of which is a long preamble to a central question: Do you have the drive to be an academic?

Many academic expectations have not changed since 1971, when Arlie Russell Hochschild published her famous essay on "Inside the Clockwork of Male Careers." The model for a committed academic career is still a man who may have a wife and kids, but the wife is THE WIFE. She is his support system, his nurturer, his housekeeper, his servant, his fender-off-of-all-distractions, and his sex slave.

Departments rarely expect "the wives" to pour tea at fall socials anymore, but the assumption is still that a faculty member's support system will be competent, smooth-running, and invisible.

Which brings Ms. Mentor, again, to the question of your missing spouse. In the absence of a wife to do it all, why isn't he doing at least his half-share? Why are the children and house "your" work? Why are you working *two* shifts?

Instead of support, you appear to have a veto system, in which your husband's need for evening attention sabotages your need to meet professional obligations.

What is to go?

Ms. Mentor would like everyone who wants to to be happily mated (she always roots for Elizabeth Taylor in her pursuit of the perfect husband). But Ms. Mentor also knows that in academia half the women professors are either single or childless, and rare is the tenured academic woman with two or more children.

You can be that woman, but only if hubby will pitch in. Maybe you can lure him into child care, at least, by promoting the notion of the modern, sensitive man, He Who Cares. (Some men, alas, still do need to have their egos manipulated.) Maybe for evening entertainment, he can let go of you and subscribe to cable TV. Millions of Americans do.

Or you may decide you would rather care for just the three children, instead of the four you now seem to have.

If you must choose, Ms. Mentor devoutly hopes you will keep the career. In these troubled times, that may very well last longer, bring you more satisfaction and challenge, and be far more pleasurable than butting against a wall of immovable sexism, an entrenched and seemingly tenured enemy within.

A Woman Who Writes Too Much

Q: My department chair told me I publish too much and write too much. Should I adopt a pseudonym, as Joyce Carol Oates does? Should I stifle my ideas until I get tenure? I would have thought that publishing a lot, and having a lot of ideas, and trying to write well, would be a plus.

A: Ms. Mentor thinks having ideas and writing well are marvelous and rare things. In fact, she withdrew to her ivory tower when she could no longer stand listening to droned academic papers at conferences. Not only did the presenters lack a sense of drama, but their prose lacked all life, or ideas. Cadences were predictable and word choices, inevitable. Clichés abounded (everything was "worthy of further study"). Science and social science presenters wallowed in the passive voice; literary critics attacked literature; historians hated the past. Few seemed to care passionately about what they were studying. Overall, academics seemed to get revved up only when they were denouncing each other.

Which leads Ms. Mentor to applaud your choice to write a lot, practicing your craft. That is the road to recognition and self-confidence. But it also attracts envy.

Without knowing your field, Ms. Mentor can nevertheless sketch out a likely scenario: You are in a humanities or social sciences department in a regional comprehensive university, such as Eastern Michigan, Western Washington, North Texas, or Southern Maine. All are examples of fine universities considered "second tier" by the elitists of Research I universities. They are also places that pride themselves on good teaching as well as a modicum of research and publication.

Further: your department at Regional U has been virtually "tenured in" (all professors with tenure) for the last five to ten years, or perhaps longer. Those with tenure were hired with the expectation of some publication, but a concentration on teaching. Most published a few articles before tenure, but many have not published at all since. More than a few disdain those who publish, considering them poor teachers and bad colleagues.

Unless the publishing scholars' work is absolutely mainstream—on Shakespeare, for instance, or presidential politics, or Civil War history—it will be attacked as "trash" or "high-flown" or "out of touch with the way we do things here. We pride ourselves on following fine old traditions."

In short, you do not fit the norms of the institution in which you've found yourself, and you have a choice. You can conform enough to get tenure, or you can resist.

Ms. Mentor's advice is to conform. Save some of your ideas for later, or give them only in conference papers. Write the articles you want to, but don't brag about them: by publishing a lot, you are embarrassing those already in your department. You can mollify them in the usual ways (lunch, coffee, buttering up), while you work on writing a book. Regional U may not love it, but others might.

Once tenured, though, you may decide you like being a big fish in a small pool at Regional U. You'll get good raises; you can meet like-minded colleagues at conferences and on the Net; and you needn't publish except when you really want to. You may also genuinely like your colleagues for being unpretentious appreciators of good teaching.

That can be a special kind of academic freedom.

Should I Tell Her?
To Let Her Go on Trusting Is Unfair

Q: My boss is a lively, enthusiastic young woman, thirtyish, only a few years out of graduate school, with a Ph.D. in biology. She's in her second year as an assistant professor, and she does cancer research.

I'm her research associate, about fifteen years older than she is, and I know my way around academia far better than she does. Mainly, I know she's putting her energies into the wrong things. She's setting up a wonderful cancer screening program that will be great for public health, but it won't lead to publications. Ours is a research university, and I know that "service" (what she's doing) and teaching don't count much toward tenure. Research and publication are the only things that get everyone's attention, and so far she doesn't have anything in print.

How can I tell her she has to scrap what she loves, do what she likes much less (she doesn't like to write), or she'll lose her job? It's not just that I'd lose my job, too—I'm hired on her current grant—but academia would lose yet another woman who couldn't say no.

How do I, as her underling, tell my boss what she should do?

A: Not easily. Ms. Mentor knows well how hard it is to goose people into taking the advice they need the most. Especially one's boss.

Yet you do know things that Dr. Boss needs to know, and you can't convey them with vague notes or hints. You might try nudging—not nagging—her a bit about publishing the research on which your name appears: "Do you know when it'll be in print? I'm looking forward to seeing it."

In academia, a very hierarchical universe, you're a satellite who can't mentor your boss, but you may be able to find someone else who can. (Yes, this is convoluted, but you're trying to save the career, and the psyche, of a young woman who's both pleasant and deserving. Academia needs her.)

Ms. Mentor advises you to seek out a favorably inclined full professor. If there's someone congenial who's working on the same project, that would be excellent. If yours is a cutthroat department, you may have to go to an approachable dean, or to the director of Women's Studies. Find someone who wants women to succeed.

Tell the Chosen Mentor that you're concerned about Dr. Boss: you want her to do well and stay at Our University and continue on the project, but you're not sure that Dr. Boss understands how important quick publication is. "Do you think you could speak to her about it?"

Unless the Chosen Mentor really hates Dr. Boss (or you), s/he will take on the mentoring—maybe taking Dr. Boss to lunch and telling her what's needed. Meanwhile, the Chosen Mentor will also be very flattered by your request. (Everyone loves to be asked for advice. It's so rare.)

Finally, Ms. Mentor compliments you on your wisdom. Only the wisest know when mentoring is needed.

Skirting the Issue

Q: I have this friend who has this problem. She's a young assistant professor in my department, and her skirts are much too short. She's very cute, has good legs, and looks "fine," as some of the students say, but the boys aren't really listening to her. They're looking up her dress, or trying to. (When she notices them, she squirms and tugs at her hem.)

I'd considered this just fashion and being oneself. But today my department head told me I should get Jennifer to stop wearing micro-miniskirts. "It's—ah—not ladylike," he said.

"Shouldn't you be speaking with her about it?" I asked, inwardly seething. "You're her boss, not I." (I should mention that I'm a few years older than Jennifer, but also untenured.)

"It's something a lady should tell another lady," he said, flushing a bit. "Surely you understand."

Well, I don't, really. If Jennifer needed a tampon, I'd be the one to deliver it, but it seems to me that any messages about professionalism can be delivered by anyone. I resent my chairman, and Jennifer has the right to wear whatever she wants to. I'm tempted not to say anything at all. I don't want to collaborate in his repression of our department's one free spirit.

Surely you agree with me, Ms. Mentor?

A: Ms. Mentor does not agree, and she also questions your motives in keeping silent. Women friends do often shield each other from criticism and shy away from conflict. But if you do not speak up, you may be responsible for destroying Jennifer's career.

For the students, whether they listen to Jennifer or not, do not vote on her tenure. (And if they're preoccupied with her legs, what is she teaching them?) Her colleagues do decide on her tenure, and rare are the academics who think fashion more important than professionalism. Women will resent her for seeming to trivialize her work. Men will think she's a cute little girl and assume she hasn't a brain.

Tactfully or not, you must be the bearer of bad tidings now—not later, after a tenure denial. Break it to Jennifer any way you want, but tell her she must go dowdy, by her standards.

And if you don't want to take the responsibility yourself, feel free to blame Ms. Mentor. She never shows her legs at all.

Odd Old Fellows

Q: I'm untenured, in a liberal arts department, and a group of older men (I'm thirty-four; they're in their late fifties) has been meeting for some years to discuss such topics as death, injustice, guilt, and envy. They've invited me to their group several times, and I've found it totally boring. They don't have a clue about real life at all, but as a woman two decades their junior, what can I possibly contribute? Should I just call them all dumb old codgers, slam the door, and go home and watch MTV?

A: Ms. Mentor thinks not, and proposes instead two other strategies. (1) Attend the group, observing it as a social anthropologist, and perhaps intervening now and then with an issue that *does* interest you, or (2) thank them kindly for inviting you but say (with an apologetic smile) that you need to spend more time on your research, to be sure you'll get tenure.

Ms. Mentor recommends (2) as the better move, for it's more apt to retain their good will. She also reminds you that someday you will be fifty yourself—and then you'll know just how annoying the "I'm young and I know best" routine can be.

Stop it. Now.

Devoted to the Dean

Q: As an undergraduate, I had a tempestuous affair with a married man. Now divorced, he's become the dean who'll pass on my tenure. Ours was a very passionate relationship, and I still can't see him without imagining him thrashing nakedly in my bed. Does Ms. Mentor have any suggestions for appropriate deportment? What can I do with my foolish heart?

A: Ms. Mentor was at first tempted into a diatribe about sexual harassment. How *could* the dean take advantage of a vulnerable young woman? Why did your college allow such conduct? He should be tarred, feathered, and—and—well, at least fired.

But all that is in the past, and Ms. Mentor's wrath availeth not. She does hope, however, that you will work to ensure that strong anti-sexual harassment policies exist at your university. And not only actual harassment, such as stalking, "lay for an A," and the like, but also fraternization. Faculty should not be dating (or mating with) students.

That said, Ms. Mentor turns herself to the more intriguing question: How does one discipline one's imagination? Indeed, she wonders if you *can* keep your mind on budgets, faculty lines, student credit hours, and other subjects characteristic of deanly presentations when you know the man so intimately. Even Ms. Mentor, who prides herself on her *sang-froid*, might be tempted to pant.

But the younger generation is, of course, always "cooler" than its elders, and Ms. Mentor presumes that you do not want to be out of step with your peers who have successfully (they claim) separated the personal and the professional for several decades.

You do not say whether the dean, now divorced, has indicated any desire to resume the relationship. Ms. Mentor fervently hopes not. She suggests, nevertheless, that you do what any exes do: see one another only in public, and discuss only professional matters. Avoid being alone with him, even in a corner at a cocktail party, and do not yield to low-voiced conversations along the lines of "Don't you remember . . . ?" and "Whenever I see you, I think about . . ."

You were a teenager or barely out of your teens; he took advantage of you; and now it's over. He may be your dean now, but he will always be a cad in Ms. Mentor's book (the only book that matters).

You do not say whether he has been replaced in your heart: Ms. Mentor hopes so. Tenure is far more important than temptation, and she hopes you will engrave that on your heart.

Never diddle a dean.

Fools Vie for High Office

Q: Why do bozos get tenure?

A: That question has troubled many a brilliant feminist mind over the last half-century, and even Ms. Mentor will not presume to have the definitive answer.

She will observe, however, that virtually all such bozos are white and male and have learned to play the academic game.

There may be a pattern there.

Turn-Down Day

Q: I've been turned down for tenure at my research university, even though my record of publication is the same as that of the last person (a man) who got tenure in my department. My teaching evaluations are better than his, and I've done more service (committee work). Should I file a university grievance, or go straight to a lawsuit?

A: Ms. Mentor advises you to do neither, at first. Be quiet and dignified, prudent and canny, and do background research.

How much better is your overall record than Mr. Last Tenured? Would every observer say that yours is better, or is there wiggle room? Can it be claimed (by his friends, and your foes) that he taught harder courses, or served on more important committees? Or that his publications were in better journals, or had more impact on the field?

Ms. Mentor is describing the unfortunate situation where it might look like a matter of professional judgment. If Mr. Last Tenured's supporters can claim that his work is of higher quality than yours, you will probably lose.

(It should be no surprise—though it is galling—that academic men are often rated more highly than women, and paid better, for the same work. Ms. Mentor calls this "the penile increment.")

Did anyone screw up? Your chances for winning a grievance or lawsuit will be much better if there were egregious violations of written procedures. Did someone fail to give you documents you were supposed to get, such as annual evaluations? If you got them, were they late, or incomplete? Were you given only a few days, and no instructions, for assembling your tenure dossier? If you were supposed to get a written warning (according to university policies) about what you needed to get tenure, did you get that warning? Were confidential papers kept confidential?

Also: Were your outside referees (recommenders from other universities) picked according to university policies or randomly? Did your recommenders disagree about your merits? Were any papers somehow lost or misfiled? Was your record inaccurately described in documents? Were there split votes along the way in the university process?

Some universities allow for an "administrative appeal" to discover all this. Check your Faculty Handbook. Have a friend read it with you, and discuss what it seems to mean.

Further: Is there evidence that anyone in the chain of tenure decisions was obviously biased against you? Were negative and biased statements made against you during your career at this university? Were there sexist remarks, and perhaps racist ones as well? If you have a disability, were you insulted or mistreated because of it? Were reasonable accommodations made for your disability?

Are all these things documented in writing?

On a different plane: Are there tenured women in your department? If not, why not? Is there a pattern of discrimination?

Here's where you haul out your carefully kept Tenure Diary. In it, write down all the procedural violations you've found: every policy violated; every bias shown.

Should you file a grievance (the internal university procedure to re-examine a decision)? If your list of violations is short, and it can look like you were turned down because the people judging you thought you lacked merit, your case is not strong.

But whether you can win a grievance often depends on who's on the grievance committee, and on the university's climate toward women. Is the grievance committee elected by the faculty, or appointed by the ad-ministration (in which case it's hopeless)? Is there a tenured senior woman on the grievance committee, or anywhere, who can give you an honest assessment?

Finding a lawyer can be hard. Most courts will expect you to "exhaust internal remedies" (grievance procedures) before suing. Few attorneys have much expertise in academic processes and peculiar byways; most know that such cases are time-consuming and difficult to win. Often lawyers in small states and towns are reluctant to sue the university whose law school they attended, but sometimes those lawyers can get fired up to sue a differ-ent university. (One attorney in New Orleans specializes in suing Tulane University.)

Groups you can ask for advice include: The Task Force on Academic Dis-crimination of the National Women's Studies Association (1056 Larchlea, Birmington, MI 48009); the National Organization for Women (NOW); the American Association of University Women; the American Association of University Professors; your own faculty union; discussion groups on the Internet (addresses are available in public libraries, or on the Net). If you need to raise money, try every women's group you know—including alum-nae associations, sororities, churches and synagogues and sisterhoods of all kinds. You may need to beg cash from your female relatives (and their husbands).

Read, read, read. Ms. Mentor especially recommends George LaNoue and Barbara Lee's book, *Academics in Court* (1987), and Shirley Nelson Garner, Vèvè Clark, Ketu H. Katrak, and Margaret Higonnet, eds., *Anti-feminism in the Academy* (1996). About grievances versus lawsuits, the

February 1996 issue of *Women's Review of Books* (13:5) has valuable material, as does every issue of *Academe* (journal of the American Association of University Professors).

Virtually every woman who sues has to do her own legwork, on her own time, with her own money.

A legal battle is long and expensive: $100,000 is often the minimum to start. It may take a decade to resolve, and you may not win: women win only 20 percent of academic discrimination lawsuits, although there are also out-of-court settlements. Plaintiffs often sacrifice marriages, friends, health, and self-esteem. Having to tell and retell a painful story of hopes dashed and dreams denied—and then hearing, over and over, that you are mediocre—can be devastating.

Unless you have a very smart, knowledgeable, and committed lawyer and an outstanding case, Ms. Mentor says bluntly that it is often not worth your while to sue, even though the thought of letting an injustice pass makes you feel like your heart is on fire. Ms. Mentor knows, too, that some of her righteous readers are now itching, squirming, and fuming. They're about to call her a Mindless Dupe of the System. They're about to tell you that if you don't fight back, you'll be allowing evil to flourish in the universe.

But Ms. Mentor's counsel, which comes much more cheaply than legal advice, is to make the best use of your life. Most people, even women attracted to the idea of throwing everything into a fight for justice and revenge, do not really want to be martyrs. If you want an academic career at another university, filing a lawsuit (or even a grievance) may work against you. Other universities, making their routine background calls, will hear that you're a "troublemaker."

If you want to continue your career, first try to get another job. (Network; self-promote; offer to write reviews; make yourself known everywhere; flatter powerful people.) If you cannot get another post, you can try filing a grievance in hopes of getting your original job back. But be aware of timetables: Is there a deadline for filing a grievance or a suit?

All depends, really, on the future you envision for yourself. When Professor Anne Margolis was denied tenure at Williams College, for instance, she went to law school, and was a practicing attorney by the time her case was concluded. The same was true for Shyamala Rajender, who won a sweeping sex discrimination victory against the University of Minnesota.

That took seven years. Janet Lever's unsuccessful suit against Northwestern University took twelve years, and current legal actions take even longer: Cynthia Fisher began her suit against Vassar College, for discrimination against married women, in 1985. As of mid-1996, it was still in the courts.

A lawsuit is rarely a good way to spend one's prime.

Only you can decide whether to put your time and energies into a suit, or into a new life, in which you can teach and mentor other women and protect them from what happened to you. You may not get revenge against your original university, but you must think in larger, more global terms. Only women who have tenure can make real changes in any university. There will always be evils to correct. Ms. Mentor feels sure of that.

And even a tenure denial is sometimes the gateway to a new life. Many a recovering academic has discovered a talent for fund-raising, humanities councils, speechwriting, journalism, advertising, polling, translating, public relations, or activism. Some write computer manuals or novels, ghost-write the autobiographies of country singers, create designer drugs, work in literacy programs, or start think tanks and institutes promoting nutrition, women candidates, or environmental causes. Some recovering academics, for better or worse, turn to politics (the dreaded Newt Gingrich was once denied tenure). A few liberal arts Ph.D.s have gone on to great success in law and medical schools.

Still, Ms. Mentor grieves when any woman is denied tenure: the world of possibilities for women is diminished, downsized. But in your one life to live, you do not have to live it as an academic. You do, though, have to be a supporter of women.

Ms. Mentor insists on that.

Tenure Denied

Q: How, in a job application, does one finesse a tenure denial? I don't want other schools to think I'm at fault just because the Neanderthal clowns in my department haven't appreciated me or any other assertive women. They call me "The Bitch of R University," in fact.

Do I say anything about that in my application letter?

A: Ms. Mentor often receives letters from women who are considered bitches, and she feels a particular kinship with them.

As all but the most benighted know, there is a double standard for energetic professional behavior: A woman should be assertive, not aggressive; a man may be aggressive. A man may be forthright and hard-driving; a woman who is the same is—A Bitch.

(One of the stranger flowers of the early 1970s rebirth of the women's movement was a book called *I, B.I.T.C.H.*, by one "Caroline Hennessey," possibly a pseudonym for a man, in which "Caroline" described the ways she tormented men. In the same era, "Joreen" (Jo Freeman) published in radical circles "The Bitch Manifesto," in which she called for women's being aggressive, forthright, hard-driving, and honestly critical—i.e., Bitchy.)

You, though, are probably too young to know your own lineage. So much of women's intellectual genealogy is buried by the other sex, most of whom would hate to be called what some of them are: Sons of Bitches.

But enough bitching.

You presumably have already been denied tenure, or you think the ax is about to fall, and you are preparing your escape. What you need, then, is some way to prevent future employers from thinking that your firing—your de-tenuring—was your fault. And yet you cannot also cast aspersions, however honest or soul-cleansing they may be, upon your former colleagues. If you do, you will appear to be a difficult colleague (i.e., a Bitch).

And so you need to orchestrate what future employers may hear about you. You will begin with your application letter and dossier, the contents of which you will know thoroughly. Have your confidental placement service dossier sent to a friend, who'll either send it to you or pick through it for negative references or insinuations and advise you to omit the bad or weird reference from Professor P.

Your dossier should be fine: it should consist of letters from hand-picked sources, people you know from conferences and perhaps an ally from your current school. Then you have to anticipate what background calls or e-mail or other inquiries might be made. You cannot know entirely who knows whom in academia, but if you have a nemesis, you can either subtly undermine him or praise him to the skies, whereupon any negative comments he makes will seem either outlandish or churlish.

Mostly, though, you must focus on the positive: what you've published, your teaching record, your professional service. You needn't mention the tenure denial at all—but if asked, say there were university politics or quotas involved, or a shift in the courses students were seeking, or a loss of funds . . . In short, soften the situation to make yourself a bravely smiling survivor, not a Bitch.

But if another job doesn't materialize, there's always an alternative career, a field that's also overcrowded but one that's historically been very congenial to Bitches:

Go to law school.

Post-Tenure

Hilda was five, sturdy and short-legged, when she hopped off to school for her first day in the first grade.

Hilda was forty, chubby and graying, when she finally stopped going to school.

Hilda had, of course, done other things with her life. After college she'd raised three children and worked at odd jobs to put her husband through medical school. She'd taken some graduate courses, but dropped out to follow her husband who, after his internship and residency, decided to relocate in another part of the country, where Hilda knew no one.

She'd made friends, and finally rooted herself in the community, and when Rob left her, she decided to go back to school "for myself."

She got her Ph.D. at forty, was one of the rare birds to get a tenure-track position right after graduate school—and at age forty-seven, Hilda is now tenured at a very good university in the South.

What will she do with the rest of her life?

The years of preparation, and the endless trek to tenure, create great expectations in those who survive that very long march. Now, at last, they will . . . what?

Few in fact can tell Ms. Mentor, or anyone else, what they expect to happen once they do achieve the holy grail of tenure.

Sometimes they're so tired they can hardly speak.

Sometimes they expect the heavens to open up, somehow—although if they did, the lucky tenurees might see nothing more than what the hapless Felicity sees at the end of Gustave Flaubert's story "A Simple Heart": a huge green parrot.

Or even a toad.

For tenure can be, and is, the reward for decades of hard work and discovery. It can also reward diligence and mindless toadying. And, like all commencements, it is also the end of a road, which can mean a kind of post-partum depression.

Which is where Ms. Mentor steps in.

Breaking Up Is Hard to Do

Q: I've just gotten tenure, and I've heard that means I have lifetime job security unless I get caught running naked on campus, selling drugs to students. Is tenure ever broken for any other reason?

A: Ms. Mentor knows the story you refer to: that somewhere, sometime, a tenured professor was seen dashing and flapping about campus, thoroughly naked, selling hallucinogens to students at cut-rate prices. A Japanese tourist with a camera happened to capture his folly on film, as an example of curious American academic rituals, and that made the acid prof's caper impossible to deny. He was stripped of his tenure, and fired.

Ms. Mentor suspects all that is an urban legend. But she knows that tenure can indeed be broken with less sensational scenarios. For reneging on tenure, most universities either have no written policies, or very vague ones citing "moral turpitude" or "dismissal for cause" or "insubordination" (that may appear more in the handbooks of church-related schools).

It is true that tenured faculty cannot be dismissed because of administrators' whims. No chancellor or university president, however autocratic, has the power to do what Richard Snyder, former CEO of Simon & Schuster Publishing Company, used to do: fire people in the elevator if he didn't like their looks. (Eventually, of course, Snyder himself was canned.)

The breaking of tenure in academia, however, is shrouded in mystery and legal fogs. Sometimes groups of tenured faculty lose jobs because of financial exigency (if a department or unit is closed, for instance). Otherwise, Ms. Mentor, who has spies everywhere, does know of some individual professors whose tenure was taken away. To wit:

- A political scientist who used to take students to see a waterfall and talk over their "classwork." Eventually one student told her father, a state legislator, about her professor's unusual "teaching methods"—which included encouraging the student to take off her clothes and "free her psyche" by running through the waterfall. The professor was fired for sexual harassment.
- A philosophy professor who had a habit of opening his colleagues' mail in the department mailroom. He was caught doing so on video camera. Not only did he throw out mail he found uninteresting, but he sometimes changed addresses and forwarded mail to new and different recipients. He lost his tenure, but is reportedly now teaching in Australia.
- A math professor who held two full-time faculty jobs, in Minnesota and North Carolina. He seemed to be teaching quite well in both colleges, but when his colleagues found out, they fired him.
- An agriculture professor who persisted in racist slurs during his lectures, even when a university administrator audited his class. (The professor hated "all gooks and Chinks," but reserved particular scorn for Koreans as "the niggers of Asia.") He was fired after a year-long investigation.
- An English professor whose daughter became ill with meningitis. The professor was so distraught that he stopped going to the university. He was offered a medical leave, but refused to take it.
- Commuters who overdid it: faculty who contrived to get one- or two-day-a-week teaching schedules, then lived far away and were rarely available for anything but class times. Their colleagues were forced to pick up the commuters' share of committee work, student advising, and the like, and eventually rebelled. Sometimes the commuters were not actually stripped of tenure, but strongly induced (or threatened enough) to take early retirement. Their commuting gigs included Columbus to Bowling Green; New York to Virginia; Duluth to Baton Rouge; and Baltimore to central Pennsylvania. Ms. Mentor once knew a man, an expert in rubber tubing, who used to commute between Hong Kong and Budapest, but she does not know what finally became of him.
- A biology professor who was an alcoholic. He took medical leave sev-

eral times and was in rehab, but could not stop drinking. After he fell down several times in class, he was let go.

- An education professor who taught photography and fondled students in the darkroom. He was fired for sexual harassment.

All of these were cases of "dismissal for cause." Some involved long legal maneuvers; others, such as the case of the state legislator's daughter, were settled overnight. But none of these cases really involves "academic freedom," which tenure was designed to protect. Most, in fact, are abuses of power and authority.

And so Ms. Mentor feels fairly safe in saying that tenure is lifetime job security.

But.

She knows that tenure is under review—even under assault—in some right-wing quarters. As she was completing this book (in mid-1996), word came that, in North Dakota, lifetime tenure might be abolished in state universities. Instead there would be periodic faculty reviews, and faculty doing badly in several annual reviews might be dismissed. And no one in North Dakota seemed to be making the fuss Ms. Mentor thinks ought to be made over such a change.

Not that Ms. Mentor defends incompetence, or teaching from yellowed notes, or laziness, or all the other sins that tenure supposedly protects. She believes that teachers should be seriously evaluated every year, and if their evaluations are awful, they should be prodded (with no raises, for instance) to work seriously on their pedagogical skills.

But Ms. Mentor wants tenure to survive, for it allows faculty to teach about, for instance, Communism (some could not in the 1950s). Academic freedom means the right to tell students all about such perennially controversial ideas as socialism, state-funded day care, or women's control of abortion rights. She wants students to know about atheism, sexual harassment, and gay and lesbian lives.

Tenure also encourages professors to do long-term research that doesn't have immediate payoffs or results: cures for cancer; monumental biographies; dictionaries of Hittite and Tokarian; longitudinal psychological studies following girls from adolescence through menopause. Such projects sometimes show up as "Nothing" in annual publication lists, but their eventual contribution can change the world.

Tenured professors should also be organizing for faculty rights: joining and creating unions; making the Faculty Senate really powerful, and obnoxious when it needs to be. Tenure cannot be broken when people use their power in the right directions.

The directions designated by Ms. Mentor, of course.

Taking Nothing for Granted

Q: I happened to be on a grant panel of full professors, giving money to worthy research projects. One of the applicants was a young, untenured woman I don't know at all, whose project sounded interesting and valuable.

But in her packet of "supporting letters" from confidential referees was a hostile, negative letter from her department chair. I'm sure she didn't know he would write that kind of confidential letter, and I think it was wrong of him to do so. (If he didn't want to write a positive letter, he should have declined to write at all. That's what I do, rather than sabotage an applicant behind her back.)

And so I photocopied the letter and sent it to her, anonymously, mailing it from a city I passed through on my way back home. She'll never know I did it. Was I wrong?

A: No. Ms. Mentor thinks you should be quite proud of yourself, for having risen to the pinnacle of academia while retaining a subversive, antiauthoritarian streak and a strong ethical sense. And a loyalty to women.

Ms. Mentor salutes you.

Taking a Chance on Love

Q: Now that I have tenure and don't ever have to write boring critical theory "discourse" anymore, I'd like to churn out a trashy romance novel and make lots of money.

How long will it take?

A: A very long time, if ever, says Ms. Mentor.

Doing "discourse" is much, much easier than writing romances, says Emily Toth, that rare author who has written and published both. (See Emily Toth's *Daughters of New Orleans* [1983].)

Few people, and even fewer academics, have the sensibility or the talent to write a romance that will sell. Scholars are wordy; novelists must be pithy. Scholars write abstract generalities; novelists have to *show* emotions, through dialogue, rather than just *tell*. To write a successful novel, you need to be able to do what Charles Dickens used to talk about: Make 'em laugh, make 'em cry, make 'em *wait*.

Further, academics have been trained to be elitist: if the masses like something, it must be no good. Scholars too often hold negative, stereotypical ideas ("trashy") that have nothing to do with what today's romances actually say. The big sellers now are about strong, feisty women and written by authors who are outright, committed feminists. (Alice Walker's *The Color Purple*, for instance, fits all the definitions for current popular romances.)

And now Ms. Mentor asks you: Are you a romance reader? Many academics think they know the field without reading any of the books, but they would never make such assumptions about "literature." Susan Larson, book editor of the *New Orleans Times-Picayune* and coauthor of ten contemporary romances, adds that you should not attempt to write a romance until you've read and analyzed at least a hundred current ones. If sex scenes make you fidget, for instance, romances are not for you.

Ms. Mentor also bristles when she hears romances disparaged, for that disparages women. Along with soap operas and country music, romances are the stories that feature women, women's emotions, and women's problems: unlike stories of crime or sports or war, romances put women at the center. Ms. Mentor feels that the general public, and academics, need to honor romance writers as polished, hardworking professionals who use their talents for an ancient and noble purpose: to tell stories that entertain, instruct, and celebrate women.

If you want to pursue, seriously, the possibility of writing romances, Ms. Mentor directs you to the Romance Writers of America (13700 Veterans Memorial, Suite 315, Houston, TX 77014; phone 713-440-6885; fax 713-440-7510; hotline 713-440-8081). They can refer you to your nearest RWA chapter, which will include monthly programs, information and newsletters, and critique groups. Unique among professionals, published romance writers regularly mentor would-be writers and teach them the skills, in effect training their own competition. But they do this out of a desire to improve the quality of the genre, and out of sisterhood.

Ms. Mentor also advises you to read *Dangerous Men and Adventurous Women: Romance Writers on the Appeal of the Romance*, edited by Jayne

Ann Krentz, one of the most popular and prolific of current romance writers. In the collection (put out by Ms. Mentor's very own publisher, the University of Pennsylvania Press), some two dozen romance authors talk about how they write and what they mean, including such subjects as virginity, the role of the hero, and "romance and the empowerment of women."

If you've never heard of Jayne Ann Krentz, Ms. Mentor suggests you hie yourself back to your library, your study, or your office, and resign yourself to doing what all authors do best. Write about what you know.

Unknown and Unmentored

Q: I need your advice, for I've made some career errors as I have danced through the minefields for the past decade. I'll soon be applying for development leaves, grants, and promotion to full professor. All these require recommendation letters from colleagues outside my university, and I don't have anyone to ask. What do I do now?

When I was a junior faculty member, there were plenty of people to ask: former professors, colleagues who'd moved on to other institutions, people I'd met at conferences, and so on. But now it seems ludicrous to ask former professors and unseemly to ask former students for letters of assessment. I am very active in research and teaching, and am involved with professional organizations in my specialization, but most of the people I know and trust are at or below my rank, and at this point my outside letters need to be from full professors.

I am geographically isolated due to the location of my university; I am intellectually isolated within my department because I am the only person in my specialization; and I am also isolated within my community because of my concern for women's issues. I might also note that I have never had a mentor.

Do you have any suggestions as to what I can do at this point? How might other women avoid such a situation?

A: Ms. Mentor, despite her quick wit and ability to pierce to the heart of all problems, was at first flummoxed by your query: What are you asking?

You seem to have plotted your career narrative impeccably. You are tenured; you are a conference-goer; you have colleagues and friends and cronies. You seem unhobbled by PTS (Post-Tenure Slowdown), a common ailment in which the tenuree is blue, burned out, or suddenly overwhelmed with real-life adult woes (prolapses, pregnancies, crab grass, crab lice, mange and musk, pills and piles—plus children, elders, death, taxes, and right-wing loonies). You say that you are isolated from others sharing your interests, but, as Ms. Mentor has often noted, virtually all feminists believe that wherever they live is politically and intellectually backward.

And so Ms. Mentor strode around her ivory tower, plaguing herself with the question: What is awry with this daguerreotype?

Finally she spotted the underlying, perhaps unconscious, motive in your missive. You want Ms. Mentor's permission to curry favor with powerful people, so as to get recommendations for promotion, grants, and the like. Or, as less tactful people might put it: You Want an OK to Suck Up to Big Cheeses.

Ms. Mentor hereby grants permission, and now she will explain.

Verily, Ms. Mentor declares, too little is said about post-tenure in the academy. Rare is the sage counsel for those who've more or less Made It—past tenure—and now ask, "How do I scale the heights of full professorhood?" (Or "How do I kick my way through the glass ceiling of perpetual associate professorship?")

You need a campaign to make yourself better known among the powerful. Luckily, you do not need buttons or funny hats, and you can use the research skills you already possess to make two bibliographies. The first will list those already among your admirers: readers who have complimented your writings; conference-goers who have praised your papers; on-line pen pals; positive book reviewers. Your second list will be those who might help now. With them, the campaign kicks off.

Through e-mail, you may seek out your powerful targets for a chat, although many influential senior professors remain electronic Luddites. ("I don't want to be reached easily," says one famous anthropologist.) Most Great Ones do eventually appear in the flesh at conferences, however, where they can be accosted and complimented on their work.

You are reminded that even when flattery is transparent, the effort is flattering.

And so, you should have business cards to exchange at conferences, where you must strive for Visibility. (And if you have to pay your own way to conferences, well, it's a career investment.) You should appear on the general, lofty, wide-ranging panels on "The Profession" or "The Future of . . ." or "New Directions in . . . ," rather than narrow readings of a single text. You should be the first to volunteer to be section chair, for often no one volunteers at all.

You should lurk at cash bars and book exhibits and seek opportunities to compliment Big Names on their work—and exchange cards. You can set up conference goals: to distribute twenty cards, for instance. But you will, of course, be charming and try not to be obvious. Ms. Mentor considers "Are you anybody, and should I be sucking up to you?" an inappropriate conversational gambit.

Other strategies might be part of your campaign. You may create your own conference, with university and state humanities funds, and invite Big Names as speakers. Few things make hearts flutter more than invitations and checks, and few settings are more impressive than free dinners. Afterward, only churls will decline to write nice notes on their hostess's behalf.

In essence, Ms. Mentor advises you to improve your S.Q.—your Schmooze Quotient. Schmoozing means not just networking or gossiping or being mentored, but the whole gamut of conversational relationships: information, jokes, small talk, preliminary identification of hopeless boors, and character assassination. Schmoozing will net you friends and allies to make you feel less isolated. Your schmoozees may also turn out to be the powerful people you need to know.

Finally, you ask, "How might other women avoid such a situation?" Ms. Mentor answers bluntly: Reach those who matter, and cultivate friends in high places (which means all manner of intellectual aeries, not just Research I institutions). But, of course, Ms. Mentor now hears rumblings and murmurings about "sellout" and "hypocrite" and "two-faced" and "careerist." She hears readers hissing, "How uncouth."

But one cannot be sufficiently appreciated in academia unless one is well known: if not well liked, at least feared. Women are, of course, often ambivalent about power, but if the opposite of power is powerlessness . . .

Ms. Mentor recalls her own days as a young duchess, new to academia, at a time when some feminists were claiming that it was "wrong" to "pull strings" to get friends and students hired. "If they're good enough, they'll get jobs" was often the optimistic mantra. But Ms. Mentor learned, they all learned, that the men then in charge of academia rarely acted in accordance with motives of fairness and the pursuit of meritocracy.

Rather, they hired their friends, or students of friends, or guys they happened to meet when they were with their friends.

They needed to be shown who the best women were.

You, wisely, are beyond thinking that merit will inevitably be rewarded. You know that you cannot sit back, like a good girl, and just be a fine tenured associate professor. You need to do for yourself, and let the world know who you are.

And so Ms. Mentor encourages you to pursue your full professorship, your fellowships, and the other—sadly, too few—goodies that academia makes available.

May the best woman win, and may she be you.

Glass Ceiling

Q: I seem to be stuck as Associate Professor. I watch as male colleagues without my teaching experience or publication record sail by to being Fulls—yet I'm not even put up for consideration. What should I do? Should I sue?

A: Ms. Mentor congratulates you on seeing clearly what's what: you are indeed stuck in the middle, with security but without honor. A glass-ceilinged woman often has a job title like yours: associate manager, assistant to the chairman of—, associate director of—. In short, you're in the women's "A-ghetto," where all the titles begin with *A*, and all the salaries and perks and powers are much less than they should be.

What to do?

Sometimes the solution is incredibly simple, as Judith Martin ("Miss Manners") discovered with the *Washington Post*. She was the lowest paid member of her department when she went to complain to her boss, who said (Ms. Mentor is paraphrasing): "It's about time you asked for a raise. Everyone else asked, and got one, a long time ago."

Which also reminds Ms. Mentor of "Dee," an English associate professor whose salary lagged way behind the men's. Dee finally decided to confront her chair, railing at him about all she'd accomplished and how it wasn't reflected at all in her "pitiful" wages and her lack of promotion to full professor.

To which he said: "Why didn't you tell me you'd done all that?"

Your first step, then, is to talk with your chair (or whoever else determines your salary). Bring along an up-to-date list of publications and other accomplishments (awards, honors); your teaching evaluation scores (if they're good); and notes about your committee service. (Of course, only research and publication truly *count*, but tributes to teaching and "service" are part of professional manners.)

For, as Dee found out, the rules are the same as at a high school dance: the big boys have to notice you before they can ask you to twirl around the floor with them. Being a good girl, holding back and expecting to be noticed, is a sure way to be a wallflower.

Academic women must self-promote. Anytime you publish a book, you must give copies to your chair, your dean, your Women's Studies Director, and anyone else in a position to reward you. (And no whining about costs: you don't want to look cheap.) Notify the faculty and staff newspaper, the campus newspaper, the college news bureau, the town newspaper, your alumni bulletins, and anyone else who'll trumpet your achievements. Likewise with awards and honors, and any publications and presentations that are not routine—that are in foreign journals, for instance, or make breakthroughs, or garner you trips to Sweden to collect your second Nobel prize.

You must make an irresistible case. After all, the whole town's talking about your accomplishments; your fans follow you down the streets, begging for autographs; students cry and scream and beg to get into your classes; you have to get an unlisted e-mail address because of all the adulation . . . Or whatever.

You may not always win easily: your chair may still be reluctant to put you up for promotion. A decade ago, one chair said of two brilliant and accomplished young women at his large research university: "We won't promote them this year—these girls need more seasoning." Even now, there are chairs who'll say, "Your children need you at home" or even, "Why do you want to be a full professor? You'll never find a husband that way."

And so you also need allies. Among the full professors, there should be some who'll speak with the chair, or write memos asking for you to be considered. Your dean may help, and if you've taught in another program (Women's Studies, African American Studies, American Studies), the head of that program can write a supporting memo.

If all that fails—if the chair simply won't put you up for full professor— then you can consult the faculty grievance committee, and also the Affirmative Action/Equal Employment Opportunity office at your university. You may also want to contact the National Women's Studies Association's

Task Force on Academic Job Discrimination (1056 Larchlea, Birming-ham, MI 48009).

All the while, though, you'll be keeping precise records. After each meeting, send a memo thanking whoever you met and describing what was said, in as neutral language as possible. Continue to keep your Post-Tenure Diary up to date, at home.

Should you sue? Ms. Mentor hopes you will not have to. Suits drag on for years, and women often do not win. Universities have lawyers on staff, and they have deep pockets.

The other alternative, which sometimes works niftily, is to get yourself a job offer from another university. That's the quickest way to get a raise, and sometimes it's the goosing that your original place needs to initiate a pro-motion. Possibly the other offer, which should include a full professorship with tenure and a big raise, will prove so enticing that you'll decide to decamp entirely, leaving your original department with egg on its face, the probable loss of a faculty line, and a lot of explaining to do.

You, though, will be walking away a winner.

Sabbatical Sorrows

Q: I am almost at the end of my sabbatical (my first one), and almost at the end of my rope. I've logged more hours with my TV than with my com-puter. And though it's hardly my field (I'm an art historian), I've become an expert on the birds outside my kitchen window. I've also found myself crying a lot. Meanwhile, I haven't worked on the project I said I'd work on during this time—at all. When I first listed all the things I'd have to read (it was on Mycenean art), I felt overwhelmed, and just started crying again.

What's happening to me? Is my life as an academic over?

A: Not at all. Wise Ms. Mentor knows exactly what you are feeling. You no doubt began your sabbatical with the vision of most new sabbaticaleers. To wit: you'd awaken refreshed each day, full of ideas, and sit at your computer or in your study, where you'd expand your horizons, take notes, draft chapters, and rediscover the intellectual thrills that first enticed you to become an academic.

As you imagined it, you'd be reinvigorated. You'd find again the plea-sures of the mind that had been plowed under during your years devoted to paper grading, committee work, and bureaucratic trivia. Each morning you would take a deep breath—after, perhaps, running a mile or two (though you've never been a runner), eating a wholesome and nutritious breakfast that you cooked yourself (although you've never been much of a cook)—and then you would reimmerse yourself in fabulous intellectual work.

Only it didn't happen.

Instead, a black mental curtain descended, bearing on it in big letters: YOU ARE A FRAUD.

You may have started having those old academic anxiety dreams: that you signed up for a course but never attended it, and now it's the end of the semester. Or that you were supposed to teach the class, but never showed up. Now it's finals time and you wonder if you can bribe the students into silence by giving them all A's.

Maybe you've even expanded to other classic anxiety dreams: you're trying to run away, but your legs won't move; you can't find a working toilet; you're suddenly onstage but you don't know your lines, or even the name of the play; or you're naked while everyone else is dressed. (If you happen to be a graduate of Swarthmore College, you may have the Swarthmoreans' unique and curious anxiety dream: you can't remember the combination to open your campus mailbox.)

All that is normal, part of "The Fear of Being a Fraud," named more than a decade ago by Peggy McIntosh at the Wellesley College Center for Research on Women. As McIntosh points out—and Ms. Mentor agrees—all academics know the Impostor Phenomenon: *I'll never be good enough; I'll never know enough; I'm thoroughly worthless, so I'll have to toady my way through graduate school—and They'll find out anyway, find out at the next stage.* At the final dissertation defense, when They say, "You've passed," every grad student's first thought is: "I got by again."

(The lone exception is Ms. Mentor, who has never suffered a flicker of self-doubt. Her first thoughts were: "It's about time" and "Where is my endowed chair?")

Still, Ms. Mentor knows that a sabbatical allows all those self-doubts to resurface: *I'll neglect a vital piece of evidence, and this time They'll finally find out I'm no good.* Because sabbatical seems to offer time to Read It All, you think you must—rather than skimming, skipping, and doing it all quickly, as you've taught yourself to do for teaching, when you've never had enough time to prepare classes perfectly.

And so, to escape the inevitable fear and self-loathing bubbling up, your psyche prefers to watch TV, listen to the birds, or weep. Other sabbaticaleers have been known to develop ulcers, or to have sudden and inexplicable attacks of vomiting, coughing, or piles, boils, or warts. All are convenient ways to avoid being unmasked as a fraud, again.

In any case, the sabbatical syndrome always cures itself: sabbaticals end. For many academics, the return to teaching at first seems draining, with endless demands on one's time. Students and committees claw and howl for attention again, and there's scarcely time for laundry, haircuts, or grocery shopping, never mind whining. The goal of physical fitness is abandoned; the exercise bike gets dusty again.

Yet the return to teaching is also a return to the well-honed skills of skimming, skipping, and quick note-taking—a return to Adequacy rather than Perfection.

It's also a return to being an adult, making choices and using time wisely—rather than being a child, refusing to choose, thinking there's too much to do, and bawling to the universe, "I don't know what you WANT!"

And so, Ms. Mentor says: Not to Despair. The post-sabbatical year is often the most productive in an academic's life, for the results of rest, refreshment, reflection, and relaxation only gradually become apparent.

(It should be noted that Ms. Mentor's book, the tome you are now reading, was written during Emily Toth's post-sabbatical year.)

Post-sabbatical, you'll return to adulthood; you'll take shortcuts; and you'll learn what you need to know and write about Mycenean art.

You won't do it all. You'll do it well.

And then, perhaps, you'll earn the only approval that matters: your own. And, of course, Ms. Mentor's.

Dickering for More Money

Q: My salary is abysmal, and when I asked my vile research dean what I could do to improve it, he said, "Grow a dick."

Meanwhile, my department head says I can't get a significant salary increase unless I get a job offer from another university. Why should I go through such a charade?

How do I grow a dick? It seems like that would save time.

A: Ms. Mentor has always been bemused, and amused, by the academic male's preoccupation with what other men think of him. He worries about whose research is "substantial" or "thin" or "seminal"; he can recite the "thrust" of one argument, and the "penetrating" qualities of another. As Emily Toth has written elsewhere, this is a grown-up version of "Whose Is Bigger?" and it pervades the entire scholarly world. (Women faculty can draw attention to this syndrome by calling their graduate courses "ovulars," rather than "seminars.")

But virtually the only way to get a raise in the current system is to show that one can get a bigger offer of money from another university—in other words, Another University's is bigger. Then the Home University, feeling it must compete, can prove that it is bigger after all, by raising the extra money.

This competition is, of course, a displaced form of *phallomachy* (the competition over penis size), and Ms. Mentor agrees that it is absurd.

In fact, she once considered setting herself up as a mythical school ("Noble University"), and selling job offers. Noble U, she felt, would save everyone money. She even sent an essay to that effect to the *Chronicle of Higher Education* (which refused to publish it).

But she digresses.

If you want a raise, you ask, must you participate in this charade, waving about your vita to sundry suitors, so that there can finally be an antler-crushing battle over your services?

Yes—until there's a feminist revolution, after which salaries will be determined collectively and equitably. (That will be long after Ms. Mentor has fallen from her ivory tower, she suspects.)

It may indeed be faster, if you can manage it, to grow a dick.

The Real World

Q: I'm pretty much assured of getting tenure, but I'm not so sure I want to be an academic. Would I be happier in the real world?

A: Possibly.

When Martha Ward, professor of anthropology at the University of New Orleans, leads workshops on tenure, promotion, and academic politics, she always begins with an unexpected declaration:

"You don't *have* to be an academic. It's not something that you *have* to do. It has to be something you *want* to do, and something that you *can* do."

She goes on to talk about Ph.D.s who've become New Orleans jazz pianists, activists, politicians, jailbirds, and the like—and her presentation is quite convincing. Hearing her, Ms. Mentor almost wanted to quit academia. But the life of the ivory tower—the opportunity to hector the youth, and write about the follies of her peers—is too choice for Ms. Mentor to resist.

But that was not true for Peggy Rosefeldt, a young theater arts professor who attended one of Martha Ward's workshops in the spring of 1991. That fall, Peggy Rosefeldt would be coming up for tenure, the decision about whether she'd be granted lifetime security as a teacher at the University of New Orleans.

Peggy Rosefeldt cogitated and meditated about whether she wanted to be an academic. A few weeks later, she quit.

Everyone who heard about it applauded her decision. She had not chosen the path of those before her; she had not done her homework just because it was assigned. She had decided what was right for Peggy Rosefeldt.

Ms. Mentor wishes there were more Peggy Rosefeldts.

During the Vietnam War, American soldiers stationed there often talked about "the world," meaning the United States, or at least that part of the planet away from the conflict.

Today, students in such tucked-away enclaves as State College, Pennsylvania, home of Penn State, often talk unself-consciously about "the real world," meaning the world of work, or at least the world beyond the university cocoon ("Happy Valley"). Students everywhere talk about "getting out" and "getting over."

Meanwhile, burned-out tenured faculty sometimes gripe that they'd like to "get out of this rat race, to the real world." A chemist at the University of North Dakota once calculated that he'd make more money in a month as a craps dealer in Las Vegas than in eight months at his academic job.

But he stayed in North Dakota.

Few academics leave their profession voluntarily.

Those who do, are often spectacular successes—as heads of foundations, or grant writers, or ghostwriters (General Norman Schwartzkopf's autobiography was ghosted by a Johns Hopkins University Ph.D. in comparative literature).

The greatest achievers among recovering academics seem to be English majors, who have a way with words. Pamela Miller, a Penn State Ph.D. who used to write learned critiques of whaling narratives, went on to writing technical manuals, at three times her former salary. Deborah Martin, a

Tulane Ph.D., was first a technical writer, and is now a best-selling writer of historical romances.

"But I have my heart set on being a professor!" Ms. Mentor hears her learned readers wailing. "I have to be an academic! I need to teach! I . . ."—whereupon Ms. Mentor, if she had a hearing aid, would turn it off.

There are many places to teach successfully and happily outside colleges and universities. Besides kindergartens, nurseries, and public schools, there are adult education and literacy programs, and academies that teach people how to do well on Scholastic Aptitude Tests in spite of themselves.

For those who must write: no one is stopping you. Academic journals now routinely publish the work of "independent scholars" alongside that of tenured professors, and journalism and public relations often pay better.

For those who must have labs, it *is* trickier. Government money for science is being cut back everywhere, and nonacademic scientists may also be shut out of industry. Ms. Mentor cannot be sanguine about their prospects.

But academics in general do well in "the real world," because they know how to be thorough and punctual. They do suffer from image problems (old maids and fuddy-duddies) and from some of their own prejudices: that grubbing for a living is bourgeois and slightly contemptible.

Still, most of the stereotypes about professors are about *male* academics. (As are, for that matter, most group stereotypes: goose-stepping Germans; singing Italians; drunken Irishmen.) The major barrier for women is—as always—sexism. Increased education does not improve women's income as it does men's: college graduate women still earn no more than men with high school diplomas.

But you asked Ms. Mentor if you'd be happier in the Real World. Ms. Mentor finally replies that happiness is intangible, except that money helps. Buy lottery tickets.

Now for My Next Trick . . .

Q: Hurray for me! Having assiduously followed all Ms. Mentor's advice about putting research first, getting role models and mentors, and being charming to old farts and young, I've just been awarded tenure. This will be my reward for some twenty-eight continuous years in school.

But except for full professor, which I can make with a second book, what mountains are left to climb? I've had straight A's, fellowships, fine teaching evaluations, and sundry honors (including my book's honorable mention for the prestigious Emily Toth Award, given by the Popular and American Culture Association). I look around my department and see some senior faculty zestfully writing and publishing and learning new things, while others do little but drone and fulminate on impotent committees. The most excruciating teachers are rarely seen at all.

Ms. Mentor, what do I do now for role models? How do I keep the competitive energy that's sustained me for nearly three decades when there's no real competition and no threat of failure?

A: Ms. Mentor's sage readers will no doubt recall the cautionary tale of Alexander the Great, who at age thirty sat down to mewl and carry on because there were no new worlds to conquer. He is one of our earliest examples of poorly handled midlife burnout.

Today Alexander, who had lifetime tenure as an emperor, could make a midlife change. He might become an artist or an astronaut or join Greenpeace. He could come out, have a sex change, start a cult, get a makeover. But instead he died young, bored, and depressed. Although he was in many ways a credit to his mentor, a quite excellent fellow named Aristotle, Alexander the Great is not an appropriate role model for the tenured woman.

Nor are most men. They are much more apt to have staked their self-esteem, in a linear-phallic way, on one goal, such as tenure. Once that is achieved, the wise ones find a new goal. But others wither.

Women, generally, lead more varied lives, with more responsibilities, interests, and changes. Fewer than half of professorial women have children, but virtually all have huge networks of friends: conference cronies; sisters, mothers, aunts, cousins; high school and college gossipmates; plus new friends among neighbors, secretaries, hairdressers, sales clerks, librarians, waitresses, nurses, and activists. Especially if they're in Women's Studies, academic women know other women all over the country, as well as throughout their own universities.

All these women friends form a constellation of role models for growth, achievement, and pleasure, throughout a woman's life.

But so what? says Ms. Mentor's correspondent. *Hurry up with your answer. I'm ambitious, and I want to forge ahead.* Ms. Mentor, a recovering Type-A herself, sympathizes with your impatience, but also insists on her own main point: Academia Is Not the Whole World.

You should, though, complete your academic cycle. Ms. Mentor advises you to keep writing and publishing. Finish your second book as soon as possible, for making full professor will quash forever any residual academic anxieties.

Also, if you aim to go into academic administration (often the graveyard of great minds), you must be a full professor to get beyond the A-ghetto and the glass ceiling, into a position of real power. If you must administer, Ms. Mentor hopes you will aim to be chancellor, or president. Or Pope.

From now on, Ms. Mentor wants you to study only what really interests you, especially if you've been pursuing DWEMS (Dead White European Males) out of obedience to authority. It's time to write about yourself, your life, your roots, your mother, and forget about trying to recuperate, for instance, misogynistic psychoanalysts. Feminism is not about women's being handmaidens and hostesses, devoting exquisite care and kindness and interpretive skills to dead men who, fundamentally, had contempt for women. Living women should not be cleaning up their messes.

Ms. Mentor says you should devote the rest of your intellectual life to women.

Do not, however, be a total lab or library drudge, no matter how much the smell of formaldehyde or old leather excites your senses. Midlife is the time to look around and sniff the roses. Give up on boring committees, especially powerless ones. Mentor only those students who appreciate you.

If you hate *Moby-Dick*, stop teaching him. Drown your copy. Harpoon it.

Eat the foods you like, and don't worry about cholesterol or fat. Reward the foods that taste good. Tenure them.

That will leave you more time and enthusiasm for lunching with all those wonderful, fascinating women you know, and learning about their lives. You can choose friends to laugh with, not just moan to. You should be joining activist community groups and working for abortion rights, or women candidates, or child-care centers, or battered women, or whatever else will make the world a better place. You should get outside academia, and outside yourself (Gail Sheehy's books, *Pathfinders* and *New Passages*, are good guides).

Midlife, post-tenure, is also the time to jump into those long-postponed emotional adventures: getting married; quitting your church; getting divorced; having a baby; reconciling with your parents; having a passionate fling (with someone outside the university). It's the time to consider coming out, if you've been a closeted lesbian. You may be a savior for younger closeted colleagues.

It's also the time to reveal—and celebrate—anything else that's been dormant, hidden, or latent. You can trumpet your ethnic roots and your politics; you can admit that you prefer *Married with Children* to PBS. You can read historical romances and sing country music. And buy a red car.

If you have a hidden disability, post-tenure is the time to come out with it. Ms. Mentor knows women academics who have heroically concealed crippling rheumatoid arthritis, intestinal horrors, dialysis, and even artificial limbs until after tenure. They know that they would not have been hired had their disabilities been known. But after tenure they're able to say to the world, "I am strong! I am invincible! I am Woman!"

The happiest midlife academics are those who keep up their energies and interests, preferably in ways that benefit their students and colleagues. That is what tenure is supposed to encourage. It is not supposed to protect those who dry up and withdraw, emerging only to snarl at the sunlight, or to go for the gold.

Ms. Mentor knows tenured faculty who have opened restaurants, bars, art galleries, or travel agencies. Some spend budgeted research hours poring over investment newsletters or hunkering down with e-mail, hoping for road kills along the information superhighway. A few have even run afoul of the law—among them some university-based weather forecasters who used their privately obtained data to invest in orange juice futures.

Ms. Mentor supports all efforts to extend the frontiers of knowledge, and believes that restaurants are manna from heaven. But she deplores the above-mentioned entrepreneurs, for they are ripoff artists who use the free time tenure allows for their own gain. They may be rich, but they are often sour and indifferent teachers, and irresponsible and surly colleagues.

Midlife, Ms. Mentor declares, is a time to improve one's teaching and one's ability to communicate life's truths (and to find out what the truths are). It is your opportunity to mold young minds, to mentor them, to show them the pleasures of the intellect and the joys of gossip. Freed from the fear of tenure denial, buoyed by a gaggle of feisty feminist friends, a midlife woman can be witty and clever and anecdotal, and even foul-mouthed if she'd like to be.

She cannot be Ms. Mentor, of course, but she can be someone almost as wise and fine. She can be herself.

Emerita:
The Golden Years

Ms. Mentor, who knows all the familiar images of women, can summon up few, if any, mental pictures of retired women.

Women do not retire.

When the laws on taxing retirement income were changed a few years ago, Phyllis A. Whitney, the author of more than forty books, wrote to writers' magazines in high dudgeon, dismay, and disgust. "Writers do not retire," she declared. As of 1997, well into her nineties (she was born in 1903), Whitney published a new novel. She wasn't done making her point.

Married women are famous, of course, for not retiring. Ms. Mentor has seen many a worried wife's face at her mate's retirement party. She knows all too well the next step: hubby is at home all the time, fidgeting and puttering and offering unsolicited tips to improve the routine that his wife has honed perfectly over the previous forty or fifty years. A husband at home is often not conducive to domestic felicity.

But what of academic women, only half of whom have husbands or children? Don't they get to *really* retire?

Sort of. But as always, with little quirks and hurdles.

In 1991 the retirement "cap"—the rule that academics must retire at seventy—was lifted. Meanwhile, many university campuses started noticing they had some very expensive senior faculty who might, since longevity is ever increasing, be there forever, gobbling up salaries and positions that might otherwise have gone to younger (and cheaper) new blood.

And so some schools began to offer early retirement "packages." Scads of highly paid, mostly pale male profs at the University of California bailed out, often to take creamier slots at other universities. The less well known remained as teachers, and the released faculty lines were often chopped up into several "adjunct" positions—ill-paid, temporary, part-time instructors and lecturers.

Those were usually women.

Of course, some senior faculty women have retired from academia. Some are pushed; others jump willingly when they no longer feel useful. Women full professors at, among others, the University of Louisville, the University of Massachusetts, and Columbia University have chosen to retire out of annoyance and aggravation with the younger generation. The older women, in their golden years, have felt bullied and patronized by younger partisans of "discourse," who discount the contributions of their feminist predecessors and believe that opaque jargon is profound, not just poor, writing.

Healthy retirement, and turning to dynamic social activism, is an alternative Ms. Mentor heartily supports. Annis Pratt, for instance, retired early as an English professor at the University of Wisconsin and now spends her days working against racism in Michigan and cochairing the National Women's Studies Association Task Force on Discrimination in Academia.

Many other academic women have retired quietly, asking that farewell parties *not* be given, and slinking off into the rest of their lives. But maybe it only seems that way.

Perhaps the quiet retirees have really gone on to something else they don't want their former, straight-laced, prudent colleagues to know about—something raucous, kinky, colorful, dangerous, or thrilling. Or they've embarked on new activities (terrorist sewing circles?) that will create a better world for women.

Ms. Mentor fervently hopes so. She wants them to send photos.

Sage or Scourge?

Q: Assuming I can afford to retire at age sixty-five (or seventy), should I? Or should I hang around and happily annoy younger folks until I drop dead in the classroom? So far, I do enjoy my role as old fart.

A: You also seem quite tactless, a quality that Ms. Mentor applauds in the chronologically gifted. For after a certain age, she believes that tact is mostly wasted. Maturity should have its privileges, including the right to be eccentric and to say exactly what one thinks.

Assuming you can do it financially, what will happen when you retire?

Students will not have access to someone so wise as you. Most likely your hiring line will be split into two, three, or four adjunct positions, and low-paid young female instructors will be overworked and harried to death on far less money than you'd have to work for.

You can save them the pain by not retiring. And maybe the absence of any job at all will encourage them to retool and go into some other line of work rather than hanging on, forever hoping.

Or you can try what some aging activists have been pioneering in the mid-1990s. You can refuse to retire until, and unless, you're assured—in writing—that your faculty line will be kept, and that you'll be replaced by a tenure-track person.

This strikes Ms. Mentor as one of the best forms of extortion she has ever witnessed.

But failing that, and assuming you still have enthusiasm for teaching and have your wits all about you (do ask others if you're in doubt), Ms. Mentor decrees that you do not have to retire.

In truth, retirement for academics varies greatly. Scientists able to keep their labs may scarcely notice that they are no longer formally teaching; humanists who have always read a great deal and written articles and books can continue to do so. According to one very eminent, highly published, and recently retired professor from Michigan: "The only thing that's missing are whiny, sullen teenagers who don't want to do the reading or think about the past. Retirement is paradise!"

Retirees of all kinds also have more time to write to Ms. Mentor and plot strategies for their own future intellectual development. I. F. Stone, the gadfly publisher of *I. F. Stone's Weekly* and the tormentor of those in the power throughout the 1960s (and before and after), sat down to learn Greek at age seventy. It went swimmingly, and he decided Plato was awesome.

Those who reveled in academic politics, though, may feel cut adrift. People do not hang on the words of someone who has little power and no stake in whether course 2593 is required or 3481 is not. Faculty Senate gadabouts can go through terrible withdrawal pains, unless they throw their formidable energies into local activism. Some have revved up their local chapters of the American Association of Retired Persons, or revived the local NOW, or loudly lobbied parks and preservation commissions. Others, now describing their profession as "full-time meddler," have become the scourges or saviors of small-town city councils.

Finally, Ms. Mentor feels obliged to repeat the one risk you mentioned for faculty who do not retire: the possibility of dropping dead in the classroom, perhaps in a middle of a lecture on the follies of youth. That is not a pretty picture. But up to that point, the pleasures of heckling young students, and patronizing one's younger colleagues, can be intense and immense.

Ms. Mentor recommends hanging around, haranguing, and being a busybody old biddy wherever you feel like it. You've earned the right.

Final Words

Final Words

Q: What kinds of reviews does Ms. Mentor expect to get for her first book?

A: Excellent ones, from the wise. She expects readers to find her book a thundering good read, with fabulous plot and characters, as well as wit, wisdom, sagacity, substance, and great pith.

She also expects people to give *Ms. Mentor's Impeccable Advice for Women in Academia* to one another for major holidays, job hunting, and tenure struggles. A copy of *Ms. Mentor's Impeccable Advice for Women in Academia* will always be an appropriate graduation gift.

Some reviews will vary, of course. Some will say that Ms. Mentor is too harsh on academia; others will consider her too generous; still others may damn her as a "feminist radical," a charge she agrees to thoroughly.

In fact, Ms. Mentor agrees to all reviews, for she knows that the only bad self-promotion is—none.

Q: How is Ms. Mentor mentoring future Ms. Mentors? Can I grow up to be Ms. Mentor?

A: Certainly not.

There is only one Ms. Mentor—and she was born with all the skills, talents, and gifts necessary to her exalted profession.

Nevertheless, you are free to admire Ms. Mentor, engrave her every word on your heart, and send missives to her via her channeler, Emily Toth, at Louisiana State University: *etoth@unixl.sncc.lsu.edu.*

Ms. Mentor's many admirers are also invited to read her monthly column on the *Chronicle of Higher Education*'s Career Network site: *http://www.chronicle.com/jobs.*

Bibliography:
Women in Academia and Other Readings Sampled by Ms. Mentor

Note to Sage Readers: Ms. Mentor is a wide-ranging reader with an eclectic flair and an impeccable intelligence. If a source is not listed here, it may not yet have made itself known to Ms. Mentor. Or it may be no good.

Abramson, Joan. *Invisible Woman: Discrimination in the Academic Profession.* San Francisco: Jossey-Bass, 1975.

Adams, Hazard. *The Academic Tribes.* New York: Liveright, 1976.

Aisenberg, Nadya, and Mona Harrington. *Women of Academe: Outsiders in the Sacred Grove.* Amherst: University of Massachusetts Press, 1988.

Allison, David B. "Destruction/Deconstruction in the Text of Nietzsche." In *The Question of Textuality: Strategies of Reading in Contemporary American Criticism*, ed. William V. Spanos, Paul A. Bové, and Daniel O'Hara, 197–222, esp. discussion p. 218. Bloomington: Indiana University Press, 1982.

Basow, S. A., and K. Howe. "Evaluation of College Professors: Effects of Professors' Sex-Type and Sex, and Student Sex." *Psychological Reports* 60 (1987): 671–678.

Basow, Susan A., and Nancy T. Silberg. "Student Evaluations of College Professors: Are Female and Male Professors Rated Differently?" *Journal of Educational Psychology* 79:3 (1987): 308–314.

Bateson, Mary Catherine. *Composing a Life.* New York: Plume, 1990.

Belenky, Mary Field, Blythe McVicker Clinchy, Nancy Rule Goldberger, and Jill Mattuck Tarule. *Women's Ways of Knowing: The Development of Self, Voice, and Mind.* New York: Basic, 1986.

Bergmann, Jörg R. *Discreet Indiscretions: The Social Organization of Gossip.* Trans. John Bednarz, Jr. and Eva Kafka Barron. New York: Aldine de Gruyter, 1993.

Bernard, Jessie. *Academic Women.* Cleveland and New York: World Publishing Company, 1966.

Bioscience 43 (April 1993). Special issue with articles on two-career couples.

Bruce, Mary Alice. "Mentoring Women Doctoral Students: What Counselor Educators and Supervisors Can Do." *Counselor Education and Supervision* 35 (December 1995): 139–149.

Caesar, Terry. *Conspiring with Forms: Life in Academic Texts.* Athens and London: University of Georgia Press, 1992.

Caplan, Paula J. *Lifting a Ton of Feathers: A Woman's Guide to Surviving in the Academic World.* Toronto: University of Toronto Press, 1993.

"Careers '95: The Future of the Ph.D." *Science* 270:6 (6 October 1995): 121–146.

Conway, Jill Ker. *True North.* New York: Knopf, 1994.

Cornillon, Susan Koppelman, ed. *Images of Women in Fiction: Feminist Perspectives.* Bowling Green: Popular Press, 1972.

Culley, Margo, and Catherine Portuges, eds. *Gendered Subjects: The Dynamics of Feminist Teaching.* Boston and London: Routledge and Kegan Paul, 1985.

Culotta, Elizabeth. "Industrial R & D: Women Struggle to Crack the Code of Corporate Culture." *Science* 260 (April 16, 1993): 398–400+.

Cyrus, Virginia, ed. *Experiencing Race, Class, and Gender in the United States.* Mountain View, Calif.: Mayfield, 1993.

Davis, Barbara Hillyer, ed. "Feminist Education: A Special Topic Edition." *Journal of Thought: An Interdisciplinary Quarterly* 20:3 (Fall 1985).

Davis, Gwen. *Ladies in Waiting.* New York: Macmillan, 1979.

Deats, Sara Munson, and Lagretta Tallent Lenker, eds. *Gender and Academe: Feminist Pedagogy and Politics.* Lanham, MD: Rowman & Littlefield, 1994.

Delaney, Janice, Mary Jane Lupton, and Emily Toth. *The Curse: A Cultural History of Menstruation.* New York: Dutton, 1976. 2d ed., Urbana: University of Illinois Press, 1988.

DeNeef, A. Leigh, Craufurd Goodwin, and Ellen Stern McCrate, eds. *The Academic's Handbook.* Durham, NC: Duke University Press, 1988. 2d ed., 1995.

DuBois, Ellen Carol, Gail Paradise Kelly, Elizabeth Kapovsky Kennedy, Carolyn W. Korsmeyer, and Lillian S. Robinson. *Feminist Scholarship: Kindling in the Groves of Academe.* Urbana: University of Illinois Press, 1987.

Dziech, Billie Wright, and Linda Weiner. *The Lecherous Professor: Sexual Harassment on Campus.* Boston: Beacon Press, 1984. 2d ed., University of Illinois Press, 1990.

Ellmann, Mary. *Thinking about Women.* New York: Harcourt, Brace, Jovanovich, 1968.

Erdman, Cheri K. *Nothing to Lose: A Guide to Sane Living in a Larger Body.* New York: HarperCollins, 1995.

Faludi, Susan. *Backlash: The Undeclared War Against Women.* New York: Crown, 1991.

Fiedler, Leslie A. *What Was Literature: Class Culture and Mass Society.* New York: Simon & Schuster, 1982.

Fine, Michelle. *Disruptive Voices: the Possibilities of Feminist Research.* Ann Arbor: University of Michigan, 1992.

Freedman, Diane P., Olivia Frey, and Frances Murphy Zauhar, eds. *The Intimate*

Critique: Autobiographical Literary Criticism. Durham, NC: Duke University Press, 1993.

Freeman, Jo, ed. *Women: a Feminist Perspective*. 5th ed. Mountain View, CA: Mayfield, 1995.

Friedan, Betty. *The Feminine Mystique*. New York: Norton, 1963.

Gabriel, Susan L., and Isaiah Smithson, eds. *Gender in the Classroom: Power and Pedagogy*. Urbana: University of Illinois Press, 1990.

Gammie, Fiona. "Report Confirms Obstacles to Women Scientists." *Nature* 367 (February 24, 1994), 675.

Garner, Shirley Nelson, Vèvè Clark, Ketu H. Katrak, and Margaret Higonnet, eds. *Antifeminism in the Academy*. New York: Routledge, 1996.

Gehrke, Brad C. "Gender Redistribution in the Veterinary Medical Profession." *Journal of the American Veterinary Medical Association* 208 (April 15, 1996), 254–255.

Gilligan, Carol. *In a Different Voice*. Cambridge, MA: Harvard University Press, 1982.

Ginzberg, Eli. *Educated American Women: Life Styles and Self-Portraits*. New York: Columbia University Press, 1966.

Godwin, Gail. *The Odd Woman*. New York: Knopf, 1974.

Goetting, Ann, and Sarah Fenstermaker, eds. *Individual Voice, Collective Visions: Fifty Years of Women in Sociology*. Philadelphia: Temple University Press, 1995.

Griffin, Gail B. *Calling: Essays on Teaching in the Mother Tongue*. Pasadena: Trilogy Books, 1992.

Hall, Roberta M., and Bernice R. Sandler. *The Classroom Climate: A Chilly One for Women?* Washington, DC: Project on the Status and Education of Women (Association of American Colleges, 1818 R Street N. W., Washington, D.C. 20009), 1984, and updates.

Hall, Roberta M., and Bernice R. Sandler. *Out of the Classroom: A Chilly Campus Climate for Women?* Washington, D.C.: Project on the Status and Education of Women (Association of American Colleges, 1818 R Street N. W., Washington, D.C. 20009), 1984, and updates.

Hamel, April Vahle, with Mary Morris Heiberger and Julia Miller Vick. *The Graduate School Funding Handbook*. Philadelphia: University of Pennsylvania Press, 1995.

Harragan, Betty Lehan. *Games Mother Never Taught You: Corporate Gamesmanship for Women*. New York: Warner, 1977.

Hartman, Joan E., and Ellen Messer-Davidow, eds. *(En)Gendering Knowledge: Feminists in Academe*. Knoxville: University of Tennessee Press, 1991.

Heiberger, Mary Morris, and Julia Miller Vick. *The Academic Job Search Handbook*. Philadelphia: University of Pennsylvania Press, 1992. 2d ed., 1996.

Hennessey, Caroline. *I, B. I. T. C. H.* New York: Lancer, 1970.

Hennig, Margaret, and Anne Jardim. *The Managerial Woman: The Survival Manual for Women in Business*. New York: Pocket Books, 1976.

Hensel, Nancy. *Realizing Gender Equality in Higher Education: The Need to Integrate Work/Family Issues*. ASHE-ERIC Higher Education Report No. 2.

Washington, DC: The George Washington University, School of Education and Human Development, 1991.

Hillyer, Barbara. *Feminism and Disability*. Norman: University of Oklahoma Press, 1993.

Hochschild, Arlie. "Inside the Clockwork of Male Careers." In *Women and the Power to Change*, ed. Florence Howe, 47–80. New York: McGraw-Hill, 1971.

Hochschild, Arlie, with Anne Machung. *Second Shift: Working Parents and the Revolution at Home*. New York: Viking, 1989.

Holland, Dorothy C., and Margaret A. Eisenhart. *Educated in Romance: Women, Achievement, and College Culture*. Chicago: University of Chicago Press, 1990.

Horwitz, Elinor L. "Speaking Out for Justice." *AAUW Outlook* 90:1 (Spring 1994): 22–25.

Jong, Erica. *Fear of Flying*. New York: Holt, Rinehart & Winston, 1973.

———. *Here Comes and Other Poems*. New York: Signet, 1975.

Joreen. "Bitch Manifesto." In *Radical Feminism*, ed. Anne Koedt, Ellen Levine, and Anita Rapone, 50–59. New York: Times Books, 1973.

Kaiser, Jocelyn H. "NIH Discrimination Case Thrown Out." *Science* 272 (April 5, 1996): 21.

Kirschner, Elizabeth M. "Alternative Careers Lure Chemists Down a Road Less Traveled." *Chemical & Engineering News* (October 23, 1995): 51–52.

Koedt, Anne, Ellen Levine, and Anita Rapone, eds. *Radical Feminism*. New York: Times Books, 1973.

Kolodny, Annette. "Dancing Through the Minefield: Some Observations on the Theory, Practice, and Politics of a Feminist Literary Criticism." *Feminist Studies* 6 (1980). Reprinted in Elaine Showalter, ed., *The New Feminist Criticism: Essays on Women, Literature, and Theory*, 144–167. New York: Pantheon, 1985.

Koppelman, Susan, ed. *Two Friends: And Other Nineteenth-Century Lesbian Stories by American Women Writers*. New York: Penguin, 1994.

———, ed. *Women's Friendships: A Collection of Short Stories*. Norman: University of Oklahoma Press, 1991.

———, ed. *Women in the Trees: U.S. Women's Short Stories about Battering and Resistance, 1839–1994*. Boston: Beacon, 1996.

Krentz, Jayne Ann, ed. *Dangerous Men and Adventurous Women: Romance Writers on the Appeal of the Romance*. Philadelphia: University of Pennsylvania Press, 1992.

LaNoue, George R., and Barbara A. Lee. *Academics in Court: The Consequences of Faculty Discrimination Litigation*. Ann Arbor: University of Michigan Press, 1987.

Lever, Janet. "Reflections on a Serendipitous and Rocky Career: The First Twenty Years." In *Individual Voices, Collective Visions: Fifty Years of Women in Sociology*, 87–108. ed. Ann Goetting and Sarah Fenstermaker, Philadelphia: Temple University Press, 1995.

Lewis, Lionel S. *Scaling the Ivory Tower: Merit and Its Limits in Academic Careers*. Baltimore: Johns Hopkins University Press, 1975.

Lurie, Alison. *The War Between the Tates*. New York: Random House, 1974.

MacIlwain, Colin. "NIH Drops Survey on Discrimination, Claiming Questions 'Ill-Designed.'" *Nature* 372 (November 3, 1994): 3.

Magner, Denise K. "The New Generation: Study Shows Proportions of Female and Minority Professors are Growing." *Chronicle of Higher Education* (February 2, 1996): A-17, A-18.

Martin, Josef (pseud.). *To Rise Above Principle: The Memoirs of an Unreconstructed Dean*. Urbana: University of Illinois Press, 1988.

Martin, Judith. *Miss Manners' Guide for the Turn-of-the-Millennium*. New York: Simon & Schuster, 1989.

———. *Miss Manners' Guide to Excruciatingly Correct Behavior*. New York: Atheneum, 1982.

Mervis, Jeffrey. "NIH Task Force to Examine 'Culture' of Discrimination." *Nature* 363 (May 13, 1993), 105.

Millett, Kate. *Sexual Politics*. Garden City: Doubleday, 1970.

Miner, Valerie, and Helen E. Longino, eds. *Competition: A Feminist Taboo?* New York: Feminist Press, 1987.

Mitchell, Margaret. *Gone with the Wind*. New York: Macmillan, 1936.

Nelson, Nancy Owen, ed. *Private Voices, Public Lives: Women Speak on the Literary Life*. Denton, TX: University of North Texas Press, 1995.

"News from LAF" (Legal Advocacy Fund). *AAUW Outlook* (Fall 1995): 32–34.

Orenstein, Peggy. *SchoolGirls: Young Women, Self-Esteem, and the Confidence Gap*. New York: Doubleday, 1994.

Orlans, Kathryn P. Meadow, and Ruth A. Wallace, eds. *Gender and the Academic Experience: Berkeley Women Sociologists*. Lincoln: University of Nebraska Press, 1994.

Penelope, Julia. *Speaking Freely: Unlearning the Lies of the Fathers' Tongues*. New York: Pergamon, 1990.

Phelan, James. *Beyond the Tenure Track: Fifteen Months in the Life of an English Professor*. Columbus: Ohio State University Press, 1991.

Pratt, Annis. *Dancing Through the Mine Field: Columns from Concerns, 1982–1992*. Women's Caucus for the Modern Languages. Available from Annis Pratt, 1056 Larchlea, Birmington, MI 48009.

Price, Jill. "Guest Comment: Gender Bias in the Sciences: Some Up-to-Date Information on the Subject." *American Journal of Physics* 61 (July 1993): 589–590.

Primack, Richard B., and Virginia O'Leary. "Cumulative Disadvantages in the Careers of Women Ecologists." *Bioscience* 43 (March 1993): 158–165.

Reagon, Bernice Johnson. "Coalition Politics: Turning the Century." In *Home Girls: A Black Feminist Anthology*, ed. Barbara Smith. New York: Kitchen Table Women of Color Press, 1983, 356–368.

Richardson, Betty. *Sexism in High Education*. New York: Seabury, 1974.

Roberts, Robin. *A New Species: Gender and Science in Science Fiction*. Urbana: University of Illinois Press, 1993.

Rosser, Sue V. *Female-Friendly Science: Applying Women's Studies Methods and Theories to Attract Students*. New York: Pergamon, 1990.

———. *Teaching Science and Health from a Feminist Perspective: A Practical Guide*. New York: Pergamon, 1986.

————. *Women's Health—Missing from U.S. Medicine*. Bloomington: Indiana University Press, 1994.

————, ed. *Feminism Within the Science and Health Care Professions: Overcoming Resistance*. New York: Pergamon, 1988.

Ruffner, Sara S. *A Liberal Education*. Santa Barbara, CA: Fithian, 1991.

Russ, Martin. *Showdown Semester: Advice from a Writing Professor*. New York: Crown, 1980.

Sadker, Myra, and David Sadker. *Failing at Fairness: How America's Schools Cheat Girls*. New York: Scribner's, 1994.

"Salaries and Advancement of Women Faculty in Atmosphere Science: Some Reasons for Concern." *Bulletin of the American Metereological Society* 77 (March 1996): 473–490.

Sandler, Bernice. "Women as Mentors: Myths and Commandments." *Chronicle of Higher Education* 39 (March 10, 1993): B-3.

Sapiro, Virginia. *Women in American Society: An Introduction to Women's Studies*. 3d ed. Mountain View, CA: Mayfield, 1994.

Schoenfielder, Lisa, and Barb Wieser, eds. *Shadow on a Tightrope: Writings by Women on Fat Oppression*. Iowa City: Aunt Lute, 1983.

Selvin, Paul. "Sex Discrimination: Jenny Harrison Finally Gets Tenure in Math at Berkeley." *Science* 261 (July 16, 1993): 286.

Sexton, Anne. *All My Pretty Ones*. Boston: Houghton Mifflin, 1962.

Sheehy, Gail. *New Passages: Mapping Your Life Across Time*. New York: Random House, 1995.

————. *Pathfinders*. New York: William Morrow, 1981.

Shipman, Pat. "One Woman's Life in Science." *American Scientist* 83 (July–August 1995): 300–302.

Simeone, Angela. *Academic Women: Working Towards Equality*. South Hadley, MA: Bergin and Garvey Publishers, 1987.

Smith, Barbara, ed. *Home Girls: A Black Feminist Anthology*. New York: Kitchen Table Women of Color Press, 1983.

Sonnert, Gerhard. "Gender Equity in Science: Still an Elusive Goal." *Issues in Science and Technology* 12 (Winter 1995–1996): 53–58.

Spector, Barbara. "Woman Biologist's Success in a Discrimination Suit Adds Weight to Findings on Science and Parenthood." *The Scientist* 8:15 (July 25, 1995): 1, 4.

Spender, Dale. *Women of Ideas and What Men Have Done to Them*. Boston and London: Routledge and Kegan Paul, 1982.

Stephenson, June. *Men Are Not Cost-Effective*. New York: HarperPerennial, 1995.

Stringer, Patricia A., and Irene Thompson. *Stepping Off the Pedestal: Academic Women in the South*. New York: Modern Language Association, 1982.

Syfers, Judy. "Why I Want a Wife." In *Radical Feminism*, ed. Anne Koedt, Ellen Levine, and Anita Rapone, 60–62. New York: Times Books, 1973.

Tannen, Deborah. *Talking from 9 to 5: Women and Men in the Workplace: Language, Sex and Power*. New York: William Morrow, 1994.

————. *You Just Don't Understand: Women and Men in Conversation*. New York: William Morrow, 1990.

Theodore, Athena. *The Campus Troublemakers: Academic Women in Protest.* Houston: Cap and Gown Press, 1986.

Thompson, Irene, and Audrey Roberts, eds. *The Road Retaken: Women Reenter the Academy.* New York: Modern Language Association, 1985.

Tobias, Sheila, and Daryl E. Chubin. "New Degrees for Today's Scientists." *Chronicle of Higher Education* (July 12, 1996): 1–2.

Tokarczyk, Michelle M., and Elizabeth A. Fay, eds. *Working-Class Women in the Academy: Laborers in the Knowledge Factory.* Amherst: University of Massachusetts Press, 1993.

Toth, Emily. *Daughters of New Orleans.* New York: Bantam, 1983.

———. "Developing Political Savvy—Many Misadventures Later." *Women's Studies Quarterly* 18:3–4 (Fall–Winter 1990): 147–152.

———. *Inside Peyton Place: The Life of Grace Metalious.* Garden City, NY: Doubleday, 1981.

———. "The Job Hunt, MLA Style." *Johns Hopkins Magazine* 25 (November 1974): 29–33.

———. *Kate Chopin: A Life of the Author of "The Awakening."* New York: William Morrow, 1990; Austin: University of Texas Press, 1993.

———. "Women in Academia." In *The Academic's Handbook*, ed. A. Leigh DeNeef, Craufurd Goodwin, and Ellen Stern McCrate, 36–45. Durham, NC: Duke University Press, 1988. In 1995 2d ed., 38–47.

Treichler, Paula, Cheris Kramarae, and Beth Stafford. *For Alma Mater: The Theory and Practice of Feminist Scholarship.* Urbana: University of Illinois Press, 1985.

Wallich, Paul. "Having It All." *Scientific American* 274 (March 1996): 31.

Ward, Martha C. *A World Full of Women.* Boston: Allyn and Bacon, 1996.

Weimer, Joan. *Back Talk: Teaching Lost Selves to Speak.* New York: Random House, 1994.

Weissmann, Heidi. "Insults and Injuries." *Women's Review of Books* 13:5 (February 1996): 21–23.

West, Martha. "Gender Bias in Academic Robes: The Law's Failure to Protect Women Faculty." *Temple Law Review* 67 (1994): 67–178.

———. "Women Faculty: Frozen in Time." *Academe* 81:4 (July–August 1995): 26–29.

"What's Good for Women Is Good for the Country." *Chemtech* 25 (October 1995): 33–34.

Whicker, Marcia Lynn, and Jennie Jacobs Kronenfeld. *Dealing with Ethical Dilemmas on Campus.* Thousand Oaks, London, New Delhi: Sage Publications, 1994.

Women's Review of Books, February 1996 (13:5). Special issue on academic women and the law.

"Women Scientists Lacking in Industry Jobs." *New York Times* (January 18, 1994): C-5.

Yentsch, Clarice M., and Carl J. Sindermann. *The Woman Scientist: Meeting the Challenges for a Successful Career.* New York: Plenum, 1992.

Index

penis, 66–67, 83, 93, 101, 106–107, 195–196. *See also* Cards, chemically treated; Phallomachy; Whose Is Bigger
"permission to pee," 88–89
phallic language, symbols, 138, 195–196
phallocrat, 153
phallomachy, 196
plagiarism, 134–137
Plato, 204
politically correct/incorrect, 6, 137, 138–139
pomposity, 130–131
Pope, Alexander, 31
Popular Culture Association, 53
pornography, 100–101
post-tenure, 78, 182–183, 189, 198–201
"Power to the People," 142
Pratt, Annis, 203
publishing, importance of, 18–19

Queer Theory, 67
quotas, 22

racism, 106–107, 113–114. *See also* African Americans
Rajender, Shyamala, 178
rape, 91–92
Reagon, Bernice Johnson, 109
Real World, 26, 56, 80, 196–198
regional stereotypes, 116, 125–127
research agenda, 61
responsibility magnet, 61
retirement, 202–205
revenge, 40–42, 50, 55, 64, 178–179
Rich, Adrienne, 117
role model, 143, 199
romance novels and novelists, 186–188
Roseanne, 84, 117
Rosefeldt, Peggy, 197
Rosser, Sue, 34, 114

salaries, 15, 38, 39, 144, 145, 153, 161, 191–193, 195–196. *See also* Competing offers
Sandler, Bernice, 102
Santayana, George, 60

Sarton, May, 149
Schwartzkopf, Norman, 197
science, 38–40, 76–77
secretaries, 62, 80, 81–82, 110, 133
Selena, 99
self-promotion, 61, 79–80, 138, 161, 166, 167, 189–190, 191–193
Senate, Faculty, 204
sex, 50–51, 174–175
sexism, 132–133
Sexton, Anne, 89
sexual bribes and favors, 34, 145
sexual harassment, 5, 39, 62, 68, 71, 79, 87, 97, 106–107, 112, 119, 130, 140–141, 149, 150–154, 161, 174–175, 184, 185
sexual orientation. *See* Heterosexuality; Homophobia; Homosexuality; Lesbians
Sexual Politics (Millett), 4
Shadow on a Tightrope (Schoenfielder and Wieser), 12
Sheehy, Gail, 200
Silverstone, Alicia, 117
size. *See* Fat; Women of substance
sleeping one's way to the top, 128
Snyder, Richard, 183
social life. *See* Collegiality
Spock, Jane, and Dr. Benjamin, 137
S.Q. (Schmooze Quotient), 190. *See also* Networking
standup comedy. *See* Teaching
Stanton, Elizabeth Cady, 13
Stein, Gertrude, 13
Steinem, Gloria, 117
Stephenson, June, 159
Stewart, Walter, 136
Stone, I. F., 204
Swarthmore College, 194

Taylor, Elizabeth, 30, 37, 169
"Teacher, The" (Jong), 85
teaching, 69, 75; awards, 85, 94; like standup comedy, 15, 24, 25, 74, 84, 89; not talked about, 70, 85; perils and pleasures, 83–104; valued, 7–8, 72. *See also* Authority